CHILDHOOD
OF AN
IDIOT

DOM HARVEY

CHILDHOOD OF AN IDIOT

ALLEN&UNWIN

SYDNEY · MELBOURNE · AUCKLAND · LONDON

Allen & Unwin
Level 3, 228 Queen Street
Auckland 1010, New Zealand
Phone: (64 9) 377 3800
83 Alexander Street
Crows Nest NSW 2065, Australia
Phone: (61 2) 8425 0100
Email: info@allenandunwin.com
Web: www.allenandunwin.com

A catalogue record for this book is available
from the National Library of New Zealand

ISBN 978 1 877505 43 0

Internal design by Alissa Dinallo
Set in 11/16 pt Sabon by Post Pre-press Group, Australia
Printed in Australia by McPherson's Printing Group

10 9 8 7 6 5 4 3 2 1

To Jay-Jay and Seven, two of the most awesome (and tolerant) people I know. I annoy myself on a regular basis, so I'm not sure how you guys put up with me!

To the Harveys—Mum, Dad, Bridget, Charlotte and Daniel—sorry for not clearing any of this stuff with you guys first. If you don't like it or you remember things differently, go and write your own bloody book.

To the extended family—the cousins, uncles, aunties, nieces and nephews—thanks for having a hand in making life more interesting. I hope the next family get-together won't be too awkward after you read this book!

CONTENTS

Harvey family portrait. All seven of us (Dad's handlebar moustache was pretty much a family member).

MEET THE HARVEYS

All things considered, I think I turned out fairly normal. The odds were stacked against me, because I am surrounded by madness—have been all my life. 'My family are a strange bunch.' A lot of people say this, but my family actually ARE a strange bunch. You'll be hearing a lot about these guys who I didn't get to choose. Isn't that the saying? You can choose your friends but not your family?

If I DID get to choose, would I have picked this family? Well, no. Don't be stupid. I would have picked far wealthier people to be my parents. Imagine being born into ridiculous wealth? That sense of entitlement and superiority from day one, without even having to work for it. I would have no problem with that.

Instead, I got a middle-class family. We had all of life's basic necessities, with the occasional luxury thrown in at birthdays and Christmas. It wasn't an easy upbringing, though, because both Mum and Dad were really strict. I even thought so at the time, when I compared myself with my friends and the freedom they enjoyed, but I could never raise the issue. Bringing it up would have been considered disobedience. Disobedience was punishable by the belt. And since my purpose in bringing it up would be to reduce the amount of time I spent bent over the end of my parents' bed waiting for my buttocks to feel that red-hot searing pain, it all seemed a bit counterproductive, so I let that one slide.

My upbringing would definitely have been way easier with the ridiculously wealthy parents I would have chosen if it were an option. Rich kids get punished by having something taken away:

'Madison, please put all your toys away and tidy your room or we won't take you skiing in Queenstown this weekend.'

Middle-class kids like us never had too much stuff that could be taken off us, so the ultimatum usually went along these lines:

'Dominic, put all your toys away and tidy your room or you'll get the belt.'

And if there were tears that didn't pass the 'reasonable reasons to cry' threshold, we would get this one:

'Stop crying or I'll really give you something to cry about.'

Still, it was all character building. And as much of a contradiction as this will sound, every blow was delivered with loving intentions. So it gives me great pleasure to introduce you to some of the nicest freaks I know . . . my family!

There was Dad, Stuart Harvey, a man whose clicking jaw could be heard from anywhere inside our three-bedroom house whenever he decided to eat. Without a word of a lie, you could be in the shower down the hall, with the water running and the bathroom door shut, and you could hear Dad's jaw as he walked past.

Then there was the way he banged his plate with his spoon to get every last little bit of Weet-Bix. Clink! Clink! Clink! Clink! Us kids would all sit there sighing and thinking, 'Arrrrrrrgggghhh! You've got every last little bit—can you stop before you smash the damn plate!'

These sounds seemed to get louder and louder as we got older. In hindsight, the volume may not have changed—it was just so fucking irritating that over time we became hypersensitive to it.

Mum, Susan Harvey, was a woman who would pluck her bikini line, with tweezers, in the front passenger seat of the car, with four of us kids crammed in the back seat. There were more kids than seatbelts in the back seat . . . but it was the 1980s, so seatbelts were a bit of a take it or leave it thing. We would go on these family road trips every December as we headed away for the New Year's holiday up to Whangamata. Every year, Mum would put her feet up on the dashboard of the car and wind the window down a few centimetres, then pull out pubic hairs one at a time and wave the tweezers outside the window, giving any motorist following too closely a windshield of unwanted black hairs.

Since it happened every single year and we grew up with it, none of us kids ever really paused to think about whether or not it was normal behaviour.

Then there was my older sister, Bridget, whose claim to fame was winning a celebrity look-alike photo contest in the *Woman's Weekly*. Bridge was chuffed with this, and rightly so. On top of the fifteen dollars prize money, Bridge got a lifetime of bragging rights that she looks like famous New Zealand model Rachel Hunter. Now, I don't want to take anything away from Bridget—with her looks I'm sure she could have married an elderly has-been pop star. But it is worth a mention that in the photo she sent which won the contest, she did have an ice-cream in hand and was wearing the same clothes that Rachel wore in the ad she did for Trumpet ice-creams. So in my slightly-mean-spirited-but-mainly-just-honest opinion, a lot of the similarities came down to the props used in the photo. It would be like me drawing a lightning bolt scar on my forehead and putting on round black glasses before telling people I look like Harry Potter. I didn't think my sister looked anything like Rachel Hunter . . . but once it was published in a nationwide magazine, that was all the proof she needed that I was wrong and that she did, indeed, look like a super model, or at least the closest thing New Zealand has ever had to a super model.

Bridget is two years older than me. Then, two years after I was born, Daniel arrived. I've never looked into all the traits of the condition known as 'middle child syndrome' but maybe I should. Whatever the hang-ups of a middle child are supposed to be, I've probably got them.

Dan and I were cellmates. We shared a small room with bunks for our entire childhoods. When Dan was fifteen, we moved to a new house that was big enough for all four children to have their own space. Bridget had left home a while before we moved to this big house, and I was not far off going flatting too. Yep, that's my family—upsizing to a good-sized home suitable for a family of six just before they end up dropping down to a family of four.

5

Dan and I hated each other, and we fought most days as two people who mutually hated each other tend to do. Being two years older than Dan, I had superior strength and size, but I didn't really have the mongrel in me that Daniel did. Sometimes I wondered if he could somehow have been the spawn of the devil, because he just seemed so angry and calculating. When we had a really big fight, it would often end with Dad using violence to stop the violence. We would each be made to lie face down on his bed for a lash with 'the belt'. This thing hurt like hell. The skin would throb and sting for quite some time afterwards. I was petrified of it and would often start crying and pleading for a stay of execution, trying to cover my bottom with my hands and making it near impossible for Dad to get a clean shot at his fleshy target.

Young Devil Spawn Dan, on the other hand, would lie down on the bed without any fuss or fanfare and, as cold as ice, turn his head and look up to Dad and say something bone-chilling like 'You don't scare me . . . bring it on!' On his really angry days, he would even heckle Dad afterwards: 'Pfft, is that all you got? It didn't even hurt.'

Finally, there was the baby of the family, Charlotte. A woman who has had a lifelong obsession with the scent of earwax. She would have been six or seven when she had this delicious but disgusting epiphany. The whole family was in Dad's car going somewhere. Probably Whangamata. I can't recall if Mum had already waxed her bikini line or not. Out of the blue, young Char put her finger in her ear and scratched an itch or did whatever it was she needed to do. Then, after removing her finger from her ear, she waved it under her nose for a second or two before putting her hands on her lap with a 'thinking' look on her face. She then went back for seconds, sliding her finger in the ear again and beneath her nostrils, this time for a far deeper inhale.

And that is the moment in time that Charlotte Marie Harvey made the discovery that the inside of her ear canals smelt identical to . . . PEACH PUDDING.

She still does it now. It would seem the peaches are never out of season in ear land. I even caught her doing it at her own wedding, while her brand-new husband was making a heartfelt speech. She is quite stealthy about it these days—I doubt any other guest even noticed. When she was still in single figures, Charlotte was quite open about the scent in her ears and even offered her freshly 'eared' finger to other people for a sniff so they could see for themselves, an offer that was seldom taken up. But as she has grown older she has also grown more subtle. After a quick ear scratch, she will pause with her hand away from her face for at least ten seconds, then raise it to her nose to scratch her upper lip area. All the while she will be breathing in the scent of her finger.

And that's the Harveys. All six of us. We love each other, sometimes. We are embarassed by each other, sometimes. We frustrate each other, sometimes. But if the shit ever hits the fan we are there for each other, all of the time.

Now that you have met the core cast of the book, we can crack into the story of my childhood . . . and probably yours too, if you grew up in New Zealand in the 1980s. If you don't relate to any of these stories, count yourself lucky.

This is the childhood of an idiot. And it gives me absolutely no pleasure to say that idiot is me, Dominic Harvey.

AN IDIOT IS BORN

I don't remember much about the beginning but I believe it went something like this:

I was just hanging out in the rather humid environment of my dad's scrotum when, with very little warning, I was propelled through the tip of his penis, like a tiny version of the circus stuntman who gets shot from the cannon. Then the race was on, an ocean swim of unimaginable proportions. It must have been like one of those photos you see of crowded beaches in Japan during summer . . . only a bit less sticky.

Myself and 100 million other sperm all racing for the egg.

For the winner? Bragging rights in the sperm community and a crack at becoming an embryo, then maybe a foetus, and eventually a human.

It was a fierce contest with a tonne of hoops to get through but I nailed it. Come to think of it, so did you! We all did. Each and every one of us has achieved greatness just by being born. Since this awesome achievement is one we all share, it is not something we go around bragging about, but it doesn't hurt to give yourself a wee pat on the back from time to time.

Mum was a smoker, and pregnancy didn't stop that, but it's not like she was one of those pregnant ladies we occasionally see but always flash a judgemental glance at these days. You know the type, usually spotted out the back of a Westfield mall or a PAK'nSAVE car park.

My mum was pregnant with me in late 1972, back when nobody knew that smoking was bad for you— or knew it was bad but just did not give a shit. Mum even tells me that she and the surgeon who performed my circumcision shared a smoke as they chatted about how to care for my mutilated genitals right after the procedure. It was probably to help them relax as I wailed in the corner with a nappy that started to resemble the flag of Japan. Smoking was still a rather glamorous activity back then. Instead of filthy glances, Mum was possibly given a thumbs up for exposing her foetus to such luxury—the seventies equivalent of playing Mozart to the unborn child these days.

Mum was a menthol smoker, too, so perhaps it gave her womb a rather pleasant minty aroma.

I've been told I cried a lot after I was born. Like, nonstop waaaaaahing for months and months on end. My guess is I was just hanging out for a good solid nicotine hit instead of the passive smoke I was receiving now that I'd been born. It was a lot to ask of a newborn baby, to go cold turkey after nine months of getting me and my tiny lungs hooked.

Mum even told me a story about my crying which she remembers with regret to this day. One day she was so frustrated by my relentless crying that she thrust me down into the bed with such aggression that I bounced up from the mattress and banged my head on one of the wooden corner posts with quite a thump. I stopped crying, though, and there were no visible marks, so no professional medical opinion was sought.

She has confessed that she used to breastfeed me while sipping on a coffee and smoking her fags. What Mum lacked as a responsible parent she certainly made up for with her impressive displays of multi-tasking.

This multi-tasking carried on through the years, too. Toilet-training was done in conjunction with another of her favourite activities—watching *Days of Our Lives* on her new colour TV.

By the age of three I had the voice-over to the opening credits of that show down to a fine art and could speak and hum along with perfect timing. While other kids my age were singing along to the *Wombles* song, I was sitting on a potty in our lounge in a haze of nicotine, saying, 'Like sands through the hourglass, so are the days of our lives,' in perfect time with the bloke on the telly.

I would remain on my potty for as long as it took to produce a stool. The payment for a poo? A jellybean. I loved jellybeans, so this was a reward worth pushing for. And, boy, did I push hard to produce the brown gold. It was a sheer miracle I didn't push out one of my vital organs during a potty-sesh.

*

Levin is not a big place. But when you are a toddler, everything is huge. The gum tree in our front yard by the letterbox was huge. The caterpillars that ate the leaves of this gum tree were huge. Everything seemed bigger than me. My life revolved around a bunch of familiar locations—our house in Liverpool Street, my grandparents' homes and my Uncle John and Aunty Robyn's house, and that was it. Robyn and John lived about a kilometre away from us, but it seemed like an impossible distance to me.

I wasn't included in most of the fun stuff Bridget got to do because she was two years older than me. It was not uncommon for me to be left at home, bawling, while Bridget went off to do big four-year-old stuff, like hopping on Uncle John's pushbike to be doubled.

You don't see too many people doubling anymore, but it was a big thing then, a way to turn one bike into two by giving someone a lift. It's not called doubling anymore—it's more commonly known as an accident waiting to happen.

There were numerous ways to give a passenger a lift on your bike—it all depended on the style of bike. They could sit up on the handlebars or on the bar if you had a ten-speed, or on the carrier at the back if you had a bike like a Cruiser or a Raleigh Twenty.

I was envious beyond belief that Bridget was old enough to go for rides on the back of Uncle John's bike. I was promised I'd get a turn when I was old enough, but that day never came, because my selfish, attention-seeking sister ruined it for everyone forever when she didn't listen to Uncle John's very simple instruction to keep her feet away from the spokes.

She ended up in hospital with bandages covering her badly mangled ankle. Then she got presents and attention as a reward for her stupidity. I should have been the one getting presents and sympathy—I had just found out that I would never get to be doubled by Uncle John.

I can't remember many specific details of my first few years, apart from being bossed around. By Mum. By Dad. But especially by my big sister, Bridget. Imagine that—from king sperm to the lowest ranking member of a four-person family. Being two years younger than Bridge she had a massive size and control advantage. I was one of her toys. But what made me more awesome than any toy then available was that I didn't require pesky double A batteries that would power a device for just twenty minutes before going flat.

I did get revenge on Bridget years down the track when I found the secret hiding place where she stashed her intimate personal teenage diary. She kept it right at the back of her undies drawer. I read that diary on a regular basis, but I could never use Bridget's secrets against her, because that would have meant answering the question: 'What were you doing rummaging through my undies in the first place, you sick fuck?'

The truthful answer is I WAS searching for her diary when I ventured into that particular drawer, but it would still have cast a shadow of suspicion over me. And since I was already a gawkish pre-orthodontic thirteen-year-old, the last thing I needed was my family thinking I was a potential sexual deviant.

It was incredibly frustrating, sitting on all this incriminating evidence but being unable to use it, though I did manage to play some psychological mind games with the intelligence I had gathered:

> **Bridget:** Mum, can I borrow the Rav4? I just want to pop round to Sonya's.
> **Mum:** Sure, Bridge. But drive carefully. Go straight there and back—I don't want you driving in the dark.

Hearing the negotiation taking place in the kitchen I would, at this point, appear from wherever I had been, to join the conversation.

> **Me:** But make sure you DO actually go to Sonya's and not to Michael McKenzie's place instead.
> **Bridget:** You are such a dick. I hate you.
> **Mum:** Bridget, that's no way to speak to your brother.
> **Me:** Yeah, Bridget.
> **Mum:** And Dominic, you stay out of this.

So Bridget would bunny hop off in Mum's Toyota Rav4 with the big yellow L-plate blue-tacked into the corner of the back window, thinking, 'How the fuck does that annoying little shit know about my mad, obsessive and almost unhealthy obsession with Michael McKenzie?'

AND as a small added bonus—the icing on this sibling-rivalry-flavoured cake—Bridget would get a telling-off for calling me a dick. My older sister might have silenced me as a toddler, but I was now bigger and stronger than her. I was the ugly duckling who was transforming into a beautiful swan. Albeit a beautiful swan who went about reading other people's private documents to try and use their secrets against them.

When I was about four, my parents had me tested by various medical and psychiatric professionals. They wondered if I had learning difficulties, because I was such an awkward, clumsy, quiet and introverted kid. No one talked about 'learning difficulties' back then. The language they used wasn't quite so friendly. In a 1977 nutshell, they wondered if I was retarded. Just mildly. Kind of a low end of the scale retard. That would be okay. I could still go to a normal mainstream school—I'd just be put in the dumb class each year.

In the end, the tests revealed I was completely normal but just very quiet; I never really had the opportunity to speak because of my bossy older sister . . . and I was probably hanging out for a smoke, too.

By the time Bridget was five and off to school, I was three and Daniel was one. Then when I turned five, Charlotte arrived so I never really had that opportunity to be Mum and Dad's favourite. (Spoiler alert:

that bit does come . . . much, much, much later in the book.)

I have a theory about my mum and her parenting technique. She never wanted us to enjoy our childhoods too much, because hers was incredibly strict and hard. In a way she would have felt short-changed if her own children had it way more awesome than she did. She would remind us how spoilt we were whenever we got to experience something she had missed out on, either because it had not been invented when she was little or because her own parents couldn't afford it. I'm not talking big things, either, but things like: 'You kids are so bloody lucky to get your own towel. When I was your age I had to share a towel with my five sisters!' She had grown up in a family with fourteen kids.

So even though we were a middle-class New Zealand family with our own three-bedroom home in a pleasant enough suburb, Mum still lived like it was the Depression.

She even regarded fresh bathwater as a treat. To avoid fights, the oldest always had the first bath, and everyone else had to jump into their soupy water, so I only heard how spoilt I was to be cleaning myself in this pristine virgin tap water if Bridget was away somewhere. I'm surprised Dan and Char are not more messed up after a lifetime of bathing in disgusting third or fourth hand bathwater night after night. The inmates in one of those notorious Bali prisons would have a more sanitary approach to personal hygiene than that!

We never had fresh orange juice, either. It was always packet powder stuff, usually Raro. One sachet of Raro was supposed to be mixed with one litre of water for optimum taste, but Mum would just pour the contents of the sachet into the biggest empty vessel she could find and then fill it up to the brim with tap water. Sometimes this faux-juice was so diluted you could have served it to visitors as actual water and they wouldn't have questioned it. The biggest vessels we owned were occasionally unavailable, either because they were already full of some other liquid or because one of the neighbours had borrowed them. (This was not uncommon at the time. Neighbours would borrow all sorts—milk, flour, sugar, utensils, partners.) On these very occasional occasions, my poor young mum would have no option but to follow the instructions and put the packet of Raro in with one litre of water. The taste would be amazing, like a gift from the orange-juice sachet gods. But even as our tastebuds came alive with delight, we would be reminded just how spoilt we were. Sometimes Mum would drive the message home with a story from her own childhood, which was often a wee bit hard to believe, even for a gullible kid. It might be something like, 'We didn't have water when I was your age. One week the taps broke and your granddad made all us kids use his old bathwater as our drinking supply for the week.'

When we looked unconvinced, she would go into defensive mode and say, 'You ask Nana next time you see her! You just ask her! She'll tell ya.'

Nana's memory was sharp as the teeth of a piranha, and when we asked her she usually had no recollection of these events—including the one about children drinking water full of my grandfather's dead skin particles!

There's another story Mum loved to tell us growing up and still repeats to this day, the details unchanged through the decades. It's about a special needs kid she rode the school bus with every day in Levin. His name was Owen and, according to my mum, he had 'a head the size of an orange'.

Now, as a kid, you believe this. You can vividly visualise some kid who looks just like you . . . except this one has a ridiculously tiny head.

As you get older and hear the story a few more times, you realise that your mum is exaggerating—shrinking this poor kid's head measurements down to make the story a bit more attention grabbing. I mean, have you in your own life ever seen someone with 'a head the size of an orange'? These people just do not exist! Except babies, of course, but their orange-sized heads don't stand out, because they are in proportion with a body the size of a Vogel's loaf and toothpaste-tube-sized limbs. If you Google it, you might be able to find an image of someone somewhere sometime who had a head the size of a ripe satsuma, but it's highly unlikely you would have seen it on a school bus in very small town New Zealand in the 1950s. Chernobyl maybe . . . not here.

As the story goes, my mum and Aunty Robyn were

being mean to this poor wee fella Owen on the bus one afternoon. Presumably, they were drawing attention to the size of his head and comparing it to a piece of produce high in vitamin C. Owen gets off first. He tells his mum what happened. His mum phones my granddad. When the bus arrives at home, granddad is waiting at the letterbox with a leather belt in hand and gives the girls such a thrashing they never bully anyone ever again.

I have no doubt that the parts of the yarn involving my granddad are true. He was a big fan of discipline. Granddad had to be strict with fourteen kids to keep under control. He loved being strict almost as much as he loved having sexual relations with my nana—and the twenty-eight little shoes on the front doorstep were a good indicator of how much he loved these encounters.

Although our own Dad was strict, when he went off to work each morning I remember waving goodbye then waiting impatiently for him to come home again in the early evening. Often he would arrive during the day for unannounced visits.

These surprise visits were because Dad needed to use the toilet to, ummm, how can I put this delicately? To download the new album from Snoop Loggy Log. He couldn't go anywhere but home. Being a preschooler, it didn't occur to me that this was weird. I was still getting paid in confectionery for shitting in the plastic bowl in the lounge, so I was not the right person to be judging the toilet habits of anybody else.

Years later, when I started working in radio, I met a Samoan DJ called Nickson. Like my dad, Nickson was unable to handle 'away games'. But Nickson was even worse—if he went on holiday, he would avoid going for the entire time he was away. Imagine that—his sphincter muscle must have the strength of an Alsatian's jaw.

We ended up moving from Levin to Hastings when I was four. Dad had secured a work promotion so we were told we were leaving. I think I was happy about it. It's funny how a brain that young processes things. I remember being excited about the big move for two reasons:

1) Hastings had a theme park (well, it was no Disneyland but by legal definition it was known as a theme park) called Fantasyland.

2) Family friends Ben and Daphane lived in Hastings. On a previous visit Daphane, who worked as a check-out girl at the Co-op supermarket chain, had let me put groceries into a brown paper bag at the checkout.

In short, Hastings held out the tantalising prospect that I would pack some more groceries. I was four and it was the late seventies and this was the sort of event that would qualify as a positive memory.

I also hoped that fleeing Levin would spell the end of haircuts by Granddad Williams. Granddad owned a pair of hair clippers and made himself available for free boys' haircuts every weekend. Given the number of sons and grandsons he had, the waiting line would often be busier than a Just Cuts on a Saturday morning.

It is worth noting that Granddad was a school head-master with no actual hairdressing experience, so the only cut he was able to do was the 'number 1'. To this day I am not even sure what this means, but I was sick to death of being called a 'Kina Baldy'. The thought of a fresh start in Hastings was exciting. At the age of four I would get the chance to let my hair grow to its full mousey-brown potential and pack groceries. I was getting old . . . and I could not have been happier.

THE HASTINGS YEARS

We moved from Levin to Hastings not long before my fifth birthday. Our house was in a cul-de-sac called Galway Place. Dad worked within walking distance at a place called AHI. I have no idea what his job was—an accountant, maybe? That's just a guess, because he loves money so much. He doesn't need it or spend it—he just likes it—so working as an accountant would suit him. I can recall all of Dad's workplaces, although I have no clue what the hell he did at any of them. All I know is that they were roles flexible enough to allow him to pop home for a poo whenever he was turtle-heading.

As well as being incredibly strict and never shy of using his leather belt for disciplinary purposes, Dad was also incredibly playful. I remember standing on the driveway of our house in Galway Place at lunchtime and waving goodbye as he went back to work for the rest of the afternoon or until his next bowel movement, whichever came first. Dad would put the apple he was holding between his teeth and do a walking handstand up the road. I thought it was hilarious. I think Dad stopped doing this after a twenty-cent piece fell out of his pockets and got lost in the grass.

Dad's frugalness may be the reason why we never got to have KFC despite years and years of pleading and nagging. Shit, we went on about it. Why Dad didn't just attempt to suffocate us all by jamming potato and gravy down our throats like polyfilla is a mystery to me. Our obsession with KFC was because it was just so shiny and new compared to every other food place. And it was American. American things just seemed way more exciting than New Zealand things. Fast food had not really taken off in New Zealand yet. McDonald's only had two branches, in Porirua and Auckland. And pizza wasn't a mainstream takeaway yet. The only chain that had really grown to any great extent by this stage was KFC. The first KFC opened in New Zealand in 1971, in Auckland. By 1980 there were thirty-seven outlets. It was called 'Kentucky Fried Chicken' then. They dropped that name in favour of the acronym sometime in the nineties when marketing geniuses decided the word 'fried' was a negative. Personally, I don't know why they bothered. As soon as you go into a KFC and see the massive deep-fryers behind the serving counter, it's a bit of a giveaway as to how the chicken is prepared.

I don't remember ever eating KFC in Hastings. I do remember the brilliant TV ad they ran for years in the seventies, though. Everybody knew it, loved it and sang it. It's funny thinking about it now because it serves as a reminder of how few rules existed in the world at large and how uncomplicated life was, even marketing. The classic ad was a cartoon of a family of fatties in the car together—Mum, Dad and two kids. They weren't just a little bit fat, either—they were fully obese! And one of the lines in the jingle was the kids complaining about getting thinner.

These days fast-food chains tend to avoid having any fatties anywhere near their commercials. I miss that simplicity. What's wrong with chucking a chubby or two into a fast-food ad?

If you want to see it, you'll find it on YouTube. Search for 'KFC Hugo and Holly' and it'll take you to it. Unfortunately for us Harvey kids, singing the ad was as close as we ever got to experiencing KFC.

*

When I turned five I joined Bridget at nearby Mayfair Primary School. My first teacher was Mrs Crompton, who at the time was, I think, the oldest living woman in the world. She must have been at least 186. Hard to know, though, because when you're five, almost everyone looks big and old in comparison to you. At the time I thought Mrs Crompton hated teaching and hated children. Especially five-year-olds. At least that's the impression she liked to give to her class of thirty kids, whose combined age was still nowhere close to hers.

My memories from the start of school are limited. I don't recall hating it or loving it. I remember it was where I saw and got to use my first-ever urinal. Before starting school I had never been anywhere that had one, so that was exciting, having a giant wall to aim at instead of a ping-pong ball floating in the water. Mum had a reasonably tough time toilet-training me. My aim was so shocking that she took someone's advice and placed a small white ball in the water. My goal was to focus on the ball and try to wee on it. That was a lot of fun, chasing that ball around with my stream of wee. Ultimately, though, it did not fix the frustrating problem she had of the wee on the floor because it took years before I finally mastered 'the shake'. It's fairly good now, but still not perfect. As soon as I think I have mastered the shake, my penis will send me a reminder of who's the boss by sending a drop or two into the front of my undies a few seconds after I have zipped her up. I'm sure my penis is a lady because that is such a bitchy thing to do.

The urinal at school was also where I learned that you don't need to pull your shorts and underpants all the way down to your shoes to go wees. I stopped doing that when I realised all the other boys just pulled their shorts down as far as necessary, a few centimetres. I blame my bizarre technique on my dad. I was just copying the way he did it at home. It was still another few years before I found out that Dad's technique of taking all his clothes off before having a poo was not something everyone did.

I can't recall any of my friends' names, but I had plenty . . . well, three. Mum remembers things a bit differently—she loves to tell a story about coming to school one lunchbreak to drop off my lunch, which I had accidentally left at home in the morning. By accidentally, I mean entirely on purpose. The thought of going hungry was often more mouth-watering than eating ham and chicken luncheon sandwiches made by Mum. Dad's frugality meant that Mum's weekly grocery allowance was a lot smaller than it needed to be. The Harvey family grocery budget was similar to that of an anorexic senior citizen living alone. This meant corners had to be cut. Glad Wrap was considered a luxury, so we were sent to school with sandwiches wrapped in waxy baking paper, and by lunchtime the bread was hard and crunchy. Fortunately, the luncheon with its numerous preservatives and additives never expired.

So Mum turned up to school with my forgotten lunch and, after searching around the grounds, found me sitting all alone. As she walked back to the car she felt so sorry for me she claims she cried. What a lady—loving her young son so much that his lack of social skills would bring her to tears . . . but not an ounce of remorse about making me eat fucking cardboard for lunch.

It's no surprise that I chose to isolate myself from the rest of the population at lunchtime. Swapping food was a fairly popular thing to do at the time, and top currency were things like chippies, chocolate biscuits and little cartons of Zap flavoured milk. Unfortunately I was never in the game, with my lunchbox stacked with untradeable items. The only exception was Friday. This was the day we got to take jelly crystal sandwiches to school. It was such a treat I'd usually eat them in the morning during playlunch. Alongside the luncheon sandwich described earlier I usually had a box of raisins and a couple of feijoas from the neighbours' tree that overhung our property. The best thing about the raisins was the little box they came in. Once the raisins were eaten, you could blow into the box and it would make a little whistling noise. Bear in mind this was regional New Zealand in the late 1970s. There was so little to do that using food packaging as a whistle or stomping on empty Zap cartons to make a loud popping noise were considered legitimate forms of entertainment.

Mum also tells a story about arriving at school one day to pick me up for something and finding me sitting in Mrs Crompton's class with my mouth taped shut, a punishment for talking in class. It's not something schools could get away with now without it ending up as a story on *Campbell Live*, but back then disciplining children by humiliating them was sweet as. And I suspect I was quite happy to sit with my mouth sealed shut. I was unable to speak, which sucked, but it also meant I was unable to eat those ghastly things that looked a bit like sandwiches, so that was a silver lining.

The best memory I have of the Hastings years was the theme park Fantasyland. It's not there anymore. A while ago it went through an overhaul and became a hydro slide park called Splash Planet. This was before Auckland's Rainbow's End had even opened, and in those days the Gold Coast only had Sea World, so even for the rich kids who were lucky enough to a) go on a plane and b) travel overseas, it was not the theme park Mecca it is today.

For a long time Fantasyland was the closest thing New Zealand had to a theme park. And it was right on our doorstep. For a child it is hard to imagine many things more awesome than living close to New Zealand's coolest park. This thing put Hastings on the map and made it a destination.

I can see why Fantasyland's time came and went. There was no way it could cut the mustard in this day and age—kids have so many more entertainment options available to them now. The idea of going to a park where the only ride is a miniature train that does a lap of the park is what the ungrateful little bastards would probably describe as lame. But lame was not even a word in our vocabulary. We were easily entertained.

I'm not sure how often we went to Fantasyland, but I remember going there a lot, like most weekends. I suspect Dad purchased an annual family pass and wanted to get the absolute best return on his investment. We loved this place. It had its own pirate ship that you could climb around and play in, a big brick castle with a moat, a man-made pond and little rowboats, minigolf, a flying fox and a giant spaceship that we would climb up and slide down. There was also Noddy Town, a village with lots of small buildings. It was based on the Enid Blyton series of children's books. Noddy was still socially acceptable back then. Nobody seemed to care that he slept in the same bed with his friend with the large ears, called Big Ears. And hung out with a golliwog. Later this story and characters were banned due to their racism, but that didn't even cross our minds. We just liked the stories and all the characters . . . even the coloured fellow.

Noddy Town was the perfect size for kids, but back-breaking work for adults, since a serious amount of crouching down and crawling was involved in getting in and out of these tiny dwellings. Mum and Dad used to run round the park and play with us, but after an unfortunate incident on the pumpkin slide Dad eventually ended up tapping out. After that he'd just walk around the park with a newspaper tucked under his arm.

Showing off, Dad had climbed into the giant pumpkin—it was massive for a pumpkin but still way too small for a grown man to be inside. He then climbed the ladder and went down the steel slide. Because this slide was not intended for adults it was a bit narrow, so Dad got wedged and had to push his way down with his hands instead of sliding. Usually this would be no big problem, but on this particular summer's day it must have been around thirty degrees. The surface of that slide was like the hotplate of a barbecue. Dad was yelling as he painfully shimmied his way down the slide in his walk shorts. It only took him a few seconds to get down and off the slide but it was long enough for him to lose the skin on the back of his legs and leave inflamed red blisters that lasted for weeks. I reckon they would have healed faster, but there were a couple of things he did that possibly slowed things up:

1. Because this was a time when nobody walked around carrying a bottle of water, Dad had to seek comfort in the nearest body of cold water he could find, which happened to be the little man-made lake next to the castle. It gave Dad instant relief, but I'm not sure it would have helped. There were signs up informing people that the water was unsuitable for swimming or drinking, so I'm hazarding a guess that its healing qualities were limited.

2. Dad used his bum ointment on his leg burns to try to help with the healing. We called it his bum ointment,

but it was a tin of this stuff called 'Rawleigh's', a thickish golden syrup that was supposed to be a cure-all, a bit like Savlon, I guess.

No one else in the family ever used it, because we would, on a reasonably regular basis, see Dad leave the toilet and head for the bathroom cupboard where the Rawleigh's was stored. He would then get a swipe of this stuff with a couple of fingers and rub it around his bum. I'm not sure if this stuff still exists or if Dad still has issues with passing stools—when we talk these days we don't spend a lot of time discussing his bowel movements.

I could be wrong about this but it would seem common sense that the ointment used to relieve your bum inflammation should not be doubled up and used to heal the burns on your legs.

I'm not sure if it was a coincidence or not, but a few months after the slide incident a sign went up at the giant pumpkin advising that it was intended for children only. Maybe my dad wasn't the only person to lose skin and dignity at the giant pumpkin.

We were in Hastings for a couple of years before Dad got another promotion and we packed up and moved to Palmerston North. It must have been quite a lucrative step-up, because the year we moved to Palmy was also the year Mum and Dad got passports and went overseas for the very first time. They only went as far as Australia but even Aussie was still a place that only rich people got to visit.

I was excited about the move. We had already checked out the house we would be renting for a few months before the house we had bought was ready to move into. The rental place was two-storey, so that was the clincher for me. That's me, never been much of a deep thinker. I was so excited about living in a house with stairs that I had completely forgotten we would be leaving the place that had Fantasyland. It was only when we got to Palmy that I realised the flight of stairs was the best thing about the city. But this place, with a reputation for strong wind and nothing else, would be the place the Harveys would settle. And a place I was proud to call home until I was almost thirty years old.

MEET THE GRANDPARENTS

In order to get something for Christmas each year, we were required to write a letter to Santa. So every year we would write and Santa would write back. It was amazing. There were few things in the world as exciting as getting this letter, which usually confirmed if we would be granted the things we'd asked for. It was Bridget who ruined the magic for me. I was ten and she was twelve. When our letters from Santa arrived, she asked me if she could tell me a secret, but I had to promise not to say anything to Mum or Dad. She then broke the news to me that Santa wasn't real—it was just Mum and Dad who got the presents for us on Christmas day. It was quite a bombshell. A lot of kids my age had it figured out, but I was quite gullible. Had Bridge not told me, it is possible I would have continued to believe well into my twenties.

I had so many questions for Bridget. The main one was about the letter. If Santa wasn't real . . . then who was writing the letters? She presented a piece of damning evidence: a letter from Santa side by side with a letter from Granddad Williams. The writing paper was exactly the same. Granddad as Santa had written in a different style to his usual letters in a not-incredibly-convincing attempt to disguise his real identity, but he had made a fatal mistake with the stationery. What a way to have your cover blown. It was Santa 101.

After that, I started to quiz Mum a bit more about bits and pieces: the flying reindeer, the red nose, the unorthodox point of entry down the chimney and the logistics of getting so many presents to so many countries in such a small space of time. And that is when she first began to use the catchy mantra: 'If you don't believe, you won't receive.'

There is nothing like a good old-fashioned threat to restore your belief in magic.

So I continued to write to Santa, but it started to become a bit of a game. As well as writing down my wish list, I would make a point of telling Santa about Granddad and how cool he was and how much I loved him. I don't think Granddad knew I knew. He may have, though. It was about as subtle as his writing paper.

The North Pole,
November, 1983

Dear Miss Charlotte,

Thank you for your lovely letter - so beautifully written, too.
I have not received many letters from children yet, but I suppose they are leaving them for closer to Christmas. Yes - I am sure I could find a pink and pretty Barbie for you - but only if you are a good girl for Mum and Dad. Say a big Hello to your brothers and sister for me. I just can't wait to get their letters, especially from Dominic. One of my gnomes said he wanted a cricket bat but he will have to write himself.
I haven't heard from Daniel or Bridget either. Perhaps they don't want anything this year or can't be bothered writing.
I love reading children's letters, but they can't expect a present unless they write to me.
Well I must finish now and go outside to feed my reindeer. It's snowing very hard outside and I mustn't catch a cold.

Love
from
Santa Claus xxx

P.S. Don't forget to leave a bottle of beer for me on Christmas Eve - I get so thirsty delivering presents
Good bye.

As you may be able to gather from the only remaining letter from Santa I could find, I was most definitely Granddad's favourite. Though this was Charlotte's letter, Granddad managed to work in a fairly lengthy mention of me. What a champ. I think Granddad had a soft spot for me, or perhaps felt a little bit sorry for me, after he walked in on me attempting to pleasure myself by putting my genitals up against the water jet of his spa pool. After that I think Granddad accepted I was not quite right in the head, a bit different from the other grandkids. And so he would single me out from the others; he would share his absolute filthiest jokes with me. Most of them I didn't understand. Some of them I would laugh at when I thought the punchline had come. For others, where I wasn't sure if they had ended or not, Granddad would usually promise me that one day it would make sense to me. There is nothing quite as frustrating as waiting five years to find out why a joke is funny (only to discover it isn't that funny after all).

Granddad Williams died after a fairly long tussle with a smoking-related illness in 1996, when he was seventy-two. Given the quantity of tobacco and alcohol he consumed over the years, it was a fairly good life span, even if the last few years were anything but quality. It was one of those deaths where it came as a bit of a relief. This commanding man who spent most of his life as a school principal was now in constant pain and reduced to asking for help to do even basic things like getting in and out of the car.

Every time I saw Granddad Williams, for as long as I could remember, he would ask me how I was. Being a slow learner, I would reply by saying I was good. Then, in true school principal fashion, he would follow up by asking if I was 'good' or 'well'.

To this day I'm not sure why 'good' wasn't deemed to be an acceptable answer. If I asked a kid how they were and they told me they were well, I'd think they were a little odd. But that was Granddad Williams, a school principal, a father of fourteen and a bit of a stickler for detail. If he was alive today it would break his heart if any of his grandkids wrote to him using text abbreviations or acronyms. And he would call a family conference if any of his grandchildren put a K at the end of a word that should end with a G. It's somethink that a lot of Kiwis seem to do these days when they speak.

*

I reckon I did well in the grandparent lottery. I had fulfilling relationships with both sets of my grandparents and only became a grandparent-orphan at the age of forty, when my mum's mum finally passed away at her home in Levin.

On Dad's side, there was Nana and Granddad Harvey. We all loved Nana Harvey. She was hilarious—although Dad would get really mad at us for laughing at her, because she was senile. She would do outrageous things like wake up in the morning and decide to call painters in to give the kitchen a spruce-up. Dad would get a panicked call from Granddad Harvey in Levin telling him he had to come down because he'd woken up to find a team of Samoan men in white overalls painting his kitchen orange and yellow. It was hard to imagine a cooler nana than this. And her cool points would only skyrocket every time Dad got angry and told her off. In the last few years of Nana's life, Dad would get mad on most visits. He would do angry housework, lecturing her as he pushed the vacuum cleaner back and forth over the same worn spot of carpet beneath Nana's lounge chair where tobacco, which had not made the trip from her packet of Port Royal to the Zig-Zag papers in her unsteady hand, frequently gathered. Dad was one of two children. His sister Margaret was killed in a car crash before I was born and I think he felt an added burden of responsibility for his deteriorating mum.

Nana's illness got worse and worse. In her final years, she would go roaming the streets in the still of night and come home with all sorts of bits and pieces she had acquired from god knows where. Visiting on weekends we were greeted by a backyard full of prams, clothes, dolls, road cones, and anything else that wasn't locked down and that could be carried by a woman in her seventies. From 1985 until the time of her death in 1988, it is possible that the majority of unresolved burglaries committed around Levin were done accidentally by Nana Harvey. She ended up dying at home in the kitchen at the age of seventy-five. Granddad woke up in the morning and discovered her on the kitchen floor. He phoned Dad to tell him the news. Then, being a man of routine, he just worked around her to prepare his Weet-Bix and cup of tea.

Since Granddad was now in his eighties and living alone, the decision was made to put him into a retirement village. These places look like fun now, like a Contiki backpackers hostel for people who smell like urine, and where you imagine a lot of bed-hopping might go on with a lot of the widowed oldies. But until very recently, no old person willingly gave up their house for a room in a rest home. I can understand why—I suppose it felt like giving up and accepting that you were checking into life's departure lounge. Apart from the occasional daytrip in the retirement village's people mover, the only way anybody ever left these places was in a coffin.

Granddad Harvey didn't have to worry about that wooden box for a while yet. He had amazing health on his side. He was a non-drinker and practically a non-smoker—he only had one smoke a day to coincide with his bowel movement.

He was ninety-four when he died. The funny thing is I don't feel like he aged at all from the time I was born to the time he died twenty-three years later. He always had that 'granddad' look to him. This was a time when old people looked and dressed a certain way. I am certain Granddad last went shopping for clothes in his sixties, and the clothes he bought then are the clothes he wore until he died, apart from a periodic upgrade of socks, singlets and Y-fronts, I presume . . . and hope!

On special occasions we would pick Granddad Harvey up from his retirement village and take him for daytrips back to Palmerston North in the car with us. This was always fun for me, because he had this habit of reading everything he saw out loud, then following it up with a guffaw. The things he chose to read out were never particularly amusing—it could have been something as simple as a sign written on a shop window that we drove past. Granddad would say in a voice that was quiet, but still loud enough for everyone else in the car to hear: 'Pedal Pushers. For all your bikes and bike accessories. Hep-hep-hep-hep-hep.'

This was a man who was born at the end of the 1800s and had lived through the Great Depression and two world wars and spent over half of his life without television. I don't think he ever went on a plane in his life. By the time international air travel became something that regular people did, he was quite old. He said he'd seen other countries in photos in books and on the television, so he couldn't see the point of going in a plane to see them again. Because of the simple life he led, I think he was able to notice and be wowed by little things that didn't even stand out to the rest of us.

*

Nana Williams died in August 2013 at eighty-five. In the final few years she was a little bit slow on her feet, but her mind was in perfect working order. She did well to last so long given her heart was always a bit iffy. I remember going to visit her in Palmerston North hospital when she had her first heart attack—she would have been in her fifties at the time and I was still at intermediate. The fact she got another thirty good years out of that vital organ says a lot about the lifestyle she led.

Her demise was very speedy, which was, I think, a good thing. It was slow enough that everyone had the chance to say goodbye, but fast enough that our lasting memories of her would not be of her being sick, suffering or emaciated.

One day she was healthy; the next day she had some breathing trouble and was taken to Palmerston North hospital. Less than two weeks later she was driven back to her home in Levin in an ambulance, where she died in her lounge surrounded by some of her fourteen children. I am so lucky I got to have this lady in my life for as long as I did. As a child, and even as a young adult, I never fully appreciated her. I think for me she was overshadowed by her husband and the special bond he and I shared over X-rated jokes after he caught me molesting his spa pool.

I'm pleased I got to grow up and have a relationship with Nana as an adult—it gave me the chance to get to know her better and appreciate just what a truly remarkable woman she was.

Somehow Nana always managed to keep an immaculate house regardless of how many of her children or grandchildren were present.

Somehow, despite being a non-smoker and drinker for most of her life, she managed to tolerate her husband's vices, and the wall-shaking snoring that came as a result of them.

And somehow, she never forgot a birthday card for any of her children or grandchildren. It was only in my mid thirties that she finally did away with the five-dollar note that she put in the card as a gift each birthday.

Nana had eighteen good years of life after Granddad died. She travelled fairly extensively, visiting family around New Zealand and overseas. She missed Granddad terribly, of course, but after the burden of nursing him through the final few years of his life I reckon she must have enjoyed the freedom that came with being a widow (not that she would ever admit that). She kept herself busy with a daily routine that involved baking, TV, talkback radio, phone calls with her family and writing out bloody birthday cards! Church was a daily thing too—she loved it.

I loved calling in to see her, always unannounced. Whenever I was in the area I would stop by New World and pick her up a bunch of flowers, then go and visit her. She would always tell me off for not phoning in advance to say I was coming, but it was much better this way—giving her advance warning of a visit meant she would spend hours fussing in the kitchen in preparation. She would fill me in on what everyone else in the family was up to. I'd ask after an uncle, aunty or cousin and she would always know what the big news had been in their life. We would talk about movies, TV shows and talk-back radio. I don't think she ever listened to me on the radio, but she was always asking me questions about the people she did listen to—Paul Henry and Michael Laws.

I would always say to Nana as I left her house, 'See you next time, Nan.' And her reply would always be,

'God willing, Dom, God willing.' She wasn't afraid of dying, not at all. She had so much faith that she truly believed that God had a plan for all of us.

Jay-Jay, Mike and I called her up on our radio show from time to time. She was always good for a laugh. After she purchased a big new LCD screen TV, I joked with her that she should stop spending my inheritance money on these big-ticket items. She kindly informed me, live on nationwide radio, that I shouldn't get my hopes up, because I was a long way down on her list.

When my first book, *Bucket List of an Idiot*, was published in 2012, I sent her a copy. I think she thought that it was cool to have a grandson who was an author. She especially enjoyed the stories in the book about the family and growing up. The signed copy I gave her was still on the shelf in her lounge when she died. I think she would have liked this book even more . . . even the bit in this chapter where she dies. God's plan, after all!

In the middle of August 2013 she was taken to Palmerston North hospital with unstable angina, a medical condition that you would most definitely not want auto-correct to change on your behalf! She was in a fair bit of discomfort with a cough and chest pain and having difficulty breathing and eating. For the first time ever, when asked how she was she replied by saying, 'I'm not well.'

A family Facebook group was set up so everybody could be kept up to date with what was going on. A heartbreaking video was posted showing Nana as a shadow of her former self with an oxygen tube under her nose. She looked bloody terrible in it but still had her trademark wit:

> 'I'm on air, everybody. I'm on air. I just want to tell everybody that I love you. That's all. And dying's nothing to be frightened of, okay? And when I come home in two weeks' time you can say she's a proper old drama queen. Okay, God bless you all.'

There was no denying she was unwell, but I just kind of expected her to bounce back, like the time before and the time before that.

From there her health steadily declined, pneumonia kicked in and nothing the doctors could find in their bag of tricks to pump into her seemed to be able to fight it.

After my radio show on Tuesday 26 August, I flew down to Palmerston North from Auckland to see her. If this was going to be the end, I really wanted to see Nana before she died. Part of me thought it would be best to stay away, and remember her as the lady who would always answer the door with an apron on and those warm welcoming eyes, the lady who would always make me stay until I had eaten a hot meal regardless of the time of the day and whether or not I was even hungry, just because she thought I was looking too skinny.

But I owed it to her. If I had the chance to tell her just what an influence she had been on my life, I had to take it. My mum was already there along with a couple of her sisters and brothers. Mum says when I walked in Nana perked up and became more animated and alert than she had been in days. That was nice to hear. I mean, she wasn't doing star jumps or anything, but she did open her eyes and give me a strained greeting, each breathy word a considerable effort.

I sat beside her and held her hand, still warm and soft. I held her cup and gave her water. We didn't talk, just sat. I only had a couple of hours, then it was time to go back to the airport for my flight home. The other family in the room told me they would leave me alone so I could say goodbye.

I sobbed and told Nana how much I loved her. It was one of those odd situations where only one person is able to partake in the conversation. Some people are quite good at these things—not me. It was a situation I had happily managed to avoid in forty years of life.

With a cracking voice I let her know how much I was going to miss going to visit her in Levin and how much I would miss our chats. I said how much I loved and respected her and how every single memory I had of her throughout my entire life was a good one. I said I hoped she was proud of the life she had lived and the example she had set because the hole she would leave behind was a massive one, for me and so many others.

Nana squeezed my hand. It was all stuff that she probably knew, but not stuff I had ever said. It felt good to let her know while I still had the chance, though.

Nana opened her mouth and in a faint voice said, 'I love you, Dom.'

I can't imagine the effort it took her to get that out. It meant the world to me. I kissed her and left.

The following afternoon she was driven home in an ambulance and slipped away that evening with some of her children in her lounge with her. My mum described it as a beautiful death.

I was pleased about that. After living such a beautiful life it is exactly the way she deserved to go out.

KNUCKLEBONES, HOPSCOTCH AND ELASTICS

Growing up with a sister who was older than me by two years meant spending a lot of hours playing games of Bridget's choosing. I'd say this is something a majority of second children experience—I was Bridget's personal plaything and slave. She didn't want to play with me because she liked me. Oh no, it had nothing to do with her enjoying my company. Nope. I was saved for those desperate occasions when absolutely every other friend she had was unavailable. I didn't care. Even if I was being abused and bullied around, it seemed a small price to pay for the chance to play games with Bridge. The conversation usually went something like this:

Bridget: Oi, come and play elastics with me.
Dom: Really??? You mean it? Ooosh!

'Ooosh' was a saying we all used in the mid eighties. It started with everyone saying 'oooshay', but it ended up being shortened to 'ooosh'. Essentially it just meant cool, but cool was uncool at that time.

Bridget: Ewwwwww. Don't be all weird about it. You're so gross.

Dom: Sorry.

Bridget: Just don't even talk to me. Your voice is making me feel sick.

It's an odd relationship, that one—sibling situations where the eldest is real bossy but is still respected and admired by the younger kids. Maybe it's a bit like the condition Stockholm syndrome. That's this slightly fucked-up psychological thing where hostages end up feeling sympathy and empathy and warm fuzzy feelings towards their captors. I reckon that sums me and Bridge up in the single-figure years. It was like I was the people of North Korea and she was Kim Jong-il.

So whenever Bridget needed a play-buddy but had no other option, I was the go-to guy. The big three games were knucklebones, hopscotch and elastics. Mostly elastics. Because all that required was a length of elastic. The other two were not so simple.

Playing knucklebones was dependent on there being a full set of five knucklebones, which sounds a lot simpler than it was. If the bag wasn't sealed properly, or a hole had somehow formed in the bottom, one or more knucklebones would escape and go AWOL. We probably clocked up a hundred hours searching for missing knucklebones. It frequently meant emptying the junk drawer in the kitchen, which is where they were kept. Why Mum decided the third drawer down would be the best place to keep such a fiddly little item is beyond me.

Maybe it was a cunning plan specifically engineered so that we'd give the drawer a quarterly tidy-up as we searched for those little metal game pieces.

Hopscotch required chalk, which was not an item that was always on hand. Dad was never into the idea of painting a hopscotch court on the driveway, because it might put potential buyers off if we ever sold the house. Seemed like a flawed argument to me, since the carport had a massive thick oil stain that had been built up over the years by Mum's Hillman Hunter. This slick was so thick and black that for a period of time in 1983 we may have been in possession of more oil than Qatar. If a hopscotch court on the driveway was going to put off a prospective buyer, I can't imagine that an oil slick the size and shape of Australia would help to seal the deal.

Is elastics still a thing? Do little girls still play it? All it required was maybe a four- or five-metre strip of elastic, which you tie so it makes a giant loop. Ideally, you need three players—two of them stand two to three metres apart with the elastic looped around their ankles, calves, knees, thighs or waist. (The better you get, the higher the elastic goes.) The third player jumps over the elastic in a certain pattern or sequence, usually chanting a rhyme. One I remember was 'England, Ireland, Scotland, Wales, inside, outside, monkey tails.' We would chant that while jumping in and out of this elastic loop. I have no idea what the fuck it meant, but I still reckon this nonsensical chanting and jumping was a better thing for children to be doing than twerking and singing Rihanna songs . . . the exception being her song about umbrellas. Inviting a friend to stand under your umbrella on a wet day sends out a positive message about sharing.

Bridget had a bed end that was perfect to hook one end of the elastic around. My role in this game was just to stand a couple of metres away from the bed end with the other end of the elastic looped around me. She had tried using the back of a chair so she could eliminate me altogether, but that didn't work—the elastic would pull the chair down. I was her only option—but before I could play Bridget told me not to speak, move, look or even breathe in a way she found irritating. I was effectively a sturdy piece of furniture.

Elastics was banned as an inside activity in our house in December 1982, a couple of weeks before Christmas. The odd thing is that the incident prompting the ban actually had nothing to do with elastics.

It was the Christmas holidays and I was playing in the lounge with my mates Aaron and Michael. We were playing one of those games that ten-year-old boys make up when they are bored. In hindsight, the whole idea sounds like an accident waiting to happen, but at the time the three of us boys thought it was a winner.

One player stood in the middle of the room while the other two turned him around as many times as they could in thirty seconds. The player then had to try to make his way to the lounge chair without falling over.

Way harder than it sounds. And, when you are ten and there is nothing else to do, way more fun than it sounds as well. When Michael's turn came, he failed epically. He wore these glasses with lenses that must have been at least a centimetre thick, glasses that would give someone with normal eyesight a headache just from wearing them for a couple of seconds. Aaron and I spun poor Michael around at pace for his thirty seconds, then moved aside to enjoy the show as he put his arms out for balance and tried to walk to the chair. Sadly, Michael never made it. He tripped over his own ankle on the way and ended up knocking over our artificial Christmas tree, causing fake branches to fall out and decorations to go everywhere. The tree was positioned in front of the ranch slider, so had it not been December the outcome could have been considerably worse, but that's one of those things that doesn't occur to you until a couple of decades have passed.

Mum walked in to find us reassembling the tree she had spent hours assembling and decorating. She wanted answers. Fast. And since it was my house, Michael and Aaron left it up to me to do the talking. I could see exactly how this was going to end. If I told the truth about our hilarious but highly irresponsible game—if I admitted we'd been getting dangerously dizzy and stumbling around in a fairly small space on purpose—my mates would be sent home and I'd be in for a belting. A lie was the only option.

'We were playing elastics and Michael fell over and accidentally knocked the tree.'

The one glaring problem with this lie was there was no elastic anywhere near us. To this day I have no bloody idea how we got away with this one . . . but we did! I think Mum was so mad about the tree toppling over that she failed to notice that the one and only thing you need for a game of elastics was nowhere to be seen.

Mum looked disappointed with the three of us and sent Aaron and Michael home immediately. Mum and I reassembled the tree together and the only punishment I was subjected to was rather satisfying—elastics was deemed to be too unsafe to play inside. Genius!

But then I started to notice something a bit odd. This happened a bit as a kid—you would know that something had changed but could never be sure exactly what or why. Mum did her best to keep the three of us boys separated after the elastics incident. If I asked to go to one of their places to play, she would suggest an alternative. If we were going away for a road trip and there was room for a friend, Aaron and Michael were always ruled unsuitable choices. At the time I remember thinking, 'I can't believe Mum is still so mad at those guys because of the Christmas tree thing.'

In hindsight, I reckon Mum may have been concerned the three of us were gay. Or my two mates were gay and I was going to end up gay as a result of playing girly games with them.

This was 1982 and homosexuality still hadn't been decriminalised. The popular thinking was that you could spot a gay guy by seeing if he had his right ear pierced. I think Mum was fairly keen to do anything that would discourage me from being gay by association.

And in fairness to her, three young boys hanging out in the school holidays playing elastics would send anybody's eighties gaydar into overdrive. It would have been more manly for the three of us to be playing with Barbies while listening to a Culture Club cassette tape.

STEALING MILK MONEY

Everybody stole milk money in the eighties. It was a Kiwi rite of passage. One of those things we all did, along with eating Weet-Bix, running round without shoes and making prank calls in the school holidays. (Is your fridge running? I just saw it jogging past my house.) The milk money was normally used to fund our confectionery addictions. It is possible that this entry-level crime was not as widespread as I remember but just seems that way because it was a popular pastime with my hoodlum mates and me.

Milk used to be sold in 600-millilitre glass bottles with tinfoil lids. These little round foil lids were cut on a machine from big sheets of foil. The offcuts were mostly donated to school and rugby clubs to use as decorations for dances and functions. If you went to a school disco or blue light rage in the era of glass milk bottles, it's highly likely you would have walked through an entrance curtain made from milk bottle cast-offs.

We used to get what was known as 'silver top', which was full-cream milk like the blue lid stuff you buy these days. There were some other options, including milk with a striped green lid, but I can't tell you what milk was beneath those lids because we never got it. Most people just went full cream. People who got any other type of milk were seen as eccentrics—the same sort of people who didn't spank their kids or smoke in the car.

It was always a race to the fridge at breakfast time to be the one to crack open a new bottle of milk, because under the lid the first few millimetres or so was a thick cream. If you weren't into the cream a rigorous shake of the bottle would sort it out, but we all loved it on our Weet-Bix.

In 2013 Fonterra created a fancy new light-proof plastic, because apparently the old plastic two-litre bottles were making the milk bad by exposing it to too much light. Which makes me wonder how any of us survived the glass bottle years. Not only was our milk exposed to the maximum amount of light possible, once opened, it would often sit in the fridge without a lid on! Oh, the outrage!

Every afternoon, people would put empty milk bottles at the back of their letterbox. Every house in suburbia had the same letterbox—pitched roof, round hole for paper, slim slot for mail and a big space at the back for the milk or parcels. The coins to pay for the full replacements would be dropped into one of these empty bottles. The wise, the organised and those who had been victims of milk money theft before often had little plastic tokens that were used as an alternative to coins. These tokens were always left untouched, because they were of no use to us. We never got greedy and took more than we needed . . . I do use the word 'needed' very loosely, though, since we usually spent the money on fish'n'chips, lollies, bubblegum with collectable cards inside or on the spacies machines. Spacies was the abbreviated term for 'Space Invaders'. There was not a lot available in terms of home gaming at the time but Spacies that cost twenty cents a game were not hard to find; many takeaway shops had a machine or two and really lucky cities would have a spacies parlour. Stealing the milk money was quite an art. Since we were kids and there was an expectation that we would be indoors by dusk, these crimes had to be committed fairly close to home and in daylight—so you would first of all need a house with a long drive, or at the very least a house where the lounge was not looking out onto the letterbox. Once you'd selected the right property, you would have to approach the letterbox and hope there was some money to take. (Some forward-thinking folk were already purchasing their milk from dairies and supermarkets.)

Then came the hard bit—getting the money from the bottle to the safety of your palm. A sudden tilt would cause the coins to bounce against the inside of the bottle, making a jingling sound so distinct it could alert the homeowner to the crime taking place under their nose. So we would have to gently and slowly tip the bottle while making as little noise as possible—not an easy task when your adrenaline is pumping because you're shit-scared of being caught in the act by any number of people—the homeowner, other neighbours, passers-by, etc.

The punishment for being caught was too terrifying to even consider. I dare say if I was ever caught I would have pleaded with whoever nabbed me to take me to the police rather than call up my parents. Whatever punishment the cops could hand down to a ten-year-old would have been way less severe than the wrath of Dad and his leather belt.

Boy, what a thicko I was. All this risk and stress just to acquire enough money to buy a Perky Nana or bag of Burger Rings.

I lost contact over the years with my partners in crime but I've never heard any of their names on the news for being implicated in any heinous crimes, so I don't think this scheme we had going on was a gateway to bigger or more abhorrent crimes. For me, the fear of getting a hiding at home ultimately outweighed the peer pressure to fit in with these cool kids. I just found it easier to hang out with a new group—kids who didn't steal because they had generous parents who just GAVE them money to buy treats that you'd find at the very top of the food pyramid diagram. Genius! All the reward with none of the risk.

You aren't allowed to smack your kids anymore. You're supposed to reason with them, talk things through, take away their iPad for a week or put them on a naughty chair for twenty minutes. It makes me a bit nervous, though, to think how my life would have played out if the parental fear factor was not present. I could have made a few bad choices that would have screwed-up my whole life, and in the process, the lives of others. On the flip side, who knows, I could have gone on to be the world's first milk money millionaire. I was genius at it.

PITCH INVASIONS

One of the best things about going to sporting events in the eighties was the pitch-rush at full time. Like all awesome things, this had to come to an end sooner or later, but it was a shame when it was finally knocked on the head because it was so quintessentially Kiwi.

With a couple of minutes left on the clock at any sporting encounter, kids at the ground would gather at the edge of the pitch and patiently wait by the advertising hoardings that generally promoted Benson & Hedges or Rothmans, because these were the sporty smokes. This was an era when tobacco advertising was still alive and well at sports grounds.

Then, as soon as the full-time whistle was blown or the last ball bowled, the crowd would rush the field and go up to their sporting heroes. Some kids would seek out an autograph; others would just want to touch a sportsman somewhere, anywhere on his body for bragging rights. A lot of the time we would not even know whose autograph we were getting. But if there were other kids jostling to get the same person's autograph, then it suddenly made it a desirable thing to have.

Towards the last days of this New Zealand tradition, many of the players would sprint off towards the tunnel at full time to avoid the onslaught. I suspect players on the winning team quite enjoyed the post-match attention, but I imagine the losers preferred sitting in the changing room and wallowing in misery with their loser team mates to being stuck on the pitch surrounded by a swarm of autograph-hungry kids.

This is how I managed to get the signature of Martin Crowe.

It was at the Fitzherbert Oval in Palmerston North in January 1984. He was playing for Central Districts against England. All counted, I probably watched a total of five balls. We never went to the game to watch. We went to the game to find other groups of kids who we could play with. All you needed was a bat, a tennis ball and something that could be used as wickets—the forty-four-gallon drums used as rubbish bins were perfect for the job. Playing was everything; watching was boring. Then, when the proper game was a couple of overs away from ending, we would find a spot near the boundary rope and get ready to make the mad dash.

My mate Michael ended up in tears at this same game when he got the signature of one of the stars of the England side.

Michael had been given a brand-new Duncan Fearnley cricket bat just a couple of weeks earlier. This bat was his pride and joy. Nobody else was allowed to touch it. I do recall him generously letting me grip the handle on one occasion . . . but he was still holding the toe of the bat at the same time. Even though he was staying at our house that particular weekend, he was still nervous that I was going to run off and steal this bat.

When play stopped Michael ran onto the pitch, bat in hand, and sought out Ian Botham, the big-hitting, chain-smoking star of the England side.

These things were often a mad scrum. You would have one player and as many as fifty kids circled around him. Michael held his bat up in the air so Ian Botham would notice. It worked. Botham saw the bat and reached out for it. Then, using the Bic ballpoint pen he must have accidentally stolen from another kid, he signed his name on Michael's bat.

That is when Michael burst into tears and screamed as loudly as he could though his sobs:

'IAN BOTHAM! YOU RUINED MY BAT.'

Poor old Ian paused to look at this broken little boy, then kept walking and signing, probably miffed and wondering what the hell he had done wrong.

It turned out the pen had dug into the willow and was etched into the surface. I didn't see what the issue was; the bat would still work just fine and it now had the signature of one of the world's coolest cricketers on it. But Michael was inconsolable. That night his parents tried to talk him around, tell him that the bat looked good, but nothing would change his mind. From that day on, every time he played with the bat and got out cheaply, he never held himself responsible, nor did he give any credit to his opposition. It was always the fault of a cricketing legend from the other side of the world who had jinxed this chunk of wood.

TAPPING PHONES

There are still payphones around everywhere. It's a rare occasion that you see someone using them, though. The booths mostly get used these days by smokers looking for a sheltered place to light their smokes on windy days.

But before cell phones these things were big business. It was not uncommon to have to wait your turn to use a payphone. They looked very different then—they were coin-operated, rotary-dial things in red wooden boxes, much like the booths the English still use. And there was no such thing as Telecom; they were all run by the Post Office.

Despite their widespread use, they can't have been very profitable, because *everybody* knew how to use these phones without putting a coin in, a technique known as tapping.

The alternative to phone tapping was paying for the phone call, and if you didn't have any money of your own, as was often the case, you would have to steal milk money from someone's letterbox to pay for it. In other words, you could commit a crime to make a call legally—or just tap the phone, which was, I suppose, still illegal, but it was a victimless crime and it meant nobody went without their bottle of silver top.

Knowing how to tap a public payphone was essential if you wanted to be guaranteed any privacy while making your call. The majority of homes only had one phone, which sat in a central area, like the hallway or dining room, so there was no opportunity to make or take a call without everyone else knowing your business.

If the number you wanted to tap was 67816, which was our home phone number at the time, you would pick up the receiver and just tap the hook it rested on in the following sequence:

Four times.
Pause.
Three times.
Pause.
Two times.
Pause.
Nine times.
Pause.
Four times.

How anyone discovered this life hack for the very first time is a mystery to me. My guess is a staff technician at the Post Office passed the technique on to a mate and it slowly spread from there. It must have cost the Post Office hundreds of thousands of dollars in lost profit every year.

If you figured out the pattern, well done! You will be able to make a free phone call if you ever get into a plutonium-powered DeLorean car that a mad scientist has modified and driven back in time, where your mum will fall in love with you in a hilarious dilemma that could prevent you being born.

TRIVIAL PURSUIT

Board games were a big part of being a kid in the 1980s. These days? Not so much. Maybe during a beach holiday at one of those already-furnished-with-someone-else's-old-shit beach houses you book online. Or at home if the wi-fi is down. I'm guessing most homes are like ours now and have a few board games stashed away in a cupboard surrounded by so much junk that on those infrequent occasions when you have the great idea to pull out Hungry Hungry Hippos for a quick best-of-five series, you quickly change your mind. To reach the Hungry Hungry Hippos, you have to remove the Ab King Pro you only used twice, the Black & Decker dust-buster that works but just needs a new nozzle and a box of old photo albums. Then comes the hardest part—you realise that Hungry Hungry Hippos is the game at the very bottom of the stack, so to extract it becomes a game in itself—board game Jenga. You have to try to remove the Hungry Hungry Hippos box without all the games on top crashing down.

So usually the poor old board game takes a back seat to something far more enjoyable, like having a TV binge and watching eight hours' worth of *Game of Thrones* that you have recorded on My Sky.

It's a blessing and curse that board games have lost the dominant spot they used to hold in family homes. A blessing because, speaking from Harvey family experience, some of our biggest arguments were caused by board games. During one particular game of Cluedo, Daniel almost ended up killing me . . . in the hallway, with the candlestick.

We had some epic battles. Later on in school holidays, when we were old enough to be left at home alone, it was not uncommon for us to have to call Mum or Dad at work for dispute resolution advice. We tended to follow a fairly predictable pattern. We would play a game and eventually become fixated on it. Once it became an obsession, the fierce competitive gene would kick in. This is usually when the trouble started. After this it was usually not long before Mum or Dad would ban the game because it was 'more bloody trouble than it's worth'. And that's when the game in question would be taken from the eye-level shelf in the cupboard next to the hot water cylinder and moved to the top shelf in Mum and Dad's wardrobe. I loved how it was always the *game* that was banned—surely after Monopoly, Last Card, Cluedo, Battleships and Guess Who had all been banned it should have been crystal clear that the problem was not the Parker Brothers but the Harvey brothers!

Monopoly was the biggest instigator of fights. I don't think we ever managed to properly finish a game because Dan and I (but mostly Dan) had a habit of kicking the board over when it became apparent that bankruptcy was imminent. It was awesome. You could sense it coming every time. Dan would be down to his last little bit of cash, then he'd roll the dice and land on someone else's property stacked with houses or hotels, requiring him to pay vast sums of rent. At this point he would either magically stump up the cash, which we would accuse him of stealing from the money tray, or he would create an argument and then kick the board over.

To be fair, a good solid board-kick was seen as the ultimate admission of defeat by the rest of us. Had Dan just bowed out gracefully and said something like, 'I can't pay that. I'm out. You've got me this time,' it would have been a way less satisfying victory than a firm board-kick and walk-off.

The one game that went on to become the absolute undisputed family favourite was Trivial Pursuit. It was first released in 1982 and by 1984 was the world's top-selling game. Some twenty million copies were sold in 1984!

Before it was sold in New Zealand, the only Kiwis who had it were people who had gone to the US for a holiday and bought one over there, which was the one and only way you could get consumer goods that were not sold here.

It was 1986 when New Zealand retailers finally received stock. Not long after the arrival of Trivial Pursuit in New Zealand came the arrival of a brand-new shop in Palmerston North, the Toy Warehouse. And that is how the Harvey family got our own copy of Trivial Pursuit for five dollars.

As part of the store's opening celebration, they were offering the world's most in-demand board game to their first twenty customers for five dollars. I can't remember exactly how much the retail price was, but it was around the fifty-dollar mark.

The discount was so large that Mum decided she should go to the Toy Warehouse hours before the 8 am grand opening just to make sure she was one of the first twenty customers. So that is what she did—set her alarm for 4 am and made her way down to the Toy Warehouse. Surprising to nobody but herself, she was the very first person in line. A line eventually did form, but it was nowhere near the crowd of riot proportions my parents had anticipated. At the more sensible time of 6 am a couple of people arrived and joined Mum, and another handful of people came down at 7 am. By the time the doors were flung open at 8 am, there were eleven people waiting outside, so everybody got one of the bargain-priced games.

Why my parents, who are reasonably sensible people, thought there was going to be a line of thousands is a mystery to me. Trivial Pursuit was awesome . . . but it was just a board game. I suspect most people would have been happy to get a good night's sleep and pay the RRP at a time that was more convenient to them—like daytime!

Once we got it, it became the family's go-to game. It was not uncommon to spend an evening playing Trivial Pursuit instead of watching the TV. Part of the pleasure Dad got out of playing it was the satisfaction of knowing it had only cost him five dollars, while other people around town had paid full price. He would mention it with a sound of amazement in his voice every time we set up the game-board, game pieces and boxes of cards:

'Can ya believe it? Only five dollars. For all of this. Bloody unbelievable.'

Then we would play and Dad would win—or be in the lead when we decided to suspend play. The problem was it took so damn long before one person had all six little coloured pieces in their game-piece that bedtime usually arrived before a winner was found.

With the Harvey kids, Trivial Pursuit success went with age. Bridget was the eldest and the best, I was second eldest and second best, then Daniel, then Char. It makes sense, I suppose, since it is basically just general knowledge—the older you are, the more stuff you should know.

But then something really puzzling started happening in our house. Daniel started getting really, really good, like oh-my-god-how-the-hell-did-you-know-that-you-are-a-genius good.

Up until this point Dan, who was eleven, had just been on the good side of average with his schoolwork, so this sudden advancement blew everyone away. It was getting to the stage where Mum and Dad were considering having him tested to see if he was a child genius, like the kid on *Doogie Howser, M.D.*

He was nailing questions that most adults would pass on. Stuff like:

'What animal was paraded through the streets of Paris on Mardi Gras to remind people not to eat meat during Lent?'
'What woman was arrested for voting in the 1872 election for US president?'
'What became America's first organised sport, in 1664?'

If you could answer any of these questions without doing a Google search, well done. You might give Dan a run for his money. FYI, the answers are:

'An Ox.'
'Susan B. Anthony.'
'Horseracing.'

We would all ask Daniel how he knew the answers. He would just shrug his shoulders and say something like, 'I don't know. I suppose I just read a lot!' When the truth eventually came out, we discovered he was not lying about that.

Explanation—the discovery was made one evening when Mum and Dad had some friends over and they decided to play a game of Trivial Pursuit, as you did in the eighties, potentially while eating something called a vol-au-vent, a little round pastry with a filling. They were all the rage at dinner parties at this time. When Mum got the game out, they discovered only one of the two boxes of questions was inside. The game could still proceed with only one box but it would be annoying. The following day, Mum turned the house upside down looking for the missing box of question cards. She found it in the most unlikely of places—under Daniel's bunk bed.

A family inquiry was launched. It was not uncommon to find random bits and pieces under our beds—the occasional bowl with Weet-Bix residue that had gone hard and was now firmer than concrete, or a near empty mug with a couple of centimetres of Milo that had become a furry greenish solid. But never before had such an important part of the family's most beloved board game been found anywhere other than where it belonged. After an intense interrogation, Dan cracked and 'fessed up—he had been reading and memorising the cards. That cheeky little fucker! What a genius move. I was kicking myself. Firstly, why hadn't I thought of that?

And secondly, I shared a room with the guy—how the hell did I not know this scam was going on right underneath me? Oh, that's right. I was too busy attempting to masturbate myself to death to care what shameful act he was up to down below.

After that, Dan was forced to sit out any future games of Trivial Pursuit. His goal was now to use the pointless trivia he had stored to try and spoil it for the rest of us. Bridget and I would be sitting at the dining room table playing and she would ask me my next question:

'What was broken in Oxford, England on 6 May 1954?'

And that is when Dan, who was in the next room with the TV on, would yell out right on cue:

'THE FOUR MINUTE MILE!!!'

This game sabotage eventually stopped, but it took a while. Dan may have been quick when it came to memorising the questions and answers in Trivial Pursuit. Unfortunately for him and his limbs, it took him considerably longer to learn that the answer to the question, 'What happens when you try to wreck other people's games by being a dickhead?' was 'A vicious dead leg that will render you unable to walk for the next ten minutes.'

SAVING THINGS FOR BEST

Mum was a big believer in saving things for best. It's a strange idea when you think about it. What is best? I'm still not entirely sure. I can, however, tell you what 'best' was not—it most definitely was not the four children she carried in her womb for a combined total of three years!

We would dry ourselves off after a shower or a bath with towels that were so scratchy, starchy and worn that you could have used them as a substitute for sandpaper. I often wondered how Mum managed to fold these things without them snapping in half. Meanwhile, sitting up on the top shelf of the hot water cupboard were a selection of unused luxury bath towels that Mum and Dad had been given as wedding presents fifteen years earlier.

'Best' wasn't Mum and Dad, either—they never allowed themselves the treat of using the items being saved for best . . . unless we had visitors deemed important enough to cross this elusive threshold.

It was the same situation at teatime. We all ate off these bizarre yellow plastic oval-shaped plates, the sort you might take on a camping trip. Meanwhile, up on the top shelf of the kitchen cupboard sat a pristine set of dinner plates with pictures of fruit on them—an apple and a pear with some grapes and berries. How do I remember the exact pattern? Probably because I never saw these plates with any actual food on them!

We also had a set of six fancy placemats judged far too special for regular family use. Made by a firm called Jasons, these things had pictures of the best landmarks New Zealand had to offer at the time. There was the Wellington cable car, the Chateau building in Tongariro, the Pania of the Reef statue in Napier, and the rest were lakes. These things were kept in their original box in a drawer, right on top of the special cutlery that was kept in a plush velvet-lined box.

I still recall Mum's fury the day she was backed into a corner and forced to use these placemats for a friend of Dad's who didn't meet the necessary criteria.

Dad's mate Brian was up in Palmerston North from Wellington for some business meetings. They went out for an evening game of tennis, and then, after freshening up in his motel room, Brian came over for dinner.

I was sitting in the lounge with Dad and Brian when, from the kitchen, Mum yelled out, 'Dominic, can you set the table, please?'

Without pausing to think how awkward I was about to make things for the adults in the room, I shouted back to the kitchen, 'Since Brian is here shall I use the good placemats or just the normal ones?'

Brian, who had his near-full glass of Lion Brown up to his lips at the time, burst into laughter, causing a fine spray of froth to float through the air and down onto the chocolate brown shagpile carpet.

I thought he was strange. I had no idea why he was

laughing—it wasn't like I'd made a joke or anything.

After a pause for thought, Mum said, 'Ummm . . . yes, of course we'll use the good ones.'

When I was in the dining room setting the table with these photos of New Zealand's finest scenery, Mum caught my eye and shot me an evil glance from the kitchen. I responded with a what-have-I-done face. And then the penny dropped. Mum had not intended to use the best gear for Brian. Nor did she want Brian, or any other guest for that matter, to know there was such a thing as 'for best'.

After giving me 'you wait until Brian leaves' looks all night, she spelled it all out for me later that evening.

The master plan was this: guests to the Harvey house who were considered worthy of the A-grade gear would be led to believe this was normal and not anything special. So the VIPs would assume that the plush fluffy towels they were using to dry their very important bodies were just the towels we used all the time. It always struck me as odd. I thought you'd want your top-tier house guests to know you liked them enough to give them the special treatment. Evidently, it was more a scheme so these guests would think we were rich or something. It was a flawed system, though, because Mum's vehicle at the time was an old Hillman Hunter. Any illusion of wealth she was attempting to create was shattered the moment our guests turned into the driveway.

In fairness, Mum really liked Brian so was possibly okay with him getting the Royal Doulton treatment. The main concern was that us kids were going to be eating OUR meals along with the adults. And because of MY faux pas, we would now be eating over these pristine unspoiled placemats. One small blotch of gravy on the corner of the photo of Lake Wakatipu would have totally devastated her.

Mum chewed more nervously than a death row inmate having their final meal. For us kids, the entire meal was spent transporting the food carefully and cautiously from the plate to our mouths with all the precision of a brain surgeon.

Fortunately, the meal went without incident. But the biggest bonus of all? Bridget and I were spared doing the dishes after Brian left. We had a chores roster, which basically meant Mum had to do minimal housework and Dad none at all. In hindsight, the small jobs we were rostered on to do were just the smallest tip of the housekeeping ice-berg, but at the time we felt like we were exploited for free labour.

Whenever we cried foul about Dad's laziness around the house, he would remind us that he was the breadwinner. That would be considered sexist now, but at the time it was just the way it was. Dads worked, and mums, for the most part, ran the house and took care of the kids. Fathers felt they were entitled to put their feet up and relax when they got home from work in the evening because their day had been more difficult and more beneficial for the family than anyone else's.

At the time we thought we were hard done by with all these chores. On reflection, we created even more work for Mum. We did these chores to such a poor standard that she had to go and redo them later on.

It's more to do with luck than anything else that we all didn't end up horribly sick from eating off unclean plates. Dad was so frugal we were only allowed to fill the sink with hot water ONCE and the Sunlight dishwashing liquid had to be used SPARINGLY. Often Bridget would only be a couple of plates in and the water already looked like Willy Wonka's chocolate river. The dishes being washed in dirty water would then be dried by me, using a tea towel so old it would have been more effective to dry the plates with a sheer curtain!

I'm surprised I wasn't removed from dishes duty, because I was incredibly clumsy. I'd break at least one plate or a cup every week. In the cupboard where the glasses and cups were kept there was no such thing as a set of four or six. It was just a scrambled collection of bits and pieces—mostly Coke glasses from service station promotions where you spent twenty dollars and got a free glass, and old Marmite jars that we washed out and used as glasses. Lots of people did this because of the clever way the jar was designed. Once the Marmite was gone you could scrub the label off and you'd be left with a perfectly fine, slightly yeasty-smelling glass.

Ultimately, it was because of my epic clumsiness that we moved onto those yellow oval plastic plates I mentioned earlier. Finally, a set of plates that were Dom-proof.

The upside of this reputation I had cultivated was that I was considered too much of a high risk to go anywhere near the dishes on the once-or-twice-a-year occasions when the 'for best' gear was brought out of storage for our highly regarded guests.

On reflection, maybe that's why Mum liked having these nice things that she kept off limits from her children— we wrecked everything! We weren't intentionally destructive—we were just kids being kids, doing the best we could but not doing it very well. There were not too many things in the house that were not damaged, stained, chipped, ripped, cracked, torn, scratched or ruined. By keeping the few things she considered precious or important away from our permanently clammy and sticky hands, perhaps she felt a sense of control and a bit of security. Some people get pleasure from using nice things; Mum got pleasure from knowing she had nice things that she COULD use. I think that's quite sweet . . . in a fucking loopy irrational crazy cat-lady sort of way!

THE SCHOOL BATHS KEY

We had a swimming pool for most of my childhood. Actually, that's not entirely truthful. What we had was

ACCESS to a swimming pool. All schools in the eighties had their own swimming pools, where students would learn to swim and take part in school swimming sports. The Riverdale School pool was a fairly basic thing, just a concrete structure about ten-to fifteen-metres long that was plonked on the ground and painted light blue. I don't think there was any heating to take the chill off the water. And because it was outside, it sat drained for the cold months of the year . . . in Palmy that was about ten out of twelve!

Each summer, families could buy a key attached to one of those big numbered tags that you usually find inside a cow's ear. This key unlocked the pool gate and gave you unrestricted access to the school pool all summer long.

This was the cheapest way to swim in the eighties. Dad reasoned it was just the same as having our very own swimming pool . . . except it was 2.5 kilometres away in the school grounds and on a hot evening there might be another dozen families using it.

We loved swimming. What we hated was Mum's strict rule—no swimming for thirty minutes after eating food. I'm not sure where this rule stemmed from but Mum seemed convinced that any person who went into a swimming pool less than half an hour after eating food would sink to the bottom and drown, like somehow the weight of a few slices of bread with ham and chicken luncheon would be enough to sink a human. I only discovered it was possible to swim on a full stomach when I was seventeen and went to the river with a couple of mates.

We picked up a feed of McDonald's on the way. When we arrived at the swimming hole, Andrew and Clint stripped off immediately and started walking over the stones towards the water. I suggested that they should wait a bit longer for their food to settle because they might sink and drown. They burst out laughing and told me that Mum's theory wasn't true. Well, not in so many words—what they said was, 'Don't be a fucking pussy.' I was torn. I didn't want to drown, but I didn't want to look like a pussy either. Instead I compromised and only waited twenty minutes before jumping in. I'm pleased to say we all made it out of the water that day.

The other awesome thing about the school baths key was that it helped the Harvey kids to do some real life myth-busting—we found out that the school principal, Mr Richardson, was making up the story about the purple dye. Every kid lived in fear of the purple dye. Legend had it that anyone who urinated in the pool instead of hopping out and using the toilet would be found out in the most humiliating way—the water around them would turn purple . . . and then the purple dye would follow them round in the water. As an adult, this whole thing seems a bit iffy. I mean, the part about the water changing colour still sounds kinda, sorta believable. But the part about this purple water following you round the pool seems impossible.

However, when you are a kid and you still believe that a rabbit drops off chocolate eggs to celebrate Jesus being murdered under stressful circumstances, you definitely get sucked into something like the purple dye story.

One warm Sunday evening in December we went to the Riverdale pool with our uncle Matthew and, remarkably, we had the pool entirely to ourselves.

The rule of the school baths was you had to be supervised by an adult at all times. Uncle Matt was fourteen at the time, so was deemed to be old enough to look after us. Because Nana and Granddad Williams had a total of fourteen children, the age difference between the siblings is so great that Nana's last child, Matthew, came along around the same time that her eldest children started having babies of their own. So Matthew is an uncle, but definitely felt more like an older cousin.

He was a secret smoker and Granddad would have killed him if he found out, so when he was left to supervise his not-much-younger nieces and nephews, he would let us go ahead and do anything, as long as it wasn't illegal or too dangerous. And in return, we promised not to tell Granddad about his smoking. It was a sweet deal and a win-win for all concerned.

And that is how I was able to convince Daniel, who was nine at the time, to stand on the edge of the pool, pull his togs down a couple of centimetres and take a piss into the crisp water below. It was edgy stuff. Dan would be pissing ON the water rather than IN the water—so when the purple dye appeared, where would it go and who would it follow? We were determined to find out.

Even though nobody had ever seen it, we didn't think Mr Richardson was making up the story about the dye. Dan and I just wanted to watch with our own eyes as the water turned purple. Uncle Matt smoked, Dan urinated, I waited. And waited, and waited. And nothing happened to the water.

We were a bit disappointed. We thought maybe the caretaker, Mr Hodgkinson, had forgotten to put the chemicals in. We were still discussing possible reasons for the water not changing colour on the walk home when Uncle Matt finally joined the conversation with some teenage logic:

'Shit, you guys are dumb! There's no such thing as a dye that changes colour. It's just a story they make up so kids don't piss in the pool.'

It was quite the epiphany. A total game changer for Dan and me. We loved swimming but hated getting out of the pool to use the toilet for fear of missing out on some fun. Now, we could pee 'n' play without any fear of being caught out . . . or so we thought. It still took another couple of summers before either of us perfected the fine art of going for a wee in the water without looking like that is what you are doing—standing stationary in the same spot for forty-five seconds is a dead giveaway. But before too long, we were happily swimming and urinating at the same time. This act of multi-tasking is way more difficult than you would think.

*

On hot days when no adult was available to supervise, we would be forced to keep cool at home by running through the sprinkler on the lawn. This activity got very tedious very quickly, though. We did get given a slip 'n' slide as a family Christmas present one year. It was amazing! But that was boxed back up and stored at the top of the hot water cupboard after less than an hour of use because Mum decided it was too dangerous. Once something was stored at the top of the hot water cupboard, it usually remained there until a big spring-clean was held and then it would end up in a container bin or at the dump. The storage shelf at the top of the hot water cupboard was basically death row for consumer goods.

When we got the green light to use the slip 'n' slide for the first time we rolled it out on the back lawn and screwed the hose into it. The problem was our back lawn wasn't really large enough to accommodate the slide. On Daniel's third go, he wanted the biggest run-up our section would allow, so he started behind the garage and sprinted to the start of the slide. He then dived and slid along the wet yellow plastic. His run-up and dive were good . . . too good. He slid off the end before coming to a halt on the concrete path that led to the rotary clothes line. Because he had no top on, he ended up badly grazed. I was so mad at Daniel after that. Not only did he get the slip 'n' slide taken away, he also had a fantastic collection of scabs to pick all summer long.

Daniel and I loved scabs. They were awesome. This might have been due to the lack of other entertainment available at the time, but we loved following the progression of a graze as it formed a scab, then guessing just when the right time was to pick it off. If you went in too soon, it would hurt and bleed again. There was only one thing that topped the satisfaction of picking a scab off at the perfect time—getting to chew the scab. I know this sounds disgusting, but I suspect it's way more common than you think. Right up there with eating whatever we pulled from our noses and chewing toenails. We all did that as kids . . . didn't we? *Didn't we??* It's only when we get older that we learn it is gross and embarrassing to eat by-products of our own bodies . . . that's when we make sure we only ever commit these acts of self-cannibalisation in private.

PERMISSION TO SWEAR

The day we got the green light to swear without fear of being disciplined was a day of foul-mouthed celebration. We were walking around the cul-de-sac swearing at other kids in the street with reckless abandon like genuine bad-asses.

Mum and Dad were sticklers about the whole swearing thing. It was an absolute fucking no-no. The punishment for breaching this house rule would be either the belt or getting your mouth washed out with soap. Pretty sure this is classed as child abuse these days. If not, it probably should be, because it was most unpleasant. Mum or Dad, whoever happened to be assigned the task, would jam that cake of soap into our mouths and rub it around, making sure they scraped it across our teeth. Even after a good brushing and rinsing, the taste lingered for many hours afterwards. It did work, though, because the punishment was so revolting we all avoided swearing whenever Mum, Dad or soap was in the house. We also avoided it when we were playing together away from Mum and Dad, because we three older kids got a tremendous amount of pleasure out of getting each other in trouble whenever the opportunity presented itself.

If Daniel and I were playing cricket on the driveway, enjoying each other's company and having a laugh, and I accidentally hit the ball over the fence and said, 'Aww, shit!', I knew I was in trouble. Daniel would look at me with a sparkle in his devil-spawn eyes and make a loud, overdramatic gasping noise and say: 'Ummmmmmmm, I'm tellllllllllling!' Then he would sprint inside, shouting as he ran: 'Muuuuuuuuuuuuuuuum! Dominic just said a bad word!'

Why would he do such a horrible thing? Two simple reasons really:

1. Watching me have a half-used cake of Palmolive Gold poked forcefully into my mouth was way more fun than getting his arse kicked in a game of driveway cricket.

1. He knew only too well that I would do the same to him if he slipped up.

Thankfully, Daniel slipped up more often than Bridge and me, so he came out worst in this sibling snitch scheme.

Haart Place is a longish cul-de-sac, but probably not long enough to deserve two vowels. The second 'A' definitely has the feel of a clerical error at the council. From the air it looks a bit like a yard glass. We lived at number 23, which was down in the bulb end of this yardie-looking no-exit street.

When we moved in it was still a new subdivision, so there was undeveloped land behind our house and a lot of the properties were yet to erect fences. As kids we loved this. It gave us limitless places near home to roam and explore. And because there were so many young families in the street, we would share each other's toys, and often just leave them out on the street. It must have looked incredibly untidy, but nobody ever complained and nothing ever got stolen. The worst thing that happened was that the occasional frisbee or ball was run over by a non-resident who found themselves in the street and didn't know that there would be a collection of kids' toys strewn all over the road.

This was a time when kids would just play out on the street or at a neighbour's house or in one of the undeveloped paddocks until it was time for dinner, or 'tea' as we referred to the evening meal, which usually consisted of peas and something else:

Peas and curried sausages.

Peas and chops.

Peas and rissoles.

Peas and Wiener schnitzel.

Always peas. And usually a poor-quality cut of meat that had been cooked until it was about as difficult to digest as a jandal. Each mouthful of this meat had to be chewed until our jaws ached before being washed down with a generous mouthful of water.

At dinnertime Mum would go outside, and if she was unable to sight us would just shout out: 'TEEEEEEEEEEEEA'S REEEEEEEEADY!!!' So us kids, and all the other residents in Haart Place, knew that dinner had been served up at number 23, the brown faux-brick house where the Harveys lived.

Next door to us were another family called the Andersons. Brian and Meredith were the parents' names. It was considered impolite for us kids to call adults by their names, so they were always just Mr and Mrs Anderson, which must have made them feel really old, since they were probably only in their late twenties at the time. The Pettersons had kids of their own who we played with a fair bit, on the street and in each other's homes.

Mum and Dad and the Andersons became good friends, even though all they had in common was that they lived near each other and both men had substantial moustaches.

Then some falling-out occurred between Mum and Dad and the Andersons. Being a child, I was not privy to the cause of the dispute, but it happened about the same time as the side fence went up between their property and ours, so I suspect it was something to do with that. Then again, it could have been an argument about whose moustache looked more like Richard Hadlee's.

Because of the dispute the grown-ups now hated each other and it became impossible for us kids to carry on with our friendship, so we broke up and battlelines were drawn. And this was how it came about that we were given permission to swear.

I was playing on the front lawn one afternoon when Mary Anderson, who was a couple of years younger than me, rode past on her bike. We made eye contact and then she poked her tongue out at me. I was furious. I shouted out: 'GET LOST, YOU BLIMMIN' IDIOT!'

Mary burst into tears and pedalled up her drive before dropping her bike and running inside. Mum was in the kitchen with the window open and heard some of the commotion, so came marching outside to see what was going on. The story I told was truthful, but it excluded all detail that could incriminate me:

'Oh, well, you know Mary from next door? Well, she rode past on her bike and poked her tongue out at me . . . then she started crying and went home. And, yeah, that's what happened.'

Mum seemed sceptical and wanted to know why Mary had started crying. While I was in the middle of a shoulder shrug, Mrs Anderson opened her ranch slider and yelled out to Mum: 'Susan, control your children. Dominic just told Mary she was a blimmin' idiot!'

Mum asked if it was true. I gave a sheepish nod. Mum told me to wait until Dad got home. I waited, not knowing if I would get the soap or the belt. Dad got home and from my bedroom I could hear the muffled conversation between my parents. I couldn't make out what was being said, but the calm voices were encouraging. A few minutes later, all four of us were called out to the dining room and told that we were free to use the word blimmin' without being punished, especially if we were speaking to the Anderson kids. Well, Mum and Dad didn't exactly say that last bit, but we knew that's what they meant.

*

Dad is to this day a non-swearer. The only swear word he uses with any regularity is 'bloody', which he uses freely and in a number of ways. When I was a kid, the most common was a slightly drawn out and accentuated 'Blooooooody hell!' This would usually be pulled out if he was annoyed by something. There was also 'Blooooooody ridiculous' which he would use when he thought someone had done or said something ridiculous—although the thing that triggered this didn't actually have to be all that ridiculous:

> **Me:** Dad, I know the news is on, but can we change the channel and watch *Mork & Mindy*?
> **Dad:** Don't be so blooooooody ridiculous!

He also used bloody as a thinking word to fill the gaps in conversation. I think this was a bit of a nervous thing, because he mainly did it with people he didn't know well when making small talk:

> 'Yeah, the weather looks like it might . . . bloody . . . ahh . . . bloody pack in by this afternoon. I was reading the . . . bloody newspaper, and it said that some storms are on their way. Bloody ridiculous, if you ask me.'

Mum has never been a swearer. I fully remember the one time I did hear her swear, and it wasn't even one of the good top-shelf swear words she let slip, just a standard old 'shit'. In times of extreme pain, like if she got a steam burn from a pot in the kitchen, Mum's go-to words were 'blast' or 'shivers'—which I suppose were like the diet version of shit. That should give you some idea of how serious it was for her to upsize from a shivers to a shit on the day she swore.

Daniel and I were on the couch watching *Scooby-Doo* on the telly when Mum walked through the back door and down towards the hall with a basket of washing from the clothes line. The basket must have obstructed her view as she walked, because her little toe clipped the doorframe and she screamed out a single 'SHIT!' as she dropped the basket on the floor. Then she hopped around on the spot repeating it over and over, maybe five or six times.

Dan and I turned around to check what had happened and we could see Mum's little toe sticking right out at a crazy sixty-degree angle. We were in shock. Our mum had a munted foot, AND she had just said the S word! Repeatedly. It was just Dan, Mum and me at home. Dan was seven at the time and I was nine, so he looked to me for answers about what we should do. I didn't know. How would I? I was only nine. Should I go and check Mum was all right and get the frozen peas out of the freezer? Or ask her to go and wash her own mouth with soap?

In the end we did neither. Mum hobbled to the kitchen and iced her foot. Daniel and I, still a bit shocked and bewildered, just went back to watching *Scooby-Doo*. For the record, it wasn't an actual ghost in this particular episode. Turns out it was just a baddie pretending to be a ghost who reckoned he would have got away with it had it not been for those pesky kids. We should have been able to work it out for ourselves. It was a very similar outcome to all the previous episodes we had ever seen!

CAR CIGARETTE LIGHTERS

I'm not sure when these things were phased out, but growing up all our cars had built-in cigarette lighters in the dash-area and built-in ashtrays on the doorhandles.

The ashtrays in the back where us kids would always be seated were cleaned out about once a year—usually when they were so full of Sparkles lolly wrappers that there was no more room!

These ashtrays were removed from car models long before the cigarette lighters. I suppose that's because the sockets that the lighter thingy went into had so many more functions than just blazing up a ciggie. There was a big range of accessories you could buy that plugged into the lighter socket—everything from jugs, dust-busters, refrigerated chilly bins and hair dryers . . . because nothing says 'multi-tasking' quite like drying your hair while you drive to work in the morning.

It's a good thing they don't have these lighters in cars anymore, because those things were bloody dangerous when used incorrectly—although it must be said that you would have to be a wee bit simple to use one incorrectly. I am incredibly disappointed to say I fit that description. I first became curious about our car's cigarette lighter when I was eight. Mum was a car smoker but she never used this thing, because an actual lighter was far quicker and more convenient.

Me: What's that thing, Mum? (Pointing to a round sticky-out knob on the dash with a picture of a cigarette on it.)
Mum: It's a lighter.
Me: What's it for?
Mum: You use it to light things.
Me: What things?
Mum: Smokes.
Me: But why?
Mum: Because you have to light the end of the smoke before you smoke it.
Me: Yeah, I know that . . . but why?
Mum: YOU JUST DO!

After an exchange such as this a period of silence would usually follow. I had a head full of questions but I could sense Mum's aggravation. I was not a particularly perceptive child, but her shouty-shouty voice was a dead giveaway that she had given me all the explanation she was prepared to.

I would wait for a short spell for Mum's blood pressure to return to levels considered non-life-threatening before going gently back in to try again.

Me: Mum.
Mum: (Sigh) Yep, what is it?
Me: How exactly does it work?
Mum: (Sigh) How exactly does WHAT work?

I believe she knew what I was referring to. If I wanted Mount Susan to erupt again, I could have answered with something antagonistic like: 'The cigarette lighter, of course. The thing we were just talking about when we last spoke. Remember? And you got all angry about it?'

But instead it was always best to play it straight and treat it as a walking-on-eggshells situation:

Me: The cigarette lighter
Mum: (Sigh) You push it in, and once it heats up, it pops back out again. Then you light your smoke. Okay?
Me: Yep. Okay.

Now there was a natural pause in the conversation. Mum must have sensed this meant my little mind was ticking over.

Mum: But don't ever touch it or you might burn the car.

That was the first priority for parents back in the eighties—damage to property. Of course Mum and Dad were concerned about our health and safety, but the biggest concern was that we would break their stuff. Surely a more effective (and caring) warning would have been to say something like: 'Don't ever touch it. The car could catch fire and you could burn to death in a nasty explosion when the petrol tank explodes.' Descriptive, terrifying and truthful. Demonstrating concern for both the person and the possession.

For most kids, a chat along these lines would be enough. They would understand that the in-built car cigarette lighter was not something to be touched by children. Under any circumstances. Ever. For me, though, a Q and A session like that did nothing but arouse my curiosity.

Weeks later that curiosity was satisfied—though it was satisfied in a way that was most unsatisfying. I was in the car waiting for Mum, who had run into a shop, leaving me with one final instruction—don't touch anything.

I managed to obey this instruction . . . for the first few minutes. Then boredom set in and I finally got the chance to have a closer look at this lighter that I was so intrigued by.

I pulled it out of its round hole and had a look at it. It was about the size of a thumb. Half of it was the knobby handle part that stuck out; the other half was metal with a grey coil on the end that looked like a miniature oven element. I placed it back in the hole and pushed it down until I heard it click. Then I sat and watched it. This was an intense time. If Mum came back before it had popped out I would have been in deep shit. After a very long minute, it popped back out to its regular resting position. I pulled it out again and noticed the coil was now glowing orange.

Holding it in my left hand, I waved it over the palm of my right hand and could feel the intense heat coming off it. I was fascinated—there was no actual flame, so how did you use this to light smokes? And that is when I touched the glowing coil with the tip of my index finger. The pain was intense and immediate; I thought I might even pass out. My skin made a sizzling noise and smelt terrible. I quickly placed the lighter back into its slot and wound the window down, using my good hand, to get rid of the smell of burning flesh.

I could have done with some medical attention, or even just a grown-up to take a look at it and let me know I was not about to die. But there was no way I could tell Mum what I had done. Come to think of it, this may be the first she knows about my badly burnt index finger, now, as she reads this book.

She must have suspected something was not quite right, though. On the ride home from town I barely spoke, only responding with very brief answers when she asked me anything. I couldn't say much—I was in a whole world of hurt. When we got home I locked myself in the bathroom and ran my finger under a cold tap, which helped a bit. But it throbbed for hours and was a pain unlike anything I had ever experienced before.

After that, it never happened again. Lesson learned. Well, nearly. I burnt my hand three years later, far worse, in a similar act of stupidity while staying at my cousins' farm. They had a Kent log fire with a glass door. My Aunty Robyn and Uncle John constantly reminded us never to touch it, because it was hot. One winter's night when the fire was roaring behind the glass, I decided I just had to touch it to find out exactly why we were not allowed to touch it. Fuuuuuuuuuuuuuuuuck me! Robyn and John were not bullshitting. A layer of my skin remained on the glass after I pulled my hand away! There was to be no clapping for at least ten days, doctor's orders. Which made that year's school prize giving a bit awkward. I was not up for any awards myself, so I would have looked like I was sulking when I failed to participate in the numerous and ongoing rounds of applause.

Still on the subject of burns, I'd estimate I spent between twenty-five and thirty days in any given year with a burnt tongue-tip after ignoring Mum's warnings that the cheese in the toasted sandwich would be piping hot.

Daniel reminded me of a similar instance where he hurt himself but was too scared to seek medical attention. Actually, I think this story goes a long way to proving that Daniel is even more of an idiot than I am. He isn't sure how old he was at the time, but his pinky was small enough to fit into a pencil sharpener and he wanted to see if it was possible to sharpen it. Naturally his finger started bleeding profusely. Realising he would be in a world of shit when mum found out, he clenched his bleeding finger into a fist and hid it in his pocket. Sensing something was up, Mum accused Daniel of hiding something in his pocket. She asked him what was in there, and he replied quite truthfully that it was only his hand. Mum demanded he empty his pockets and his shredded finger and palm full of blood was revealed. Mum cleaned Daniel up with some Dettol and a Band-Aid . . . then handed him over to Dad so he could be given the belt.

How any of us survived childhood amazes me sometimes. Charles Darwin wrote about a thing called natural selection. Darwin's theory is that only the fittest survive, meaning that the dumbest humans will end up eliminating themselves from the gene pool due to their own stupidity. Dan and I are living proof that this is not always the case. Even with perfectly capable parents who fed us good advice, we still had to find things out for ourselves, often resulting in severe bodily harm.

THE IDIOT BOX

Dad had a way of fixing broken electronics in our house. His unorthodox repair method worked best with our old TV set, but he would also try it out on anything that was playing up that could be plugged into a wall—alarm clock radios, cassette players, toasters, whatever. We called his technique . . . the love tap.

It involved no tools other than his right hand. He would simply select a spot and give it a slap. Remarkably, it usually worked. Then, whenever the problem flared up again, as it inevitably did, he would just slap it again in the exact same spot.

The problems with the TV set as it started to age were numerous—there could be sound but no picture, picture with no sound, or it could be in black and white instead of colour.

There was no science behind the love tap, but you would swear there was if you watched Dad at work. He was the only member of the household who was allowed to beat up the television. He seemed to think he knew the exact spot that needed to be hit, like he was the TV whisperer or something.

TVs were different in the eighties. They were big and expensive things, usually in faux-wood casing. You treated a telly the same way you treated a fridge or a dishwasher—it was purchased with the expectation that it would be at least a ten-year relationship.

Very few households were privileged enough to have more than one. And, unlike today, if the telly broke down it was cheaper to get the repair guy to come over than to just buy a brand-new one. Most people used Tisco, a nationwide chain of TV repairers. The good thing about Tisco was that they had a lot of staff, so they could always come over to look at the broken TV on the day you called them. We used Tisco . . . until the day Dad discovered Brucie's TV and Radio Repair. It was owned and operated by a man named, you guessed it, Bruce. Bruce was way cheaper than Tisco, but because it was just a one-man business, we would sometimes have to wait as long as four days for Bruce to make it over and repair the TV. These periods without the TV working were excruciatingly painful. We would usually just end up going to bed real early to read because it was better than the alternative—staying up and talking to each other. Dad never cared how long it took Bruce to come over to fix the telly because he hated it. He would only ever watch it for the sports news every night and all the All Black games.

Unfortunately for Dad, five out of six Harveys loved the telly, which left him well and truly outnumbered. So most evenings Dad would sit down in his chair and read whatever book he had just borrowed from the library, while the rest of us settled in for an evening of TV from the two channels available. Oh, what a prime-time predicament—do we watch *The Krypton Factor* on Channel 1 or whatever is on Channel 2?

The Krypton Factor was a weird New Zealand game show where competitors went head to head in a series of mental and physical challenges. In one round the nerdy competitors would be in a futuristic-looking set in a TV studio, answering general knowledge questions. Then they would be outside, each in different coloured tracksuits, running over some army obstacle course. The only other option was Channel 2, which would be playing something American, like *Growing Pains* or *Family Ties*. Channel 2 was always the pick of the Harvey kids, but unfortunately our parents quite liked watching people they didn't know from a bar of soap answering trivia questions and climbing rope walls in ridiculous looking outfits. So what to watch was a choice that was usually made for us.

When we finally joined the masses and got a video recorder, we didn't have to decide anymore—we could watch one channel and record the other. These days I can sit down with my Sky remote and trawl through over a hundred channels and not find anything worth watching, but back in the eighties it seemed like there was always something worth watching, even given the lack of options. My guess is there are so many ways to waste time these days that we have all become super-discerning. Back then, we were more easily entertained.

Dad told me off about my TV addiction last time he came to visit. The conversation went something like this:

Dad: (Pointing to TV on wall) What's this?

Me: It's our fifty-inch HD Samsung. Don't you love it?

Dad: Yeah, it's not bad. Where's the smaller Sony one that was on the wall last time I came?

Me: Oh, that's in the bedroom now.

Dad: But . . . you already had a TV in the bedroom. It was a Philips one, wasn't it?

Dad always has been a big brand man. He's very frugal, but he is also all about buying trusted brands when it comes to electronics. This is one area where he would always spend a bit more to buy a brand name he knew.

> **Me:** Yeah, that's in the spare room now.
> **Dad:** How often does the spare room get used?
> **Me:** (Sheepishly) Hardly ever.
> **Dad:** So you had a perfectly good TV in your lounge AND in your bedroom, and you bought a brand-new one for the lounge just because it was ten inches bigger?
> **Me:** Ten inches bigger . . . AND in high definition. Check out the megapixels. Look at the clarity, Dad!
> **Dad:** (Walking off shaking head) More bloody money than sense.

He may have had a point too. I don't have a lot of money, but I have even less sense. I possibly have more television sets than I have money and sense combined.

THE VIDEO RECORDER

The day the Harveys bought a video recorder was one of the most significant in our family's history. To rank the arrival of the video on a scale of importance, I'd say it was right up there with the day Mum came home from the hospital with baby Charlotte. But, if I am being totally honest, we were way more excited about the video than about the new baby. We grew to love Charlotte but with the video it was love at first sight. There were other new things that came along, like the microwave oven, but nothing as brilliant as the VHS. We all got on best when we were not required to speak to one another, so an invention that allowed us to get more out of our TV could only be a major positive.

I remember when I first got to see one in action. It blew my ten-year-old mind. We were visiting the Bennetts, friends of my mum's. The Bennetts were the first people we knew who had a video. We sat down with the Bennetts kids and watched *E.T.* just two years after it had been playing in movie theatres. And because this was before video stores had started to pop up, Scott Bennett belonged to an underground video swap club where wealthy people would import movies from the US and share them with each other. I'm not sure how many of Palmerston North's elite were in this underground video library, but it can't have been many and I don't imagine the selection of titles they had was incredibly vast. But since there were just two TV channels broadcasting at the time, watching a newish movie along the lines of *E.T.* would have been a refreshing way to break up the monotony of watching *The Littlest Hobo* every afternoon during Olly Ohlson's *After School* TV show.

Olly was a legend, quite possibly the first Maori presenter on New Zealand telly. He coined the catchphrase, 'Keep cool till after school', and every kid could sing along to the theme song:

'A, F, T, E, R, S, C, H, double O, L. After schoooooool.'

If you have never seen the show, that will mean nothing to you. But for everyone else, it would be hard to see that particular passage of text written down without bursting into song. I loved *After School* as much as the next kid, but having a video machine and a blockbuster movie from some exclusive underground movie-sharing society would have definitely made me more popular with my peers. Instead, I had no video and a reputation for the worst after-school snacks. Word spreads like wildfire when your mum serves up Vanilla Wines and watery Raro as a post-school treat. It's very hard to entice classmates back to your place for a play date once the word is out that the snacks are of an inferior standard.

I think we were fairly late on the video bandwagon. I remember all four of us kids harping on and on and on for ages before Dad finally caved in to our demands. We were very persuasive and had a wonderful bullshit line that Mum and Dad started to believe after a while: 'Everyone else has got one—we are the only family out of all our friends who don't.'

It arrived in 1987 when I was fourteen. By now, video stores had started to pop up around the place, eliminating the need for those tape-swapping clubs the rich early adopters belonged to.

We got it because Mum was going on an extended trip to Italy with her mum and some of her siblings to see the Pope. I think the idea was that a video recorder would make Dad's job of being the sole carer in her absence a bit easier. (She also prepared, packaged and stored in the deep freeze a month's worth of eat-and-heat meals all labelled with microwave instructions.) And I think Mum was scared we would miss her so much that we would need something to help divert our attention. If that was her cunning plan, it worked better than expected. Mum who? Didn't even notice she was gone—too busy watching TV shows we had recorded.

Video recorders were really expensive in the early years. The prices were shocking when you consider how much they cost twenty years later—in 2007 you could pick up a brand-new one at the Warehouse for twenty dollars on a good day.

Our one, this big JVC unit, cost $999—and that must have been a sensational price, because as I think I've already mentioned, Dad was a major tight-arse.

Our JVC was one of the first units to come with a remote control. Although to be fair, the word 'remote' was used loosely back then. The remote had a cord attached that plugged into a hole on the video unit. The problem was the cord. For some strange reason that only the JVC design team would be able to answer, it was only about two metres long. This meant it could not quite make it all the way back to the sofa where everyone was seated. So even with a remote control we still had to get up off our seats to press the buttons . . . we just had to walk two metres less than before.

TOYS AND GAMES

One thing you got used to as a child of the eighties was disappointment. The toys at the time very rarely did what the TV ads and packaging promised they would do. Maybe part of this was our own fault, for building these products up so much in our minds before we got them. You see, toys were never something we were just given for the hell of it because we wanted them. We weren't given toys because we had been good, or because we had done our chores or whatever. All those things were mandatory. They were done because if they weren't done we would end up getting the belt. Toys were treats restricted to birthdays and Christmas. It was rare to acquire something new in between those dates.

The biggest let-down ever for me was the sea monkeys that I eventually got at the age of nine, a whole four years after I first decided I wanted them.

Comics were a big part of being a boy in the eighties and every comic had an ad on the back cover for sea monkeys. These things looked amazing . . . in the ad. The big illustration was of a naked family of sea monkeys all smiling while standing by their castle in the tank. Then, in a smaller drawing, there was a family of regular humans standing over the tank smiling as they watched the naked family of sea monkeys.

And if these drawings were not enough, the text of the advert was the clincher:

'World-famous Sea Monkeys are SO full of surprises you can't stop watching them. Always clowning around, these frolicsome pets swim, do stunts and play games with each other. Because they are so full of life you will never tire of watching them. Anyone who loves the company of pets will adore Sea Monkeys.'

In fairness to the scammers peddling this product, there was a little notice at the bottom of the advert warning: 'Caricatures shown are not intended to depict Artemia.' But I had no idea what Artemia was, or Caricatures, or depict. I found out, though, when my longstanding wish finally came true and I got sea monkeys. There was a little cut-out form at the bottom of the ad which you had to fill in and send away with the money to buy the world's happiest naked underwater family. It was only a couple of dollars, from memory, but the problem was you could only get them if you were in America. It is easier to buy a yellow-eyed penguin on the black market than it was to order something from the United States to be sent to New Zealand in the 1980s.

As luck would have it, a new kid from America joined our Standard 3 class during the year and we hit it off. I loved having David as a friend. It was the first time I had heard an American accent in real life. And he seemed so much cooler than everyone else, just the way he called lollies 'candy', his mum 'mom', the footpath a 'sidewalk', and other Americanisms. And, just like the moms in my favourite TV shows, David's mother always had the best afternoon snacks when you went to his house after school. David's dad was travelling back to America for business, and that is how, after four years of red-hot burning desire, I finally became the parent of a sea monkey family.

I was devastated. It was total shit, absolutely nothing like the commercial. They looked a bit like food floaties in a glass of water. There were no smiling faces or adorable sea monkey children. And as for the promise of these things 'always clowning around playing games with each other'? Never happened! My memory is a bit sketchy as to how these 'pets' ended up dying. Either I got bored and simply stopped feeding them, or Mum tipped them down the sink.

I think this feeling of being let down over and over was more of a problem for boys than girls. Popular girls' toys like Cabbage Patch dolls, My Little Pony, Strawberry

Shortcake and the Care Bears were never supposed to do anything in the first place, so there wasn't as much scope for disappointment.

Between them, Charlotte and Bridget accumulated all those things in the eighties, along with a thing called a Wuzzle that became Char's favourite soft toy. *The Wuzzles* was a cartoon on TV created by an animator who had one acid trip too many in the sixties. It starred a cast of hybrid animals. Charlotte had the Bumblelion plush toy. Bumblelion was half bumblebee, half lion, and lived in a beehive. He had a pink mane, fuzzy yellow antennae, a lion tail and stripes on his belly. The Wuzzles were very cute but also a fantastic reminder about the importance of saying no to illicit drugs or at the very least using them in moderation.

Because we had only the two opportunities each year to get something awesome, we would always put a lot of thought, study and research into our wish list. Occasionally, a third opportunity would present itself—sickness. I'm not talking just a day in bed with the flu sick. I'm talking hospital-stay-because-you-fell-off-your-bike-and-your-collar-bone-pierced-your-skin sick. Being badly hurt had a silver lining: a substantial gift would usually come your way. Much to the envy of the three healthy Harvey siblings, who would cry out in unison: 'Awwwww, that's not fair!'

As bad luck would have it, Dan did the best out of all of us in the third gift stakes. He hit the jackpot when he stabbed himself in the forehead with a knife. Dad used to buy potatoes by the sack, a big bag that weighed about twenty kilos. Presumably it worked out cheaper to buy them in bulk. This sack was stored in the washhouse in between the washing machine and dryer, and each afternoon someone was allocated the chore of going to get Mum a container of spuds for tea. On this particular day, Dan took a knife out with him to cut through the string that was sealing the sack shut. These days a task such as this would never be left up to a child, or if it was, the parents would send the kid out with a far safer tool for the job, like a pair of scissors.

Somehow Dan put the knife under the string and started cutting towards himself. He must have been doing it with quite some force, because when he broke through the string the knife, still firmly in his hand, flew up and stabbed him in the forehead. The wound wasn't overly deep, but when he came running inside screaming, the knife was still stuck in place, dangling from his forehead. We were all a bit annoyed by this one. It wasn't even that bad—the wound was so small it could be covered with a Band-Aid. But I think Mum and Dad both felt a bit guilty about it, so Daniel was taken to the Toy Warehouse and allowed to pick something he wanted. He went for the must-have item at that time, a Coke can wearing sunglasses that would move and look like it was dancing when it was placed near a speaker. Unlike most of the other toys of the time, this one did exactly what it was supposed to do.

We all got hours of entertainment out of this thing. It really made us laugh. Kids today are so spoiled for choice a product like this would not even keep them amused for the duration of a song. But for us, the dancing Coke can became like a seventh member of the family.

Dan struck paydirt again a couple of years later, when he spent time in hospital for a ball that hadn't dropped. That's not how the surgeons described it—they went for the far classier sounding 'undescended testicle'. For that hospital stay, Dan scored himself a gaming console, a thing called a Sega Genesis and a Sonic the Hedgehog game. The graphics and sounds would seem lame now, but at the time this was revolutionary in the world of electronic games. Dad must have felt really bad about Dan's ball to shell out the money this thing would have cost. Dad made a point of stressing that it was Daniel's present but that the whole family would share it. I knew Daniel would hog it, though, since it was given to him (because I would have done the same). I was spewing with jealousy. I would have given my right testicle to have a Sega Genesis. Ironically, that is precisely what Daniel had done.

SCHOOL REPORTS

Growing up we were frequently told by adults that we should enjoy being a kid and make the most of our schooldays because they would be the best days of our lives. Without exception, every adult would say it, even Mr Hodgkinson, the friendly caretaker at Riverdale School.

In fairness, since Mr Hodgkinson spent his days cleaning out rubbish bins filled with old sandwiches, apple cores and banana skins for a living, he was in all likelihood telling the truth. It is hard to imagine his childhood could have been any worse than that!

This constantly reinforced message that life was as good as it was ever going to be bummed me out quite severely because, quite frankly, life was not that awesome, so it was a depressing thought that it would only get worse as I got older.

The problem was I was average at just about everything. And that's possibly an overgenerous appraisal of my skill set. If I'm being brutally honest, I was usually on the bad side of average. I wasn't a loser, but I was never a winner, either. Kids like me got through school without much fuss or fanfare. We just existed, made up numbers. We never got our name engraved on a trophy or got a shout-out in assembly from the headmaster. Nor did we get the strap too often or spend many hours doing our work at the naughty kids' desk just outside the headmaster's office.

One thing that all kids receive nowadays which would have suited an average kid like me to a tee is a nice touchy-feely school report. These things are so diplomatic now that it's outrageous. What a parent of a school-aged kid gets to read now is a page of vanilla that has been coated in sugar THEN wrapped in cottonwool. You could be the school's biggest shithead—the kid who threatens to, say, dig the teacher's eyeballs out with a ballpoint pen then urinate in his eye sockets—and your school report will still make you look like a decent kid:

> 'Raymond excels in aggression and violence. A+ for attempting to cause grievous bodily harm to the teaching staff.'

In the eighties the school report was a document that caused a great amount of stress and anxiety, making it hard for the average kid to make the most of 'the best days of their life'.

A good report would bring rewards. The deal in our family was that for each 'A' you got on your report, you would be given a king-size block of Dairy Milk chocolate, a Harvey family favourite. I can't recall the exact number of choc blocks I managed to obtain over my eleven years at school, but it's safe to say there was never much risk of me developing tooth decay as a result of my awesomeness in the classroom.

A bad report, on the other hand, would result in punishment at home. So not only would I have to deal with the disappointment of having my entire year's worth of school work shot down by one A4 piece of paper, but there would be further disciplinary action to come .

The reports were sent home with the students in a sealed brown envelope, so I never had any idea of just how bad it was until Mum started reading it.

As she read, I would study her face, looking for subtle clues to indicate just how much trouble I was in. After a minute or two of skim reading, Mum would usually pull out one of three lines:

'Sounds like someone's been going to school just to eat his lunch.'
'Looks like a certain someone needs to pull his socks up!'

Those two, I could live with. By this stage in my life, I had got used to people being disappointed in me. After a while, letting people down becomes second nature. The third line was the one you did not want pulled on you:

'Wait until your father gets home.'

That was the worst, because it meant the report was not just a little bit bad, but full-blown bring-on-Dad bad. So on top of feeling like a total loser for having a stink report, I also had a couple of hours to sit and wait, a bit like a defendant in a jury trial, to find out what my punishment would be. This would all come down to what sort of a day Dad had at work. If Dad's mood was good, I could escape with a pep talk about applying myself better and putting more effort in. A rough day at the office for Dad would result in a 'this will hurt me more than it will hurt you' spiel followed by a belt to the buttocks which most definitely hurt me more than it hurt Dad.

I may not have been smart at school, but I was smart enough to know that my dad was full of shit when he told me it was going to hurt him more than me. Immediately afterwards he would sit down to read the *Manawatu Evening Standard* . . . meanwhile sitting down was not an activity I would even attempt for a period of time after getting the belt.

And that is why I feel a bit ripped-off by how good kids have it now. Their school reports are considerably kinder. And because smacking is now illegal, a terrible report will result in a far less scary punishment. Ultimately, I think I am just a bit jealous.

I want a friendly report. I want an easy punishment. I want to be a kid today.

My end of year report from Riverdale School, Standard three, in 1982 is a stand-out. The only positive in this entire document is my attendance—397/400 half-days. Once you read the rest of it, you get the feeling the teacher must have let out a sigh of disappointment every morning when he saw that I had bothered to turn up: 'For fuck's sake! There's that Harvey kid again. Doesn't he ever get sick?'

We did get sick, just as often as other kids. But Mum was the ruler of whether or not we were fit enough to go to school, so unless there was blood gushing out of an open wound somewhere, we would have to go.

The conversations would usually go something like this:

'Mum, I feel really sick.'
'If you're well enough to tell me you're sick, you can't really be sick.'

It was an odd theory. I think it was her way of saying that the only way we could get a day off school on the grounds of being unwell was to be unconscious. And arguing your case was a futile exercise:

'Seriously, Mum, I mean it. I honestly don't feel good.'
'No. You're fine.'

And off to school we would go. I don't remember ever being a bad kid, a shithead. I just remember being an uncoordinated, slightly shy and awkward nine-year-old. So I am not sure why my teacher that year, Mr Marshall, disliked me so much. Come to think of it, maybe everybody got a bad report. If you are sitting down writing twenty-seven school reports by hand in the evening after spending a day in a hot classroom with prepubescent children who smell of that pungent kid-sweat after running around for an hour at lunch, it's hard to imagine you'd be in an overly positive frame of mind when you get home and have to spend your evening thinking about those kids you just spent the day with.

Mr Marshall was a first year teacher, straight out of teachers' training college. He must have only been twenty-one or twenty-two at the time, but I just remember him being a mean grown-up with a light ginger moustache, the sort that some self-conscious folks might try to pass off as being 'strawberry blond'.

He looked more like a traffic cop than a teacher. This was back when there were the police and the Ministry of Transport. The police didn't deal with cars or traffic— that was done by the MOT, or traffic cops as they were known. The traffic cops had different cars and uniforms to the police and were hated by nearly everyone. For some unexplained reason, many of these traffic cops sported ginger facial hair.

My report the year I was in Mr Marshall's class had seven B's and four C's, meaning I earned a grand total of zero blocks of chocolate. 'B' meant 'Does his best on most occasions'. A 'C' was as bad as it got: 'Erratic. Insufficient effort. Parent/teacher conference called for.'

The comments make for some brutal reading:

'Often his ideas are off topic, this being related to a lack of listening. At times he speaks to show off.'
'Dominic has problems in maths and has made little effort to overcome them.'

'Dominic needs to make more of an effort in social studies. He has a tendency to be egotistical in thought.'
'Dominic has put in little effort to improve his standards of spelling.'
'Dominic displays coordination problems in PE which effect* [*sic*] the standards achieved.'

*(Yes, you saw it right. After making a dig at my spelling, Mr Marshall makes a spelling mistake of his own! And while this irony went unnoticed by my parents at the time, it was brought to my attention by the editor who worked on this book. It may have been thirty-two years later, but it was still a fist-pump moment.)

After all these little jabs peppered through the report, we get to the 'general comments' section, where Mr Marshall really gets the chance to put the boot in. I can imagine his fury while he was writing it. It was probably similar to Dad's fury when he got home from work and read it:

'Dominic has not had a very successful year, and attempts to improve both his work and work habits have only had a short-term effect. He doesn't listen well and this often gets him into trouble. Socially, Dominic is well adjusted but he has a tendency to show off in front of others. He is easily led into misbehaviour.

Then Mr Marshall closes with this wee gem:

'I feel he needs to concentrate on the present and not on the long-term future plans of the family.'

Thankfully, that last line saved me from getting the belt! That was a dig about my parents breaking up earlier in the year. Mum and Dad broke up and got back together on numerous occasions, but 1982 was the first time. By the time the report came out, they were back together and it was business as usual in the Harvey house, so I think they felt a bit guilty about that comment.

I'm not quite sure what Mr Marshall meant, because I honestly don't remember being too hung up on the long-term future plans of the family. I don't recall being messed up by Mum and Dad's break-up. I think they both did really well in shielding us kids from whatever shit they were going through. They sat us down and explained what was happening and promised us we could go to town and each get a toy we wanted. That was the clincher for me— suddenly divorce was starting to look a lot like Christmas!

Apart from Dad moving out, nothing else had changed in my life. We were staying at our family home in Haart Place. Dad did none of the cooking or day-to-day household chores so nothing changed there.

It must have been a bloody hard time for Mum, but she held it together and put on a brave face for her kids. When Dad announced he was moving back in, he asked us if we had any questions. All I wanted to know was if it meant I would have to give back the Hot Wheels track and cars that I'd been given as a divorce present. For the record, I got to keep it.

Can you imagine the world of shit a teacher would be in today if they wrote an inappropriate comment like that on a student's report? That would probably be a sacking offence.

Apart from that remark, the rest of the report is a fair assessment of my year's work.

I was not a good student. I was bored out of my mind in class. I found it hard to concentrate because I didn't have a clue what I was doing, especially in maths. Whenever I got an answer right in maths, it was a combination of luck and guesswork, and came as just as much of a surprise to me as it did to Mr Marshall. My attention span was somewhere in between that of a goldfish and a squirrel and I was a show-off. So, as brutal as it sounds, Mr Marshall was just telling the truth, and the truth is often a bit unpleasant, like having a drink of orange juice just after brushing your teeth.

No parent wants to hear that their kid is thick or a pain in the arse . . . but the truth is some kids just are! I would love to be a student now and get school reports that highlight my strengths and brush over my weaknesses. Who wouldn't want that?

I don't know if it would have been a good thing for me, though. My self-esteem was already way higher than it had any real right to be. I didn't need false praise. I think if I was pumped full of bullshit about how amazing I was, I would have ended up being one of those delusional kids who gets heartbroken and humiliated on a talent show like *X Factor* when the judges inform them that they can't sing after they've been told their entire lives how amazing they are by well-meaning family members.

What I needed was exactly what Mr Marshall gave me—a good swift kick up the arse.

| PHYSICAL EDUCATION HEALTH | B | 3- | Dominic displays co-ordination problems in Physical Education which effect the standards achieved. He has participated well in competitive sport. |
| ATTENDANCE | 397/400 | | |

GENERAL COMMENTS

Dominic has not had a very successful year and attempts to improve both his work and work habits have only had a short term affect. He doesn't listen well and this often gets him into trouble. Socially Dominic is well adjusted but he has a tendency to show off in front of others. He is easily led into mischievous. I feel he needs to concentrate on the present and not on the long term future plans of the family.

CLASS FOR 1983 Std 4.

TEACHER *Jenny Marshall*

PRINCIPAL. *Richardson* I will be looking for better results next year Dominic

ILLEGAL MUSIC DOWNLOADS—THE 1980S EDITION

Any child of the eighties has seen a lot of changes in the way we listen to music. We started with vinyl then moved onto cassette tapes. I would estimate I have spent somewhere in the vicinity of ninety hours using my little finger to reel in thousands of hours of tape that have been chewed up by old or dirty cassette players.

After that we moved on to the not-all-that-compact compact discs. We still dabble in CDs, but it is mainly digital downloads now—although there is currently a small vinyl comeback taking place. It makes me regret chucking out all the old family vinyl—Mum had quite the collection of Cilla Black LPs. It's funny how when you live long enough, you start to see old stuff going full circle and becoming popular a second time round.

Even my mum has moved with the times. She has an iPod mini that she runs with, one of those tiny little things that clips onto your singlet or shorts and holds around two hundred songs, which means, if you really wanted to, you could go for a twenty-two-hour run and never hear the same song repeated. Since Mum is petrified of computers, she brings it over to me once or twice a year and I load it up with songs she will like. I know her musical tastes well so it's not a difficult job. Then when she gets bored with that playlist, she brings it back again and I load up some new songs. A perk of this system is that I get to throw in an occasional song I know she would most definitely not like to hear while out on a run. I do this every time. It's one of those jokes that has absolutely no pay-off, because she has never called me in a state of outrage or said anything about it, but it makes me laugh every time I think of her out for an early-morning run when a combination of songs like this could happen:

Adele—'Someone Like You'
Ed Sheeran—'Small Bump'
Abba—'Knowing Me, Knowing You'.

Then, totally out of the blue, a little bit of in-your-face hip-hop:

Kanye West—'Bound 2'.

I can just imagine Mum fumbling around in a state of panic, trying to turn it off or find the right button to skip to the next track as this song pollutes her ears. Without the permission of Kanye West, I cannot print the lyrics to that song in this book. I could have asked, but that seemed like way too much effort to go through. But the central character in the song talks about the things he would like to do with his lover, or 'bitch' as he refers to her. He seems very eager to aggressively make love to her on the handbasin, after which he will happily purchase her a drink as a token of his appreciation, but he warns her that she should stand back if she wants to avoid getting his seminal fluid on her fur coat.

Somehow, he manages to make all this rhyme.

Really, as my mum's eldest son, it should be my duty to try to protect her from such vulgarity. But clearly I am far more easily entertained than the average adult.

In recent months Mum has also become a massive user of Spotify. It's not something she asked my advice on (maybe because of the unspoken joke I/we have going on with her iPod shuffle). She set up her Spotify account all by herself. The only reason I know this is because in the process of doing so she must have somehow agreed with the click of the mouse to link it up with her Facebook page. So whenever I or any friend of my mum's go onto their Facebook newsfeed, they find it clogged up with updates about what Susan Harvey has been listening to on Spotify. It never ceases to blow my mind, either. Firstly, I wonder what the hell my mother was doing up at twenty to four on a Thursday morning. And, secondly, why was she, in the middle of August, listening to Christmas carols performed by the cast of Glee?

Music is so accessible now. Everything is available on demand, and it is cheap or free—if you can live with the guilt of knowing you are depriving Katy Perry of $2.39 of income by illegally downloading her work.

It's the same deal with music videos as well. On YouTube you can watch what you want when you want. Things have never been better for music lovers. Even then, we all like to have a little grizzle about buffering videos and having to watch five seconds of an advertisement before we get to the good stuff.

It was not all that long ago that things were very different. With music videos, there was no designated music channel. On the two TV channels that everyone had access to, there were only a handful of shows that played music videos, totalling about four hours a week of music! *RTR* was a must-watch in the Harvey household. It was on every Saturday night at 6 pm and counted down New Zealand's official top 20.

Because it was only a half-hour show, they only played five or six full songs and short snippets of the other songs that made up the chart. The only song that was guaranteed to be played was the song in the number 1 position. I recall one particular period when, for what felt like 276 Saturday nights in a row, the number 1 spot was held by the Patea Maori Club with 'Poi E'. Don't get me wrong—it was a great song. And it was a fun video to watch for the first eleven months or however long it was that it spent at number 1, but after a while we started to resent it for holding other videos back. You see, it was entirely possible that you could have a favourite song and never ever get to see the video clip to accompany it.

This was an era when radio DJs were far more important than they are today. If you heard a song you liked for the first time, you would turn it up and hope the DJ would come on at the end and tell you that it was the new song from Chumbawamba. Before anybody gets too excited here, I should point out that I am just using Chumbawamba as a hypothetical example. Chumbawamba realised they had achieved total musical perfection with their 'Tubthumping' song (in which the central character repeatedly gets knocked down but continues to get up again) so have decided to release no new music.

It was a daily occurrence back then for both radio DJs and retail assistants at record stores (as they were called) to deal with listeners or customers who would sing them a line or two of a song in the hope that they might recognise it. Screw that! How awkward for the less gifted singers who were just hoping to buy a cassingle of a new song they had heard and liked.

Today if you happen to hear a song you love on the radio for the first time, you can just open up an app like Shazam or SoundHound on your smart phone. This will not only tell you what you are listening to but also ask if you wish to buy it for a couple of bucks. You can purchase, download and be listening to the song before the DJ on the radio has the chance to let the song finish and tell you who the hell it is!

Because of this constant thirst for music, we were always taping songs off the radio. This could only be done at home, so if a song you loved came on while you were out in the car, you were shit out of luck.

There was quite a science to all this entry-level musical piracy, too. We would always have a blank cassette tape sitting in the tape recorder cued up to the end of the last song we had recorded. When a DJ said they were about to play a song we loved, we would wait for them to stop talking, then hit the play and record buttons at the same time. We used to get infuriated when the DJ talked over the intro right up to when the song started—the frustration this caused us is comparable to that caused by ads on YouTube today.

Then with the song recorded, we could take the tape, place it in our Walkman portable cassette players and listen to it on demand until we were sick of it.

Even with the song recorded to cassette, it was still quite an effort to listen to it on repeat. Since a lot of Walkmans only had a FWD button, we developed a cumbersome but effective system of rewinding the tape after listening to the song.

If the song was on side A of the cassette, we would eject the cassette after listening to the song and put it in on side B. We would then hit the FWD button and count to somewhere between fifteen and twenty (it varied with the length of the song). We would then stop, eject, flip the tape so it was back on side A and play the song again. It sounds like a time-consuming method, and it was. But it was the eighties and we were kids, so if there was one thing we had in unlimited supply it was free time.

Why these early cassette decks had no rewind button is a mystery to me. Maybe it was Sony doing what Apple does now and holding back little features for future models.

If my theory is right and that is what they were up to then, boy, were they holding back a mind-blowing trump card . . . the double cassette player with high-speed dubbing! Shit just got real for the first generation of music pirates.

GOING TO THE MOVIES

One thing that has changed little in the past thirty years is the price of confectionery at the movies. From memory, a container of Tangy Fruits in 1984 was just slightly cheaper than a brand-new car. Tangy Fruits only stopped being made in 2008, along with Snifters and Sparkles. Tangy fruits were the lolly most closely connected with 'going to the pictures'. Outside of movie theatres they were not widely consumed. Most of the theatres back then didn't have the sticky carpet multiplexes have today; they had sticky wooden floors instead. In the frequent event that someone towards the back accidentally dropped a single Tangy Fruit on the floor, it made enough noise as it picked up speed on the fairly lengthy journey all the way down to the front of the theatre that it interrupted the movie. (Though I am sure most of the Tangy Fruit drops were accidental, as opposed to some smart-arse being a smart-arse, because of the cost involved in getting the damn things in the first place.)

We didn't go to the movies very often, and on the infrequent occasions that we were lucky enough to go and see a film, we would be given a cut lunch from home to take with us. It was pointed out to us that going to the movies was enough of a treat . . . so if we wanted something to eat we would have to take something from home.

I remember going to the Regent Theatre in Palmerston North in 1985 to see arguably the greatest movie ever made: *The Goonies*. This movie had everything—story by Spielberg, theme song by Cyndi Lauper, and a cast of kids including Sean Astin, who went on to a starring role in the *Lord of the Rings* trilogy, and Corey Feldman, who went on to take heroin.

I went with a couple of friends, nice normal people with nice normal parents, and they were each given enough money to buy their ticket and some food to enhance the movie experience.

There are no words to accurately express the humiliation I experienced when my friends, both eating Bluebird salt and vinegar chips and sipping Coke from special limited-edition Goonies cups, asked me if I could go and eat my sandwiches in another row because the smell was making them feel sick. Why Mum ever thought sardine sandwiches in a movie theatre would be okay is a mystery to me. And there was no sympathy afterwards when I complained about what happened. Mum just pulled out her standard line about how they were just jealous of me. That was her response to most of our social embarrassments. It was a nice line, but it wasn't believable. Had they been jealous of my sardine sandwich, they could have just asked to trade some of their chips or Coke, a swap I would have happily agreed to. Asking me to piss off and sit a few rows back because the stench from my snack was making them sick just seems like a reasonable response. There is a time and place for sardines, and a Saturday afternoon in a movie theatre is neither.

THE 10 BEST KIDS' MOVIES IN THE EIGHTIES

The Goonies
Gremlins
E.T.
The Karate Kid
Ghostbusters
Labyrinth
Short Circuit
The NeverEnding Story
Back to the Future
Ferris Bueller's Day Off.

MUM'S UNHEALTHY OBSESSION WITH LLADRÓ

My mum had an obsession with the idea of poshness. I'm not sure where it all stemmed from, but it was a bit odd. People who knew her and liked her already knew she wasn't posh, so the only people she was fooling (and I'm pretty sure these people were not fooled at all) would be strangers or people who could not yet be considered friends. Basically, anybody who didn't really matter.

There were of course the cutlery, dinner set and towels that she kept for best, only to be used on those extremely rare occasions when guests she considered worthy of using them came to visit. These guests would also be served wine from a bottle rather than the cask she usually drank from. But it was Mum's posh phone voice that gave us all the greatest joy. Since there was just one phone in the house, a landline that sat on a small table in the hallway, Mum always insisted on answering it. As soon as it rang she would scream out, 'I'LL GET IT!' Just in case anyone else in the suburb of Riverdale was planning on dropping in to answer it. She would then stand next to the phone with her hand hovering over the receiver, clear her throat, and let it ring three to four times before finally picking it up:

'Good afternoon, you've called the Harvey residence. How may I help you?'
'Yes, he is. Whom may I say is calling?'
'Certainly, please hold on and he will be with you in a moment.'

And that is when our mum would go from being one of the Queen's aides back to being a suburban Kiwi mum of four:

'STUUUUUUUUART! THE PHONE'S FOR YOU. IT'S DONALD OR DENNIS OR SOMEONE FROM WORK. MAKE IT QUICK, THOUGH. I DON'T WANT TO MISS AN IMPORTANT CALL.'

We finally got one of those clunky cassette-tape answering machines when I was fourteen. I think Dad got sick of trying to keep all his calls under fifteen seconds just in case someone important was attempting to get through at the same time.

After some months with the machine in place, Dad highlighted the fact that nobody important had called. Mum put this down to Dad buying the cheapest machine available and it must have somehow failed to record all these important calls.

As we grew older and I was about to leave home and go flatting for the first time, Mum and Dad finally moved into a posh home with more than three bedrooms and one bathroom. Meaning I got to enjoy the luxury of having my own bedroom for a total of about seventeen nights. To this day I don't know if this was unfortunate timing or a well-executed plan on my parents' part, but I'm going with the latter. Bastards!

This larger house allowed Mum to realise a dream—

Mum, at the age of forty-something, got a formal lounge. Or a complete waste of space, as Dad called it.

The white plywood double doors with swirly engravings looked like something you might find in Buckingham Palace . . . assuming Buckingham Palace was a two-storey house in a Palmerston North suburb built in the seventies with affordable materials designed to appear more expensive than they actually were.

This was where Mum kept her authentic-looking Persian rug that had been imported all the way from the People's Republic of China. Mum had purchased it years earlier at one of those giant rug importer's sales that sweep through towns from time to time. She had kept it rolled up and under the bed. She knew it was too risky to have it rolled out in the house where something terrible could happen to it . . . like someone walking on it.

This formal lounge was Mum's own special zone in the house, a room where she could have nice things and keep them displayed. It was where Mum kept her Lladró pieces in an antique cabinet.

Lladró is a brand of porcelain figurines. They are just as breakable as all the other brands of porcelain figurines in the world . . . but way more expensive.

I never got the whole Lladró thing. Still don't. I think Mum just likes it because it's horrendously overpriced. For the few minutes that Mum is at the counter buying yet another Lladró piece, the shop assistant who is serving her thinks she is posh. Mum will deny it, but I reckon that's what it is. She would never ever buy it online, because it cuts out that interaction with another human!

Don't get me wrong—it's nice stuff. But no porcelain statue of a clown's head is worth three thousand dollars!

Mum had been working towards a house with a formal lounge for the best part of a decade. Over the years, as savings allowed, she would buy a new Lladró piece. But since we were a growing family of six in a small house it was just too risky to have these beautiful pieces out on display. So Mum would purchase them and then store them in the garage, still in their boxes.

When the family finally moved out of our house at Long Melford Road, I'd say the value of assets in the garage was greater than those kept in the house.

These expensive pieces were funded largely by the government supplement Mum received known as the family benefit. For each child you had, you were automatically given a small sum of money each week to go towards raising them, something like thirteen dollars per week per child. So with four kids, Mum ended up with quite the Lladró savings fund going on. The government's contribution towards this formal sitting room was so considerable that Dad affectionately nicknamed it the Lange Lounge. Never when Mum was in earshot, though.

The rest of the cash required to finance this obsession with overpriced pottery came from Mum's resourcefulness. Daniel would be forced to wear my hand-me-down clothing. Not just the big-ticket items like school uniforms, either, but little affordable pieces that weren't really designed to be shared or passed down, like underpants.

The beautiful antique cabinet was also stored in the garage next to the chest freezer, covered in blankets for protection, just waiting till we moved into a house where it could be accommodated. Mum acquired this cabinet from an antique shop on the side of the road twenty minutes away from Palmerston North near Himatangi beach, or Himahawaii as some of the locals rather meanly called it. (It had brown water that we were warned not to swim in and advised to never swallow, and the boy racers' cars speeding up and down the hard sand made it look nothing at all like the beaches of Honolulu.)

We stopped off at this antique shop during one of our Sunday drives as a family. This shop had just popped up in an old corner building that had once been a Europa service station. This was at a time before antique shops were even a thing. Why the owners picked a stretch of the state highway in between Sanson and Foxton is anybody's guess. Seems like a bloody strange location for such a niche store, but I suppose the rent was dirt cheap. The sale of this one cabinet alone probably covered rent, rates, insurance and wages for the first year of trading.

So for some time after that, Mum would show friends this fancy cabinet in the garage and be bursting with pride when they asked where she'd found such a fine piece. She would get to tell them she'd bought it from the anti-cue shop. I am not sure who eventually put her straight and told her it was pronounced anne-teek rather than anti-cue. I wish I'd been there to witness it. On the embarrassment scale it must have been right up there with the time she found out her favourite brand of champagne, the affordable Marque Vue, was pronounced Mark Voo and not Mark View, as she'd been calling it for years, every time a bottle was popped for a special occasion.

I'm not sure what the turning point was for Mum. Maybe it came with age, and feeling comfortable in her own skin. Or maybe she just got sick of everyone else in the family teasing her about it. But sometime in between all her children leaving home and today, Mum gave up on her aspirations of poshness. She still has her prized Lladró collection and the anti-cue cabinet, but apart from these reminders, she has gone completely the other way. So much so that we kind of wish she would go back to being just a wee bit posh.

Now instead of pretending to be rich, she goes on about how poor she is. We learned just how bad she had got a couple of summers ago when we shouted her a trip to Fiji with us for a week-long holiday at the Hilton Hotel on Denarau Island.

Every morning after housekeeping had tidied up our rooms, Mum would ask if she could have any of the toiletries in our room that we wouldn't be using. So every day she would come in and take the soap and the miniature bottles of shower gel and shampoo—everything she was legally entitled to remove without it being classed as theft.

When we got home she proudly boasted that she had thirteen emergency sewing kits. I asked her when she thought she would ever need one of these kits, let alone thirteen. That's when she informed me she had already used one of them to mend a rip in the Hilton bathrobe she took as a souvenir.

GO OUTSIDE AND PLAY

When we complained of boredom in the 1980s it was a legitimate complaint. There was literally next to nothing to do. No internet, YouTube, Candy Crush, Facebook. Not even satellite TV. In fact, at this point any household that had a VHS player was doing well for themselves!

Whenever we said we were bored, Mum would reel off a list of tempting things to do to beat the boredom, like tidying our bedrooms or helping her to fold the washing. Since she knew all of these tantalising offers would be declined, it got to the point where she entirely gave up on providing us with options to beat the boredom. By the time I turned eleven, that particular complaint was met, without fail, with the same response every time: 'Go and play outside!'

It was a fine suggestion in theory. But the problem was there was nothing at all to do outside.

I think it started as a trick. Mum said it once in anger when we were annoying her too much on a 'housework day'. These days usually fell on what should have been one of the good days—a Saturday or Sunday.

If Dad was at home, we would usually do something as a family. Never anything really awesome, but usually a car ride somewhere uninspiring to do something uninteresting. (These Sunday drives get a chapter all of their own later in the book.)

If Dad wasn't at home with us, it was because he was doing one of the following things: playing tennis or golf, getting some stuff done at his work, or visiting the library. Dad loves books, but because of his frugality did not believe in book ownership. Even if a book was released that Dad really, really wanted to read, desperately, he would go on the Palmerston North library wait list and patiently wait, sometimes months, for his turn to come up. Then if the book turned out to be a stinker, he would breathe a huge sigh of relief that he hadn't paid for it.

If Dad wasn't home on the weekend, Mum would typically use it as an opportunity to get the house in order. She could have insisted that we help her, but I think she knew this would make the job even harder for her. The best thing she could do was politely tell us to piss off and leave her alone. Reading between the lines, that is precisely what 'Go and play outside' meant.

So we would all dutifully go outside. And that's when Mum locked the brown aluminium ranch slider, allowing her to get on with the chores while her unhelpful children learned to entertain themselves.

After a while the line about going outside to play was delivered as a telling-off, with a scowl, and it was clear that we were being banished as a form of punishment.

Parents today could not do this. The outside is just too risky. The child could be run over, get sunburnt, molested, or end up eating some gluten. Growing up in middle-class New Zealand in the eighties, no kid was allowed to be fussy about food. Either our immune systems were amazing or our life spans were compromised dramatically as we were slowly poisoned by being fed things that were not appropriate for our body types. There are arguments for both sides, but I can honestly say I have never been to a funeral for a mate whose life ended prematurely because he ate cheese when he had an intolerance to dairy.

Actually, it's amazing there were not many more premature deaths as a result of kids doing stuff unsupervised as a way to fight boredom. Nothing real bad ever happened to us, but when I think back about the shit we got up to I have to admit there was a large element of luck in play.

These forced periods in the great outdoors without parental supervision made us experts at killing time. Time and boredom were two things we had plenty of. We found ways to entertain ourselves, though. It was during one of these outdoor weekends that we devised the plan to move the trampoline next to the carport roof and jump off. We had a rectangular trampoline made by a Levin firm called Supertramps. They were the go-to trampoline for Kiwi families—this was a time when Dad thought anything made in any Asian country was 'Jap crap'. The trampoline was a present for all four Harvey kids for Christmas one year. Safety pads were available for purchase at the time but, according to Mum, 'Santa' had made a judgement call that they were just too expensive, and unnecessary, and that the Harvey children should be grateful to be getting anything at all. The tramps these days look more like a cage-fighting arena—big safety nets up the sides and hidden springs that no longer look anything like springs. It's all good stuff—it's to keep kids safe. But part of the fun of trampolining was the risk of breaking a limb.

Remarkably, the new game of jumping from the carport roof onto the trampoline went without incident. After a while that got boring, so we turned it into a long jump competition. We would each take a turn at jumping from the roof onto the trampoline mat, then spring off the mat and land on the grass as far away from the tramp as we could possibly go. The landing spot would be marked on the grass with a clothes peg.

The problem with all these games we invented was how quickly we would get bored with them.

This was a problem because with each new game invented the risks would inevitably increase. After the long jump game came the double bounce game. Two of us would bounce on the trampoline and take turns at double-bouncing each other, hoping to generate enough height to be propelled up onto the carport roof. We canned this game when Daniel mistimed his jump and ended up ripping off a bit of the spouting. If we alerted Mum to this, one or all of us could have been given the 'wait until your father gets home' spiel, which usually resulted in getting bent over the bed for the belt. So instead we carefully rested the spouting back in place, where it rested precariously for a couple of days until the next light shower of rain brought it down while we were all at school. Dad put it down to wear and tear and we all got away with it.

The worst injury sustained on the trampoline was by Daniel.

It was summer and we had been playing on the trampoline with the garden sprinkler underneath the middle of the mat. Safe? Not really. Fun? Yeah. And an effective way to keep cool in the heat? Shit yeah. Daniel thought it would be a good idea to take his togs off and jump around nude. It really was bloody funny. I declined his pleas to join in, though—the fence between our backyard and the Mannings next door was not very tall, and they had a daughter a year younger than me. I really couldn't afford the humiliation of her seeing my under-developed genitals flapping around. I'm fairly sure she was grossed out by me already so I doubt her seeing me fully nude, jumping up and down on a trampoline, would have done much to change her mind.

I can't recall how 'ball-gate' happened. It all took place so fast. But somehow, Daniel lost his footing on the slippery wet mat and ended up sliding off the mat onto the springs, where the skin of his scrotum got pinched in the coils of one of the springs. Panic and pain set in immediately and Daniel started screaming. I tried to calm him down, knowing that if Mum heard and came running outside we would both be in a world of trouble. I knew how these things played out. I'd get the belt for sure, just for being older than Dan and letting the activity go ahead. Daniel would possibly be spared the belt this time round on account of his genitals already having suffered severe trauma.

Freeing Dan's ball sack took considerably longer than the split second it took for him to get caught there in the first place. Attempts to yank himself away from the springs just caused more excruciating agony for him. In the end, I had to get both my hands closer to his scrotum than any brother should ever have to go and pull the springs apart, allowing Daniel to get free. That Mum never heard all this was a minor miracle. My guess is she had the old Electrolux vacuum cleaner going as well as Kenny Rogers. This combination of horrible noises would have kept her blissfully unaware of the commotion going on only a few metres away in the backyard.

It is also a miracle that none of the neighbours came over to ask if everything was okay. Every time we got away with something that would have been considered belt-worthy, it was a huge relief, a real 'phew that was close' moment.

One side of Dan's scrotum swelled up and turned purple, so it resembled a giant grape, but it went unreported and un-inspected by adults. With anything like this there was always a chance that something more serious could be wrong—internal bleeding, a ruptured testicle, whatever. But we were both gamblers. After a lifetime of being force-fed Kenny Rogers' greatest hits, we knew when to hold them and when to fold them. And on this occasion we decided it was best just to shut up and ride it out rather than 'fessing up and facing further disciplinary action. I'm not so sure this was Dan's preferred way of handling the incident but he came round to my way of thinking when I warned him that if he said anything to Mum or Dad I would go to school on Monday and tell Rachael Holloway that he had a purple ball. He liked Rachael, so a deal was struck on the spot. He would regret that decision seven years later when he asked her to the school social and she turned him down, saying, 'Sorry, I only date guys with purple balls.'*

*That last bit may not have *actually happened*.

GO OUTSIDE AND PLAY
(THE AWAY EDITION)

Mum was strict with us and knew where we were at all times. I'm surprised we weren't all leash babies—maybe those leash harness things that some kids wear these days hadn't been invented yet. If GPS technology had been around when we were growing up, Mum would have monitored our every move. When we were told to go and play outside, we were essentially restricted to a radius of a few hundred metres. Mum always liked to keep us within yelling distance in case she needed us for something urgent, an emergency. When she yelled our names it was bloody loud, and everyone in the cul-de-sac could hear it, so Mum only ever did it for real important stuff . . . like setting the table or cutting some rhubarb for pudding.

This meant the only time we got to fulfil our desire to explore was when we had play dates or sleepovers at the homes of friends whose mums weren't so strict.

One of our favourite things to get up to during these short and rare breaks away from my mother's overprotective bosom was to bike to the Esplanade and use the free playground. The Esplanade was the entertainment hub for Palmerston North—a huge park that runs along the banks of the Manawatu River, with a bush walk and rose garden, a kids' playground, a miniature railway and a bunch of aviaries with birds in them. The only bird any kid cared about was the cockatoo. If adults were around we would try to entice it to say hello. If it was just other kids around, everyone would have the same goal—to train him to say 'Fuck off!' Nobody ever succeeded in corrupting the cockatoo, but I think I speak on behalf of every kid in Palmy who tried when I say it was a shitload of fun giving it a go.

The playground was the most epic one in Palmerston North. As well as the standard swings and seesaws that all parks had, this one also had the longest slide in the city, a flying fox, trampolines built into the ground and a mouse-wheel that you ran around in until you had worked up enough momentum to hurt yourself.

When we got bored of playing, we would usually go and hide in the bush that surrounded the miniature railway track. The track runs in a 2.2-kilometre loop and weaves through the Esplanade bush. For a small charge, parents and young kids could go for a ride through the bush that took around twenty minutes.

We got hours of amusement putting a stick on the track and hiding in the bush, waiting for the train to come back round. The driver of the train, usually a volunteer from the local Rotary or Lions club, would be forced to stop the train to remove the obstacle by hand. As he did this, we would watch from deep in the bushes, nervously sniggering. Being caught and returned home by another adult would result in severe punishment, so sometimes we would not even have the courage to wait around to see the pay-off for our prank.

Another weekend highlight was the trip to the dump. We lived just round the corner from it. Most weekends Dad would load up the car boot with grass clippings and other general household rubbish and go for a drive to the dump. For the time it took him to unload all the rubbish and throw it on the pile of other people's crap, we were allowed to run around and look for stuff— shoes optional, of course. Every time, without fail, we would find something amazing to take home with us. I remember one summer feeling particularly suave as I adopted a cool walk and strutted up and down Haart Place wearing a pair of Ray Ban Wayfarers which were in perfect condition . . . apart from the missing lens in the right eye. As long as the other kids in the street only saw me from the left side they would have been impressed by my coolness. I'm not sure why Dad let this scavenging happen. It seemed like a vicious circle—he was removing rubbish from the house while we introduced someone else's rubbish. And all our findings would inevitably make their way back to the dump in due course.

Our rather pleasant little house in Haart Place was positioned very close to both the refuse transfer station and the sewage treatment centre, as the council called them, or the dump and the poo-ponds as we knew them. Obviously when Mum and Dad first inspected the house it was not a hot day with a breeze blowing in our direction, because on these days there was no mistaking the stench of faecal matter.

As well as the dump and the poo-ponds, we also had the Awapuni racecourse, the Mangaone Stream and the dog pound nearby. We could access them by jumping the back fence of our house and running through a couple of paddocks. This land is now developed and full of houses but it remained our own personal playground for as long as we lived there. It was a more carefree time than now. These days, the thought of children under ten playing near a stream unsupervised is unimaginable, not to mention that we did all of this exploration usually without footwear and always without sunscreen.

Often at weekends we would wander over to the dog pound and offer to take the impounded dogs for a walk. It seems unthinkable now, but the staff let it happen. So there we would be, maybe eight-or nine-years-old, wandering around with some homeless dog on the end of a leash. It only stopped because we got bored. Nothing bad ever happened—no dog ran away, nobody got bitten.

Remarkably, the worst thing that ever occurred on any of these weekend adventures was when I trod on something while running through a field and sliced my foot open, leaving a gash that required four stitches. I was upset, but only because the location of the wound meant I was forced to wear shoes until it had healed up again.

I hated shoes. They seemed so restrictive. I wore them on the occasions I had to, like going to church, but otherwise went without.

Even in winter I would walk to school in bare feet. This stopped after the school principal, Mr Richardson, saw me arrive one morning without shoes. A note was sent home and Mum and Dad were called into school for a meeting. The school had noticed my lack of footwear and wanted to know if the family required some financial assistance. Riverdale School had an embarrassing thing known as 'the poor fund' for families who could not afford to send their kids on school camps, pays sports fees and, it would seem, afford even a cheap pair of shoes! Mum was mortified. She never seemed too concerned about the prospect of me getting frostbite from walking to school on mornings when it was so cold that the white grass would crunch as I walked over it, but she was horrified that some of the staff at the school thought we had no money. Dad, on the other hand, quite liked the idea. His way of thinking was that if the school were offering to buy me shoes, we would be mad to turn down their generous offer. So after that Mum made sure we wore shoes she had bought from Hannahs every day for school. Even in summer.

Mum's bizarre no-trouser policy remained in place, though. I'm not sure why this was a thing, but Mum had a rule that Dan and I were never allowed to wear long pants to school. Ever. I think this was a hangover from her ultra-strict childhood, when all her brothers were made to wear shorts all year round. Another reason could have been due to the damage we seemed to cause to any pair of long pants we ever wore. The knees on all these garments would be either grass-stained or ripped and the ankles would usually get torn up in the bike chain. So keeping us in shorts all year round was the best solution for Mum. It meant more often than not we had scabs or torn skin on the knee area but Mum was much more comfortable with us harming ourselves instead of clothing. These war wounds were just a hazard of the job—being a kid in the era before kids were wrapped up in cotton wool.

Every naughty or dangerous thing we did as kids was just because we were bored. And we had time to kill. Some days seemed to last forever.

It was during a period of boredom that my mate Ian and I watched on closely as his slightly older brother inserted a felt-tip pen up his own anus. Ian's brother was eleven or twelve at the time. He invited us into his room and said he wanted to show us a really cool trick—his exact words. He then pulled his pants down and instructed his younger brother to poke the felt pen a centimetre up his bottom. Then he started to push, like he was about to fart, and the felt would just about fall out. Then, as he stopped pushing, the felt would retract and go back inside. It was like the world's grossest and most weird party trick.

I have a sneaking suspicion that this was not the first time Ian's brother had done the trick with the felt-tip pen and the puckered anus, just because of his matter-of-factness about the whole process. One thing I can tell you for certain, though—it must have been an old, dried-out felt-tip, because those things were precious to all of us and there was no way that any kid would ever treat a perfectly good felt-tip in such a disrespectful manner.

There was nothing quite like a good full set of fifty Faber-Castell or Stephens felt-tip pens. This was the golden era of colouring-in books and colouring-in competitions, so a good set of felts was essential. If you were buying a kid a gift in the eighties, boy or girl, you could never go wrong with a set of felts. I once had a fifty set. But it was some cheap Chinese knock-off brand, so each felt was only good for colouring in a surface the size of a thumb-nail before they would dry out. Once that occurred they were useless, not really good for anything . . . other than conducting lame magic tricks involving your orifices.

I DISCOVER THE OTHER USE OF MY PENIS

I was a very slow developer. I was fourteen-years-old before I finally discovered what my penis could be used for other than urination. You cannot imagine the range of emotions I felt on that fateful day. There was the extreme and instant tiredness that overcomes us men immediately when we are done. There was also elation at this ridiculously pleasurable feeling I could give myself. There was a touch of guilt, only a smidgen, though, and it was something I learned to live with in the time it takes Usain Bolt to run twenty metres.

But the main emotion was anger. I could not believe it had taken me fourteen fucking years to figure out what an erection was for. It's hard to fathom how someone could be so useless. It would be like having a roller-coaster sitting in your backyard and never pausing to wonder what it was for.

All was not lost, however. By the age of fifteen, I had more than made up for lost time. I took to this hobby with vigour and enthusiasm. It is some sort of miracle that I was never the victim of a humiliating walk-in. Unless I was caught, but Mum or Dad were generous enough to slowly walk out on tiptoes as their elder son lay on his bunk bed in a scene that must have looked like he was having a nasty fistfight with his groin and murdering his much, much smaller victim.

Due to our living arrangements at the time, I became something of a masturbating ninja. My little brother Daniel and I were still sharing a bedroom and a rickety bunk set. Dad had purchased the bunks as a kit set instead of getting the store to assemble them. There was no way he was up to the task of putting bunks together—Dad was what you would call an un-handyman—but since he could save twenty-five dollars by doing it himself, he was prepared to take a gamble and risk having one of his sons crushed due to his poor workmanship. Just climbing the ladder rungs to get to the top bunk in a cautious manner would make the bunks sway back and forwards a good ten centimetres.

This made the act of self-pleasuring a little more than a metre above my brother about as challenging as solving the Rubik's Cube in the dark. It is a feat I mastered, though. I used my free hand to hold onto the window frame, which stabilised the bunks. Was it enjoyable? No, not really. And the risk of being caught was huge. But I was so late to the self-pleasure party that I had catching up to do.

I also practised this new-found hobby of mine in the bathtub. Like the bunks, the bath came with its own set of risks. We had a 'no locking the bathroom door' policy, which made things tricky. This rule was implemented after an incident in which Dad was, in his own words, 'almost killed'. It was one of those 'almost killed' incidents where the result could have been catastrophic but, in reality, nobody came to any harm whatsoever.

Dad loved the bath. I think a large part of his love of the bath was because he could see exactly how much hot water he was consuming. And I can tell you, the answer is very little. The typical bath my father enjoys is a lot more water efficient than having a standard five-minute shower. Dad lies in no more than six centimetres of lukewarm water, only enough to cover the back half of his body.

Hanging on the wall next to the bath in our house in Palmerston North was a large round mirror with a heavy gold frame. One evening Dad stepped out of the bath and was drying the half of his body that had succeeded in coming into contact with water when the gold mirror came crashing down into the tub.

Dad had hung up the mirror when we moved into the house. He banged around the wall with his fist looking for a stud. I was in the room with him at the time and every single tap on the wall sounded exactly the same to me. But eventually Dad was happy he had found a solid wood beam to bang a nail into so the heavy mirror would hold. Evidently he had missed the stud and narrowly cheated serious injury as a result of his own poor workmanship. Still, at least he could sleep easy at night, comfortable in the knowledge that he had not built the bed that he and Mum lay down on.

The no-locking policy somehow evolved into a no-knocking policy, meaning that the door could fly open at any given moment without warning. Most New Zealand homes at this time only had one bathroom. Some were lucky enough to have their toilet in a separate room. Our place had both lumped together in the same small room. There was nothing quite like soaking in a nice relaxing bath while your dad sat next to you defecating and asking for assistance with the crossword in the *Evening Standard*:

'I need a seven-letter word that starts with the letter P. The clue is: something nobody in this family can ever get.'

AN IDIOT DISCOVERS PORNOGRAPHY

By the age of fifteen I had become a ferocious masturbator. I was excellent at it. Not just the act itself—I had also mastered the art of not getting caught. The downside was that I'd finally found something I was quite good at but couldn't skite about it to anyone. Imagine the conversation:

Mum: What a productive day. I mowed the lawns, did three loads of washing AND baked pikelets.
Me: Big deal. I masturbated four times before midday.

There was no big self-esteem boost in knowing I was an incredible wanker. I was usually full of remorse, regret, guilt and self-loathing immediately after I'd finished. I'd feel the need to wash my hands and give myself a look of disappointment and utter disgust in the mirror. But then I would get over that and be back doing it again the very next hour.

Had anyone in my family any idea of just how out of control my habit was, I'm sure they would have sought professional help. Mum probably would have gone one step further and attempted to cure me herself, much like she did when my nailbiting was at its very worst. She put invisible nail polish on my fingernails—the taste of this polish was supposed to be so revolting that I would eventually stop. The stuff did taste disgusting, but did nothing to fix my nailbiting. I just ended up with mild poisoning and was sick for forty-eight hours. Nothing to see here—just a dude with bad nails having a vom.

Much like the nailbiting, I don't think anything was going to stop me being a prize tosser. She could have superglued Goldilocks pot scrubbing pads to the palms of my hands and I still would have given it a nudge.

For these early solo sexual encounters I was reliant on the closest thing I had to pornographic material at that time—the Farmers' catalogue with the colour pictures advertising ladies' undies. And the 'Dolly Doctor' section of Bridget's favourite magazine, *Dolly*.

After that I graduated to the sketches of girls in different stages of puberty in the book *What's Happening to Me?* This book was the follow-up to *Where Did I Come From?* and most families in the eighties had a copy of it. The book saved parents the awkward task of chatting to their kids about puberty. There was a page that had really, really realistic looking pencil sketches of girls showing their development over the puberty years. There was a similar page with a bunch of guys growing from boys to men, but I doubt too many teenage girls around the country were popping into the loo with that page of the book marked for some quality alone time.

After that, I graduated to proper pornography. It was considerably harder for teenage boys to see a naked lady in the eighties than it is now. There was a little magazine and stationery shop round the corner from us that stocked adult magazines, but I was too young to buy them. Even if I was old enough, I think I would have been too reluctant to take the magazine to the counter. I had managed to conceal my hobby from everybody, so I really didn't want the notoriously grouchy old lady in the shop to figure it out. She had an excessive amount of skin that flapped loosely around her neck. It looked like the scrotum of a young boy had been placed there.

This woman was terrifying. I think she just had a thing against kids being in her store. She was always polite enough to me if I was in with Mum, and she was nice enough to other adult customers. But as soon as a child, or children, were in her store with no adults within earshot, she would turn into a dragon, with breath like Werther's Original and a stench of perfume that smelled like toilet spray workplaces get for their loos.

Any child who picked up a magazine from the shelf would not get to read more than a sentence of any article before she would yell out from behind the counter:

'Excuse me! It is not a library. You can buy it and read it
at home or get out. Thanks very much.'

She always ended with a thanks very much, as if that
somehow made her little rants seem a bit more polite.

Any kid who didn't listen and continued to read for
free would be lucky to make it through a paragraph before
she would get up from her little stool behind the counter
and snatch the magazine from them. There was a rumour
everybody knew but no one could ever verify that some
kid years earlier had gone in and folded the back cover
of a *MAD* magazine. Each month this magazine had a
picture on the inside back cover that you would fold on
a dotted line to make a completely different picture. The
legend goes that she saw him doing this, so locked the
door and kept him prisoner for thirty-five minutes until
his parents could come down with money to pay for the
magazine that he'd damaged. Who knows if it was true
or not? It does seem a bit hard to believe—but this was
the eighties, and she really was quite unpleasant, the sort
of lady even her own grandchildren would have disliked.

On the occasions that I had money to buy a magazine,
I still felt afraid. She had glasses that dangled around her
neck on a chain of fake pearls which she only ever used
to check the price of the magazines she was selling. So
my purchases from this shop were limited to a few *MAD*
magazines, *Smash Hits* and *RTR Countdown* music
magazines. Buying *Mayfair*, *Playboy* or *Penthouse* was

most definitely not an option. Thankfully this is where the kid across the road comes into the picture—Shane Attwell.

Shane was two years older than me and was like the big brother I never had. His family lived just across the road from us in Haart Place. They moved in on a Tuesday. On the Wednesday a cop car pulled up in the driveway with Shane in the back. He had been caught shoplifting from the Cut Price store (like a Four Square) just around the corner. His poor parents, Les and Hazel—what a way to be welcomed to your brand-new neighbourhood!

I don't know if this still goes on, but in the eighties when something exciting happened—like a police patrol car pulling into someone's driveway down the end of a cul-de-sac—curtains would start moving, very indiscreetly too, as everyone would want to know what was going on over at number 15. And word would spread. Fast. People were very sociable and gossipy then, always had time for a cup of tea or some home baking or a chat over the fence or down by the letterbox. These days I reckon most people would struggle to tell you their neighbour's name.

I met Shane the next day. I saw him leave on his bike for school, so I chased him. I caught up to him at the Maxwells Line intersection, which was the busy road we had to cross to get to school. And by busy, I mean Palmerston-North-in-the-eighties-busy. So we might have encountered a car some mornings.

My first interaction with Shane went something like this:

Me: I saw you in the cop car. What did you do?
Shane: Nothing much, eh? Just stole from the dairy.
Me: Ooooosssssssssssh.

And after that we were BFFs. Or more specifically BFF-WAAD (best friends forever . . . with an age difference).

Some school holidays Shane would be sent to stay with his uncle in Hamilton. And his uncle would load his teenage nephew up with dodgy magazines full of pictures of naked people to take home. At the time we thought Shane's uncle was the biggest legend ever. This transaction would be considered creepy now. Was it creepy back then? Dunno, maybe . . . but we thought it was the most awesome thing.

The magazines were always the same sort, so maybe he had a subscription to *H&E*. It stood for 'Health and Efficiency' and was a magazine for nudists. Right through this magazine could be found photos not only of hot girls in their twenties, like most of the other porno mags, but also of both sexes at any age and with any body shape. It was educational stuff—frightening even. Sometimes you would have to flick many, many, many pages before you found something appealing. But it was the best thing available at the time. And it was straight-forward, basic stuff. Fairly harmless. Looking back, I enjoyed the process of obtaining, concealing and using this contraband with the help of my neighbour.

As research for this book, I devoted a hundred hours to looking up pornography online, just to see what is available and out there for teenage boys today. Strictly for research, did I mention that? It's a completely different ball game now. The stuff anyone of any age can access now with just a smart phone would shock most people . . . and lead you to believe that a vast majority of women love nothing more than getting a face load of semen.

THE SANYO PORTABLE CASSETTE PLAYER

I can remember when we got the Sanyo portable cassette player. They were heady times in the Harvey household. I was eight when it first arrived but was not allowed to touch it without an adult present until I was ten. I was given the full this-is-not-a-toy speech. I think that was due to my extreme clumsiness—anything that could be broken when it was dropped was off limits for me.

Mum and Dad got the Sanyo portable cassette player on their first overseas trip, to Sydney in 1980. It was not cheap, either—NZ$225 it worked out to be. Hate to think how much that would be worth today.

Air travel was a bit more of a big deal back then. Mum and Dad got dressed up like they were going to a black tie event just for the three-hour flight. Being only seven, I just thought that people who flew on planes got dressed up, but now I wonder if maybe it was just my parents and not something every passenger did. Imagine that—Stuart Douglas Harvey and Susan Elizabeth Harvey, Dad in a suit and his brown leather jacket and Mum in her best dress and fascinator, sitting all the way back in row whatever-it-was while other economy passengers sensibly wore comfortable clothes like track-suit pants and uggs.

Farewelling Mum and Dad for this first overseas trip was like the flight control centre at NASA watching their astronauts take off into space. Mum and Dad were brave adventurers, travelling off into the great unknown in this big metal bird to a land of the future . . . Australia. Some day they would return (well, ten days later according to the itinerary on the fridge door) and astound us with their stories of this mysterious land they had been exploring.

And this takes us back to the Sanyo portable cassette player. This was the big purchase they made in Australia, the land of the future. They got other stuff too.

Darrell Lea lollies for us kids. We had lollies in New Zealand but these were Australian-made lollies, so they had to be better, we believed.

A giant bag with more clip-on koalas than any person would ever need in this lifetime or the next.

And clothes you couldn't get here yet. Mum was excited about these items. 'It's viry trundy,' she would tell people in her strong Kiwi accent. 'It's nixt year's fushions.'

Mum loved the Sanyo portable cassette player. It was about the size of one of those tall boxes of Weet-Bix and had these thick, clunky buttons. If you hit the eject button, the tray would spring out so suddenly and with so much of a springy-clunky noise that it could give a first-time user a fright.

Mum got one cassette to listen to in her Sanyo portable cassette player—*Kenny Rogers' Greatest Hits*, which had just come out. Mum loved Kenny. She would listen over and over. And she loved to sing. Just like the passive smoke from her ciggies, I was also unable to avoid Kenny singing and my mum singing along to Kenny, which really was a toxic duet. Maybe even more harmful to my ears than the smoke was to my lungs.

Around the time Mum finally went off Kenny was the same time she got taught a cool trick with cassette tapes. There are stories behind both these incidents.

Mum and Kenny's break-up had nothing to do with his music. She didn't wake up one morning and realise this music she was listening to was soul destroying. No, she loved those songs. So much so that when Kenny came to Wellington for a concert, Mum was not going to miss it for anything in the world. She went and got a nice spot on the grass twenty or so metres from the stage for this sunny weekend afternoon concert. During Kenny's set he paused to interact with the crowd and do some giveaways. And while Mum was looking down, carefully turning the pages in the glossy program she had just purchased, a Kenny Rogers World Tour 1980 frisbee, thrown by the man whose name was printed on it in gold, hit Mum in the side of the head. It was captured on the big screen at the side of the stage, which got a big laugh from the other evil Kenny fans in attendance. Mum got to keep the souvenir frisbee, but she was terribly embarrassed by what had occurred and blamed it all on Kenny. After that, she never bought another one of his albums and rarely listened to his tape.

So when a family friend came over and told Mum how you could record over a cassette by putting bits of sellotape over these two little grooves on the top corners, Mum jumped into action. And the first tape to be sacrificed was *Kenny Rogers' Greatest Hits*. The only thing you could record over these tapes was songs off the radio, or, if you had a built-in mic, your own voice. Since the Sanyo portable cassette player all the way from the future had a mic, Mum decided to go solo and start singing songs on her own. Without Kenny. And without any backing music.

Mum would spend hours sitting in front of this thing singing into it. She would sing until she had recorded the song bang on (well, as bang on as a non-singer could hope for), then she would start on a new song. Her plan was to repeat this process until the whole tape was filled with songs 'flawlessly' sung by her. What she planned to do with this one-off masterpiece when it was completed I have no idea, because we never got to find out. As Mum was nearing the end of the B side, her masterpiece almost complete, something terrible happened. The Sanyo portable cassette player chewed up Mum's tape. She hit the eject button and pulled out the cassette, only to find the thin brown tape was stuck in the machine. To make things even worse, it was already twisted and tangled.

Not wanting to try and fix it herself by spooling it in using a pen or a small finger, Mum decided this was a job for the professionals. She put the Sanyo portable cassette player in the passenger seat of her car, the injured cassette still attached to it, and went to Manawatu TV & Sound to see if they could salvage it.

A week later we got a call back from the repairman. Since Dad's work was nearby he went in to pick it up. The good news was they had cleaned the heads of the Sanyo portable cassette player and it was working perfectly again. They had also managed to repair the cassette tape. Then came the bombshell from the repair guy.

'Unfortunately, sir, there are no Kenny Rogers songs on that Kenny Rogers cassette. Sounds like some lady has played a joke on you by recording over Kenny with some really badly sung songs.'

Whether this incident happened or Dad just made it up, there is no way of knowing for sure. But having heard over three hundred hours of Mum singing, it definitely sounds believable to me.

After that unsolicited feedback on her singing Mum started to make better use of the fact that the Sanyo portable cassette player was . . . errr . . . portable. She would take it to a room in the house other than the dining room and sing away. Eventually the Kenny Rogers tape with its two little bits of sellotape had to be tossed. It probably just died of old age, but I am convinced that the time it got chewed up in the machine was a suicide attempt.

LIES MY MUM TOLD

Mum was a big fan of parenting by scaremongering, stopping us kids from doing anything she didn't want us to do by putting the absolute shits up us.

I can't be a hundred per cent certain, but I'm sure this was something unique to my mum and not a tactic used by other parents in the eighties.

There are those harmless little lies that parents tell their kids for good reason. Like the one about the purple dye that follows you around if you wee in the pool, or the classic one about Mr Whippy only playing his music when he has run out of ice-cream. But the lies Mum told us are real head-scratchers. I don't think she did it for a cheap laugh, either. Mum wasn't one of those crazies you see on YouTube who tell their kids they're going to Disneyland and, after a period of elation, tell them the truth, that they're going nowhere. Cruel? Yes, very. Funny? Yes, very.

I cannot for the life of me explain why Mum would have said these things. Perhaps she had heard them somewhere and was gullible enough to believe them.

I mean, it would be perfectly reasonable to use this scaremongering technique if it were in the child's best interest and based on some factual evidence. For example:

> 'Always wear a seatbelt or else you may go flying through the windscreen and be killed when you land head first on the road.'

But the scenarios Mum warned us about were ridiculous, with no basis, not even urban legend. I have managed to suppress a lot of them over the decades, but some of them frightened me so much as a young fella that I still remember them to this day. These were some of her most common lies:

> 'If you swallow chewing gum it will stick to your heart and kill you.'

There were two other variations :

> 'If you bite your fingernails and swallow them, they'll pierce your heart and kill you.'

And:

'If you get a splinter and don't get it out, it will travel in a vein to your heart and kill you.'

This was heavy stuff for a kid. We didn't have to worry about sunscreen or helmets, but we had these death threats to think about.

Having chewing gum in the first place was a rarity. Our parents never gave it to us; it was always a gift from someone else. We weren't too fussed about chewing gum either way; there were way better lollies out there. And chewing gum in the eighties was . . . what are the words I'm looking for here . . . total shit. We all loved Hubba Bubba when that finally arrived from America, but chewing gum was awful. It would go all stringy and tacky and in the hands of children it posed a huge risk of irreversible damage to car seats and human hair. I can't even remember the number of times Mum had to pull out her scissors and do a butcher job on some-one's hair after a sticky old piece of Juicy Fruit got stuck.

Juicy Fruit was the only flavour that appealed to kids. It had a delicious sugar-coated shell with the chuddy beneath it. The gum itself was totally tasteless; all the flavour was in the sugar shell. So once you chewed for about a minute, all the flavour of the shell had been swallowed and you were left chewing something that probably tasted not dissimilar to a condom. Not that anyone would have ever tried chewing on a Trojan.

Because of Mum's warning, we lived in absolute fear of swallowing chewing gum. I found it difficult to intentionally swallow a pill . . . but on the rare occasions I had chewing gum it was always consumed with trepidation. I was worried that it could kill me if it somehow went down the back of my throat.

I finally started to question this one at the age of eleven. Dan was nine at the time and was clowning around in our shared bedroom when he accidentally swallowed one of those skinny triple A batteries. He begged me not to tell Mum and Dad because of the trouble he would have been in. Since I was eleven, and presumably more responsible, I should have told on him so medical advice could be sought. Instead, not really thinking about the possible risks associated with swallowing a small tube of corrosive acid designed to power small toys, I granted him his wish and didn't tell the adults . . . right after I had negotiated a deal to take possession of his prized Hulk Hogan WWF figurine. Dan loved wrestling; I hated it. But if I had this toy that he loved so much, I knew I would be able to use it as currency somewhere down the line. World's worst big brother right here! What an absolute arsehole.

Anyway, after freaking out for a few hours about the swallowed battery we forgot all about it and life carried on as usual. Then, three days later, Dan yelled out at me from the loo. I went to see what he wanted. In his hand was some scrunched-up used toilet paper. Probably a home brand one-ply. He told me he didn't want to put the paper in the bowl until I had seen something. There in the bowl, nestled in a courgette-sized poo, was the battery. Fortunately for my brother's tiny anus, it had worked its way out lengthways. After witnessing that with my own two eyes, I reached the conclusion that if you could shit out a battery, your body would manage to sort out anything you happened to swallow . . . including chewing gum. But to this day, I still don't swallow gum! I reckon I've swallowed a total of three or four pieces of gum in my life—and I've survived.

In the eighties, if you wanted your kid to do something, or not do something, the way to go was to scare them with some outrageous and nonsensical lies:

'If you pull a face and the wind changes, your face will stay like that forever.'

Nowadays parents seem to have a bit more respect for their kids and would probably say that pulling faces is not a good idea because it's mean and you might hurt someone's feelings. The wind changing story sounded far-fetched and highly unlikely . . . but what if it was true? I'd be totally screwed then, with a permanently disfigured face and an angry 'I told ya so' rant from Mum. Not a speech I would want to sit through when I was just coming to terms with my new face. I could have had mega-squinty eyes for all eternity, just because the wind changed when I was telling a Ching Chong Chinaman joke. Unfortunately, this wasn't an uncommon impression for kids to do in the 1980s, highly discouraged now on grounds of it being racist. This new sensitivity to the feelings of others is really cool, but I can honestly say that me and my mates at Riverdale Primary never meant any harm. And Melee Joe, the only Chinese girl in the school, was one of my good friends, so I could always use the line that callers to talkback radio love to use these days about not being racist because I'm friends with someone from the ethnic group I'm about to have a crack at.

I tried this line about the wind changing on my adopted nephew, Sev, a while ago, when he was nine. Just to see what his reaction would be. At the time he was teasing one of his younger cousins by pulling his nose back with a finger so his nostrils looked piggish.

He just shot me a whatchutalkingabout glare and said: 'Dry!'

I could not believe it. Such a cynical response, delivered with superb timing at such a tender age. A response like that when I was his age would have earned me disciplinary action for rudeness, I suspect. But I thought his response was hilarious and entirely appropriate.

Sev came to live with us shortly before his fifth birthday. His father, my wife Jay-Jay's younger brother, was being sent back to prison and there was nowhere else for him to go. It was either he lived with us or went into state care. Since then we have become his legal guardians and even though he is a nephew, he definitely feels more like our son.

'If you eat your crusts, your hair goes curly.'

This used to really puzzle me. Mum definitely wanted us to eat our crusts, so maybe curly hair was seen as something to aspire to. But it was totally unnecessary. We were one of those households where wasting food was unacceptable. Even if crusts were thought to cause baldness, we would have still been forced to eat them.

'If you trip over while eating a lollipop, the stick will stab your brain and kill you.'

Okay, so this is something that could happen, at a stretch. And maybe it did even happen to somebody somewhere. But it still seems like a real long shot, about as likely as being struck by lightning while going to cash in your winning Lotto ticket. Because of this threat, whenever we were lucky enough to be given a lollipop, one of those little thin round things on a white stick, we would eat it sitting down. If we did go on the move with one, we would hold it in our hands and periodically stop to lick it, all because of the fear of falling over and having the stick—which couldn't ever have been more than five centimetres long—piercing the back of our throats and stabbing our brains. Although, given my terrible clumsiness, maybe Mum's concerns were justified. If any kid was going to be unable to manage this fairly basic act of multi-tasking, it would have been me.

'You can't swim for thirty minutes after eating or you will sink and drown.'

I've mentioned this particular warning in an earlier chapter. But Mum's argument was strengthened in the nineties by a widely believed urban myth about an intellectually handicapped adult who disobeyed the thirty-minute rule. Roly Hei Hei was the star of a popular ad campaign run by IHC, an organisation that advocates for people with intellectual disabilities. The ads starring Roly played for a couple of years and then disappeared. That's when a rumour started that he had drowned. It spread quickly, and there were a few versions doing the rounds. Depending on who you spoke to, Roly:

'Drowned when he jumped in the pool to retrieve his sunglasses, the same ones he wore in the TV ad with the fluoro arms.'
'Drowned after someone slashed his floaties.'
'Went for a swim too soon after eating heaps of bread and sank like a stone.'

Mum loved this. When news of Roly's death spread, Mum was convinced it was because of the bread. She finally had actual proof that the theory about the stand-down period after eating was true. Only it wasn't. Roly was alive and well. IHC had just finished that campaign and chosen to take a different direction.

This happened a lot before we had the internet to check up on things. All sorts of terrible rumours would be passed around and accepted as fact. Another wide-spread but completely false urban legend at around the same time was that, in a cruel twist of irony, the singer of the hit song 'Don't Worry, Be Happy' was so worried and unhappy that he had committed suicide. Like Roly Hei Hei, Bobby McFerrin is still alive and well . . . it's just his career that is dead.

'God will punish you.'

Since we were a Catholic household, this was one of Mum's favourites. She never elaborated, but we were all shit-scared of God and his ledger of punishments that he was storing up for whenever. The fear of being punished by God was nowhere near as effective as the threat of getting the belt from Dad. That is because the belt actually happened, whereas this God fella never seemed to follow up on the threats my mum made on his behalf. Mum used it on occasions where there was not enough proof to send someone down to the master bedroom for the belt. The conversation usually went something like this:

Mum: Someone opened the pack of Toffee Pops and had one. Who was it?
Bridget: Not me.
Me: I didn't do it.
Daniel: Well, it wasn't me.
Charlotte: Don't look at me! I didn't take it.
Mum: Well, one of you is lying. But God knows who did it and he can't stand children who steal and lie, so you can expect to be punished.

Poor old God. Mum made him out to be a real grudge holder, someone who would punish kids for the smallest things, like putting shorts in the wash with a tissue in the pocket or saying you used soap in the shower when you didn't.

It made me nervous every Sunday when we got dressed up in our most uncomfortable dressy clothes to attend mass. I thought that if God was going to punish me, church was the most likely place for him to dish out his punishment. I couldn't stand church. Most weekends I would end up getting a 'pay attention' arm pinch from Mum or the glare from Dad that meant 'You just wait until this is over and we get back in the car!' The worst part of the mass was when we had to get off the seat and kneel down on the wooden floor to pray. I'm pretty sure no one was praying apart from the priest . . . the entire congregation's knees were so sore that it was impossible to focus on anything but the pain.

Church got slightly better when I finally hit an age where I could have my confirmation ceremony. Instead of sitting still on a hard wooden pew for the best part of an hour, I could now break the monotony by getting up and walking to the priest for a wee bite to eat. Not that it was called a 'bite to eat' . . . the proper term for this snack was communion. The first time, I was excited. Finally I'd get to eat the thin white round thing that all the adults got. Well, what a let-down that was. It tasted like paper! I'm not sure what I was expecting. I knew it wasn't going to taste like the body of Christ, which is what the priest said it was each Sunday, but I definitely expected it to have some kind of flavour to it, maybe vanilla.

It wasn't until I was around twelve that I started to think Mum's line about God punishing us was just another of her lies. One Sunday, I found myself daydreaming during mass and functioning on autopilot, which was not uncommon for a kid in church, because the sermons were painfully boring and we were not allowed to bring in anything to help keep us entertained, not even a book. This one particular weekend I was repeatedly picking my nose and wiping whatever I pulled out on the underside of the pew. I don't even know how long I had been doing this or how many trips my finger had taken to nostril-town when Mum caught me mid-wipe and pinched my arm. I stopped, immediately. I was shitting bricks. I knew I'd get hell for this on the ride home, and perhaps even the belt when we got home. But here I was in the house of God and I had been disrespectful enough to wipe bogies on one of his seats. If God was ever going to get pissed and punish me for something, now would be the time. And you will not believe what happened next . . . NOTHING!

And that's when I put two and two together. In Bible studies we learned about forgiveness—apparently God was a real fan of it. In the Bible he even forgave the guys who put nails through his son's hands and hung him up on a crucifix. If God could get over that, I'm sure he wouldn't lose any sleep over a bit of snot beneath a seat at Our Lady of Lourdes in Palmy North. After that I stopped being so scared of Mum's threats on God's behalf. The threat of Dad's belt still remained, though.

All dressed up for church. Always in matching clothes.

AN IDIOT GOES TO HIGH SCHOOL

It was always Mum and Dad's plan to send me to Palmy Boys for my secondary school education. My plan would have been to send me to Awatapu College. Awatapu was considerably closer to where we lived, and it had girls. But that was an argument I lost, meaning that each year I rode about 1680 kilometres to get to this place I really didn't want to be. Given my awkwardness, it is highly unlikely any of the girls at Awatapu would have even liked me, but on the frosty mornings, the windy mornings and the wet mornings as I made my way to my all-boys school, all I could think about with every pedal stroke was what could have been. Naturally these fantasy sequences starred me and a bevy of hot chicks.

Come to think of it, it's almost as if Mum and Dad had made a conscious decision to send me to schools other than the ones I wanted to go to. After I finished at Riverdale Primary, all of my friends went to Monrad Intermediate, the closest intermediate in the school zone. I wanted to go to Monrad as well. Instead, my parents sent me to a religious school where I knew nobody. Mum was worried that there could be too many bad kids at Monrad from Highbury, the state housing suburb that backed onto it. So for the two years in between primary and secondary, I was sent to St Peters. St Peters was right on the other side of town, too far to bike, meaning I had to catch a bus for thirty minutes each morning and afternoon, and for the next two years that was my life. Then, at the end of form two, while all my new-found Catholic friends were staying on to do their secondary school education at St Peters, I was yanked from this school to go to Palmerston North Boys High School, where I knew nobody. Fuck my life!

I stayed at Palmy Boys for four years and one term. Coincidentally, that is also the exact length of time I overstayed my welcome at this prestigious school.

I left in May 1990 when I landed my first full-time radio job. It was an amicable break-up, school and I. We said we would keep in touch, we promised to remain friends, but both of us knew deep down that this was unlikely to happen.

The timing of this radio job couldn't have been any better. The first term was coming to an end and that meant we had 'internals'—exams set by the school to give us an idea of how we were all getting on in each subject. The problem was, I wanted my seventh form year to be kind of a gap year. I felt I owed it to myself after eleven years of gruelling hard study! So to make the year as laid-back as humanly possible, I chose the easiest five subjects I could think of. I enjoyed English, economics and art, so I picked them. I was good at English, okay at economics and shit at art . . . but I really, really loved it. I would usually get an A on my reports for effort and a C or D for the actual work. I had a great relationship with the art teacher, Mr Docherty.

I think he felt a bit sorry for me. He must have wondered how someone could try so hard and still be so bad.

For my other two subjects I stacked up my timetable with art history and classical studies. Boy, was that a dick move. They were both way harder than they sound—how was I to know that learning about the central characters in Greek mythology would be challenging?

I had somehow passed School Certificate and then Sixth Form Certificate, as they were known at the time. Well, 'passed' is a very subjective word. It would be more truthful to say I scraped through by the furry stuff that builds on your teeth overnight as you sleep. If I was a high jumper and the bar was the exams, let's just say that bar was bouncing up and down as I landed on the sponge mats. But now I was facing the most humiliating exam results of my school life . . . I wouldn't call it a fall from grace, since my results were never anything to brag about in the first place. It'd be more accurate to call it a fall from disgrace (if there is a lower place you can go to after disgraceful).

These exams are not called 'School C', 'Sixth Form Certificate' or 'Bursary' anymore. For some reason the Department of Education felt the need to take a perfectly good jacket and bedazzle it with rhinestones. So between 2002 and 2004 the old system was phased out and replaced with NCEA, the National Certificate of Educational Achievement.

I'm really not sure what the reasons were for coming up with a new system, but at a guess I would say it is a way to make the thicker kids feel better about how useless they are. The schools are big on that touchy-feely stuff and, as one of the dimmer kids in my year at school, I think I can speak on behalf of all us less gifted kids when I say thanks for helping us out. We appreciate it. You guys changing the entire system is way easier than us having to put in more effort and study harder.

*

PNBHS was character building. In a nutshell, that means it was a horrible nightmare. For those who are academically awesome or superior at sport, a school like this will be a breeze. You will be placed on a pedestal and be devastated when your five full years are over. It is not uncommon to see young men in their very late teens or early twenties around Palmerston North still proudly wearing some of their PNBHS sports gear for fun even though they have long since left school. This is because if you excel at sport, you are a rock star.

One such rugby head was Headbutt Hamish. He was so good at rugby that he was a law unto himself at school. He would just randomly go up to unsuspecting younger students and headbutt them, thus the rather obvious nickname. Reporting the incident was a futile exercise because, in flow chart form, this was generally the chain of events:

1. I get headbutted by Headbutt Hamish.
2. I report incident.
3. Headbutt Hamish gets called into the office for questioning.
4. The school's 1st XV coach steps in and promises to discipline his star player.
5. No disciplinary action is taken against Headbutt Hamish.
6. I am subjected to even more headbutts as punishment for snitching.

The alternative was far more desirable:

1. I get headbutted by Headbutt Hamish.
2. I do nothing about it.
3. No disciplinary action is taken against Headbutt Hamish.
4. All going well, my head may be spared from any more unwanted butting until the next term.

You cannot imagine my joy when I finally left school and discovered that this sort of thing did not occur on a day-to-day basis in the real world. My first radio boss, Steve Rowe, was a bloody scary man (more on him later) but after the first couple of disciplinary meetings he called me in for, I realised headbutting was not something he had in his management disciplinary toolbox. After that I didn't mind getting in trouble so much. Steve would just shout, swear, slam his fist on the desk and go red in the face. Had he resorted to physical violence or the occasional headbutt, I may have been a far more disciplined employee.

I often wonder if the sort of bullying I experienced as a kid still goes on at schools around New Zealand. I would really hope not—I'd like to think all schools have a zero-tolerance approach to this type of thing now, but maybe I'm naive for thinking that. As a grown man, if someone assaulted me it would be a criminal matter. For school-aged kids it should be no different . . . even if the attacker is, like, really, really awesome at sports.

Other bits and pieces went on that some would probably call bullying, but these things were more likely to be put down to 'boy humour', rather than anything too malicious. I mean, if you reported someone for one of these minor incidents, everybody would have thought you were a bit of a dick. Stuff like sneaking up behind a student who was standing up and whipping his pants down. The school was super strict on the uniform and how it was worn—socks up, shirt tucked in and very specific shoes. The only place a student could show a bit of individuality was in the way he wore his shorts. Many chose shorts that were fairly baggy and loose, which made them easy targets for down-trou's—unacceptable behaviour in the workplace, of course, and probably not something the human resources department would put down to 'just having a laugh'.

Another good one—and when I say good one, I mean something that was fucking annoying and not good at all, but still something that happened a lot—was the puddle-splash. The puddle-splash was usually done in winter, when it rained more, and puddles would form on the asphalt in the school grounds. When walking past one of these puddles, you would slam your foot down in the direction of your target. The shoes most boys wore were these big black things called Nomads which had a huge thick rubber sole . . . perfect for slapping down into puddles. This move, when executed effectively, would leave the person doing it completely dry and the victim of the prank drenched in water. It was one of those things where if someone got you, you would have to wait a while, sometimes even a year or two, for the opportunity to get back at them. Leroy Wolland, if you happen to read this, I have not forgotten! I may not have got you before I left school . . . but I do plan to get you one day. You have been warned.

I suppose the upside of a school like this is what an average, run-of-the-mill student can get out of it. For me, PNBHS is where I practised and practised until I became real good at being sarcastic and cynical—traits that have helped me become a bestselling author of books that include vast quantities of both those things. People will tell you that sarcasm is the lowest form of wit, but it isn't. It is right down there with fart jokes and innuendo, but if you are searching for wit's low point, it's hard to go past the last five movies Vince Vaughn has made.

It's my opinoin that Headbutt Hamish was the worst of the school bullies. Most of the school's sporting heroes were just regular young men who never exploited their celebrity status among the PNBHS teaching staff. And those who did exploit their 'fame' usually did so only for personal gain. Like Julius, who ended up being my class-mate in the sixth form. He was a year older than the rest of the guys in the class. He had failed the previous year so was what was known as a second-year sixth. Since he was older than us he automatically seemed cooler, but he was one of those guys who was just awesome without even trying—he had a cool name, a cool haircut, a cool Sex Pistols bag, and he wore headphones all the time in an era when nobody wore headphones all the time, not even Matthew Ridge. He was polite and friendly to everyone in the class . . . but always in an aloof hipster way. If I asked him what he was listening to on his cool headphones, it would always be a bootleg recording of some band I had never heard of. Looking back, I wonder if he was just listening to cassettes of the Traveling Wilburys like the rest of us but made up fancy-sounding band names to help keep up the super-cool-guy image. Since this was pre-internet, there was absolutely no way of knowing if he was making up these band names or not.

Julius seemed to hate cricket, which was unfortunate, because he was awesome at it. Having never been in a position to call myself naturally talented at anything, I can't understand how someone could hate something they are so good at. Maybe it's a case of that old saying, 'Easy come, easy go.' But I have my suspicions as to why Julius hated cricket:

1. Wearing a helmet while batting would mess up his aaaah-mazing hair.
2. Wearing headphones while bowling was frowned upon.
3. White pants were simply not his thing.

I think the only reason Julius stuck at cricket was that it made him a bit like a diplomat who had immunity against prosecution. He was in trouble often for little bits and pieces—like truancy and smoking in the school grounds. For most students, these offences were grounds for suspension and usually meant an awkward appearance in front of the board of trustees. For Julius, these matters were forwarded on to the coach of the 1st XI, who was better at making these problems disappear than world-famous magician David Copperfield. The amount of stuff this guy swept under the carpet was astonishing. By the time Julius left school, it would have been easier to climb Mount Kilimanjaro than to reach the summit of the cricket coach's lumpy rug.

Unfortunately for me, my only strength at school was an almost perfect attendance record, which did not curry me any favour with any of the staff. Mum didn't tend to believe in illness. She thought being sick was a sign of weakness, so I was at school every day without fail. The girls got a bit more sympathy, but if Dan or I complained of not feeling well on a school day, Mum would get out her thermometer, which looked like a relic from the First World War. Then, whatever number the red mercury rested on, Mum would inspect it and say, 'Nah! Nothing wrong wit ya. Put your shoes on!'

Mum's way of thinking was that if she couldn't see it, it wasn't there. A head cold meant nothing to her—even if you were so lethargic every step you took felt like a marathon, she'd make you strap on the helmet and bike the four kilometres to school. Usually in the rain, since these sorts of illnesses generally struck in winter. Hypothetically, having an arm sliced off in a chainsaw accident would probably get you the day off—although IF this happened, we'd still have wanted to go to school anyway, because we'd be in so much trouble at home for getting blood on the carpet!

Corporal punishment was still a huge thing at Boys High, usually administered by the principal, Mr Brookie. We were caned across the buttocks, or just below, at the top of the thighs, depending on Mr Brookie's aim. The school kept caning for as long as it could and only stopped when the law was changed in 1990. Lots of other schools had canned the cane or strap for good years before they had to—not Palmy Boys, though! I reckon it was a perk of

Mr Brookie's job. A little part of him may have died that day he had to throw the cane into a woodchipper.

In my four years and one term at Boys High I was unlucky enough to be caned . . . but lucky enough to only be caned once. What a terrible experience that was. A searing pain like nothing I have ever experienced. But I learned my lesson and from that day on I never again committed the heinous crime that got me into the predicament—aiming my penis up and attempting to get my urine stream as far past the top of the urinal as possible. Everyone did it—it was just my bad luck that some arsehole prefect happened to catch me in the act. On reflection, I suspect he was jealous of my height. I got way past the top of the urinal and was quite close to the louvre windows.

They say every cloud has a silver lining and I realised it was true after I made the painful bike ride home on the day of my caning. I pulled my shorts and undies down in front of the mirror, about fifteen centimetres away from it, then poked my head under my legs to inspect the damage to my buttocks. It was at this moment I discovered I had some hair growing inside my bottom. A bad day suddenly became one of the best days of my life. At the age of fourteen I had my first pubes . . . it was just a bit of a downer that they were growing where nobody apart from a bum doctor would ever be likely to see them.

SCHOOLTEACHERS: THE GOOD, THE BAD AND THE BLOODY UGLY

Palmerston North Boys High was full of interesting characters—eccentric types who made the school day more interesting—and the principal, Mr Brookie, was definitely one of them. Charismatic, hilarious and terrifying, Errol Brookie's life was the school. He was educated there and was made head prefect in 1948. Then he went away and trained to be a teacher and returned to Palmy Boys in 1955. He remained at the school until he retired in 1990, the same year I left and one year after he had stopped caning the students. An incredible man if you were not in his bad books, he was always guaranteed to say something drily amusing every Monday morning at school assembly just before he read out his list of students to meet him at the library foyer immediately after assembly to be caned. Sometimes it would be in the office foyer, but I think the slighter larger library foyer gave Mr Brookie a little bit more swing room.

He smoked a pipe and you could smell it wafting down the corridors as he walked. His loud, authoritative voice, combined with his reputation as a no-nonsense cane-lover, made everyone petrified of him. No student would so much as hoick in the quad if Mr Brookie was within a thirty-metre radius. This is really saying something, because hoicking was such a big thing at Boys High—everyone did it all the time. It seems very odd in hindsight, but maybe at the time it was just a cool thing to do in front of your peers, like the world's lamest act of rebellion ever. By the end of lunchbreak most days the quad would be like a minefield of snotty patches of saliva. The spitting thing became so disgusting that Mr Brookie even brought it up at the full school assembly one morning. He said the quad looked like it had been raining bluff oysters. Everybody laughed . . . apart from the eight or nine kids who had been called out for the cane. Since they were about five minutes away from being in a world of hurt there was nothing that could make them smile.

Mr Brookie wasn't the only stand-out teacher on the Palmy Boys payroll either, not by any stretch of the imagination. That school was (and possibly still is) rife with delightful oddballs. I would have loved to have been a fly on the wall in the staffroom at lunchtime—it must have been like a kooks' convention. I could write an entire book about the PNBHS staff, but the potential legal costs would wipe out any profits from the book sales. So Mr Wigglesworth, the PE teacher who wore those tight trackpants with the stirrups every day, Mr Thornton, the science teacher with one leg shorter than the other and the custom-made shoes, and Mr Hucker, the history teacher with the golden voice and the giant Adam's apple, can all breathe a sigh of relief—you guys are all off the hook . . . unlike this bunch . . .

Mr Tamatea

Mr Tamatea was a big Maori fella. Not fat but stocky. He had a thin black moustache and a tightly curled mullet haircut which was always black and shiny, like an oil slick. He taught Te Reo Maori and maths. Maths is where he and I became acquainted. Mr Tamatea had a reputation, and everyone who took one of his classes knew about it. He had a signature disciplinary move he'd become well known for—the Ear Pull.

This was as bad or even worse than the cane. Mr Tamatea would approach any student misbehaving, grab their ear, pull them to their feet and then escort them to the front of the class. Any resistance would just cause more damage to the ear. The best thing to do was follow his hand as fast as you could to minimise the pain.

One day he tag teamed me and my best mate at the time, Matt Cherri. We were chatting in class when, completely by surprise, he grabbed us both at the same time by an ear each and took us on an excruciating hunched-over journey to the front of the class. There, still with a firm grip on our ears, which by this stage were burning red, he knocked our heads together and then let go so we could sit back down. My ear was hot to touch and was ringing for the next two periods. It seems a bit rough now, but I don't think I even bothered complaining to my parents. Mum and Dad would never have taken my side over the school's. Their reaction would have been to say something along the lines of:

'Well, you must have done something to deserve it. Serves you right!'

Jay-Jay, Mike and I called Mr Tamatea a few years back to talk on our radio show. He was still teaching but had not given a student an ear job in decades. I can't recall what topic we were discussing, probably mean teachers or something, but he was pretty embarrassed and not keen to go on the air. Fair enough. But if I was him, I think I'd be more embarrassed about the permed mullet than the unique method of punishment.

Mrs Hackner

I'm not sure how old Sandi Hackner was, maybe late twenties or early thirties. When you're a teenage boy it's hard to guess these things—all adults just seem way older than you. Mrs H. definitely seemed like one of the cool grown-ups, though. She was Australian and had moved to Palmerston North when her husband, a surgeon, accepted a job at the hospital. They must have had one hell of a fight when they first arrived. I'm not quite sure what she had been told or what she was expecting, but in Palmy North in 1987 it was impossible to order a pizza on a weeknight after 8 pm . . . it must have been a severe culture shock coming from Sydney to this place that averaged about ten hours of sunshine a year!

Mrs H. never looked like a local either. She was definitely the teacher who looked the least like a teacher, always well dressed in clothes that were a couple of seasons ahead of what was being sold in the Palmy stores, and never without some high heels, dangly jewellery and perfume. It was never a chore to call her over to your desk to get her help with an economics problem, a task which required her to lean down. I'm sure some of the other more sensibly dressed female staff members must have hated her. Not that any of the students ever picked up on any of this animosity . . . we were far too busy ogling Mrs H.

In real-world terms I'm not sure how her hotness would have stacked up, but when you are a boy going through puberty and you spend your weekdays with 1200 other boys, any woman thrown into this mix is going to stand out.

Coincidentally, fourth form was the year that I earned my best ever marks for economics. I reckon I know exactly why this is—I worked hard for Mrs H. because she was so nice that I didn't want to let her down. That, and I also put my hand up to ask her over 1300 questions . . . some of which were related to economics.

Mr Doyle

Mr Doyle, or Digger Doyle as everyone called him , a reference to his Australian roots, was a PE teacher who looked nothing like a PE teacher. He was a lean man but barely a day went by that he wouldn't be wearing one of the most unsporty outfits imaginable—a pair of pleated corduroy trousers and a windbreaker jacket. He had a high-pitched, nasal voice, perfect for things like getting students' attention and stripping paint from a wall, and was grumpy eighty-five per cent of the time, but he was still a well-liked, funny teacher. Never scared of his material getting stale or old, he had one well-worked line that he would pull out as often as possible over many years: 'If you treat me like shit, I'll treat you like Purex toilet paper and just wipe my arse with you.'

Digger Doyle was a bit of an enigma to the students. Nobody really knew anything about him, but there were numerous rumours that swirled around, mostly to do with his frugality, and his net worth as a result of this legendary unwillingness to spend.

One favourite lingered for a couple of decades, passed through generations of school students. The legend went that he was so untrusting of banks that he had over $300,000 stashed in socks that he kept in his living quarters at College House. College House, or 'Cock House' as it was called by students who didn't stay there, housed students who boarded at PNBHS. Mr Doyle lived there and worked as a house master. I assume it was some deal where the staff who lived there got free rent or even a supplement to their salary. It all added fuel to the fire about Digger having more money than the Reserve Bank sitting in a few old Gold Top socks hidden in the back of a drawer somewhere . . . probably underneath a pair of cords.

Mr Bevan

I'll never forget the first time I saw Mr Bevan. It was at school assembly on my first day as a third former at this terrifying new school and he marched onto the stage and sat down behind the grand piano and started belting the keys. His fury had to be seen to be believed. It was like a form of assault. He must have been bored shitless—his set list was limited to a couple of hymns and the school's song, the unimaginatively titled 'On! Palmerston North Boys High', with lyrics inane enough to rival any Miley Cyrus hit:

> Come, lads, let us lift our voices
> And make the rafters ring
> While everyone rejoices
> A paean of praise to sing
> Of a school to all of us so dear
> Her fame has spread both far and near
> We'll raise a rousing, ringing cheer
> On! Palmerston North Boys High!

It is shocking that I still have those song lyrics committed to memory. These days I struggle to remember the four-digit alarm code at home and Jay-Jay's new cell phone number, yet I can still remember the words to a song I was forced to sing back in the 1980s!

To top off Mr Bevan's theatrical performance, there was his appearance—he had white bushy eyebrows that stood out a few millimetres, like an awning for his eyes, and pure-white hair that made him look like one of the great composers from the 1700s.

He was never thought of as strict or mean—he was just eccentric, a little crazy, and waaaay too into Beethoven—although I did see him snap into a rage one day. Matthew Cherri and I were in the music block one lunchtime. The school had just got new keyboards and we went in to have a fiddle around with them. We were sprung by Mr Bevan, who flew into a fit of fury and slapped Matt on the side of his face. I only escaped without being assaulted because Matthew was closer to the door that Mr Bevan came in. Poor Matt. He always had red flushed cheeks anyway—now the right side of his face was a burning red colour. As we briskly walked away from the music block, hearts pumping and adrenaline flowing, Matthew suggested we go to the office and report what had just happened.

Selfishly, I talked him out of it. Had we taken the matter further, Mr Bevan might have got in trouble for bitch-slapping a student, but Matt and I would have most definitely got in trouble for being in the music block at lunchtime. Having avoided a slap, the last thing I wanted to do was put myself in a position where I could face the cane.

But we both learned an incredibly powerful life lesson that day, something that everybody should live their life by: *You should always ask before you fondle another man's organ.*

THE TIME I CHEATED, GOT AWAY WITH IT, AND STILL FAILED

Something about my third-term result for computer studies did not compute. But not even Mr Edmonds, the ultra-smart computer studies teacher, could work out what the glitch was.

Taking sixth-form computer studies was a bad idea. I only took it as a subject because everyone kept going on about how important computers were going to be in the future. This was 1989, and every adult had a story about someone who knew someone who'd been laid off and replaced by a computer or a robotic machine. Dad's way of thinking was that I could either be the boss of the computer in the workplace—the guy who tells the computer what to do—or be destined for a life of unemployment. They were the only two options. It was a scary time, a time of change, and nobody likes change.

It was all such an unknown back then. The internet was not even a word. The grown-up world was still fizzing at the bung about this new thing called a fax machine—you could send someone a letter or document and they would get it immediately. This was mind-blowing stuff. I recall a TV commercial where some generic-looking businessman was sitting in some very generic-looking boardroom and then went back to his very generic-looking hotel room and stared longingly at some very generic wallet photo of a generic-looking little girl. And that's the precise moment the facsimile message came through with some generic-looking kid's handwriting telling her dad how much she was missing him. The grown-up world was busy talking about how the fax machine would eventually put traditional postage out of business. Meanwhile, both the fax and postal industries were blissfully unaware that something known as email was less than a decade around the corner.

I think my dad really had an expectation that by now every household would have a robot maid like Rosie from the TV cartoon *The Jetsons* and, to be fair, he wasn't the only one. This was the decade of promise. In 1984 at the Olympic Games opening ceremony in Los Angeles, a man flew into the stadium with a jet pack on his back. After that, we all thought that by the year 2000 this would be how everyone got from A to B. In the eighties, nothing seemed impossible and the magic year that we were all expecting to have this stuff by was 2000.

Palmerston North Boys High School was lucky (and advanced) enough to have a computer room with enough computers so every student could have one to use. That was a really big deal. So, under immense parental pressure, I signed up for computer studies, and it became apparent a couple of periods in that I had taken on another subject I was terrible at.

The problem was that computers were fucking boring. They couldn't do anything. Dad and TV shows like *Knight Rider* had given me the impression that computers were smarter than humans. What I found out when I finally got to play on one myself was that a computer is only as smart as the human who is using it, which in my case made the computer a $3000 pile of shit—the world's most overpriced typewriter.

It was a massive disappointment. The screen was black with fluoro green writing. No pictures or nice fonts. You know that writing that comes up on your screen these days when something really, really bad happens to your computer? The text that makes most of us unplug the cable and plug it back in to start again? Well, that was the stuff you saw on the screen all the time. All commas, semicolons and backslashes.

Terms one and two were all about the basics of computers. For the third and final term of the year, each student had to write his own computer program. This was a big deal, too. This assignment alone represented twenty per cent of the entire year's grade. I predicted I would do poorly at the end-of-year exam, which made it important that I didn't fail epically on this one.

I had absolutely no idea where to even begin. I had weathered some awful school marks in my time, but for the first time ever I was looking down the barrel of a 0/100. Before taking computer studies, my worst subject had always been maths. But at least with maths there was a multi-choice component, so I had a chance of walking away with at least a few correct answers.

I came up with a plan. I'd love to tell you I'm ashamed of this, but I'm really not. My choices were limited—not handing anything in and getting a zero, or doing what I did and walking away with at least a few runs on the board.

Joseph McIntyre was an old mate of mine from Riverdale Primary school days. He was heaps smarter than me, but we were still friends. As we got older, though, we had less and less to do with each other socially. His superior intelligence made it hard for us to remain really good friends. The gaping difference in our IQs became obvious when we were still both in single digits. I wanted to jump out of a tree down onto the lawn below with a couple of Foodtown plastic bags and some string as a makeshift parachute. Joseph already knew this was never going to work. From the ground he shouted out something about velocity and weight ratios. I wanted to try anyway but, sure enough, Joseph was right. He was always right. I didn't break anything but the landing was bloody painful and gave me pins and needles for some time afterwards. So we never had a falling-out but just drifted apart and fell into appropriate social groups for our intelligence levels.

In sixth form we found ourselves as classmates again in computer studies. This served as a reminder of why we were no longer socially compatible—he was top of the class, I was absolute bottom. I came up with a plan which I thought Joseph would be far too smart to ever accept—I would pay him to write my program for me. Remarkably, he agreed. Partly, I think, out of pity. But mainly because I offered to pay him twenty dollars, which was not a massive sum of money, but since he was so good with computers it was an easy payday for him.

We agreed the program he would write for me would have to be pretty basic, otherwise an investigation might be launched which could get us both suspended. So Joseph did my entire project for me. It was handed in on a 3.5 inch floppy disc and came with a three-page written component, which Joseph wisely suggested I rewrite in my own handwriting. These three pages explained step by step how the entire thing was operated. Even writing about it now, some twenty-five years later, I still have no clue what it was I handed in. Attempting to explain those pages of text to someone would have been like having a crack at speaking another language.

When Mr Edmonds handed back the marked assignments, Joseph got his first and was singled out by the teacher for his brilliance, which earned him a 96 per cent mark.

My heart was pounding and my mouth was dry. I sat there feeling sick with guilt. Was this the moment I would be exposed as a cheat?

Mr Edmonds walked by and dropped mine on my

desk. I looked at the red mark on the top right-hand corner—75 per cent.

As he moved on to the next student, Mr Edmonds said, 'Well done, Harvey.'

No questions, no scepticism, nothing. Joseph and I had pulled off the perfect crime. I still wasn't certain I was out of the woods, though. Part of me was expecting Mr Edmonds to call out my name to see him after the bell rang. But that never happened. Unreal!

As a result, I ended up with one of the most conflicting school reports ever written. Mr Edmonds' comments suggested he had no idea how someone could do such an incredible job creating and writing a program for an assignment yet do so poorly in the exam.

After a whole year together, Mr Edmonds finally had a question I was able to answer!

Yeah, yeah, I know cheating is deplorable, cheats never prosper and all that stuff. But the way I see it, I was doomed in this subject anyway. So if you want to use an Olympic Games analogy, I wasn't cheating so I could win a gold medal for swimming. I was cheating so I wouldn't drown in the bloody pool.

SUBJECT	EXAMINATION %	EXAMINATION MEDIAN	ATTITUDE	COURSE WORK	REMARKS	CLASS TEACHER
HISTORY	25	57	D	D	Works quietly in class but appears to be uninterested in achieving good results. Study needs to be undertaken regularly	
ENGLISH	80	55	A	A	a keen, interested student and a pleasure to teach.	WTW
COMP. STUD.	29	54	B	A	Dominic's exam results were disappointing in view of the excellent work done during the term. He must endeavor to remember what he learns	
ECONOMICS	53	56	C	B	This result is definitely below what Dominic can achieve. A less casual approach would see this improved on	

SCHOOL'S OUT FOREVER!

It's been almost a quarter of a century since I *rode* my bike out the front gate of Palmerston North Boys High for the final time. I put the word 'rode' in italics because it was one final act of defiance on my part, and shit it felt good. All bikes had to be wheeled through the school grounds. Riding them resulted in an instant detention. But since I had just signed out, I could do what the hell I wanted with my bike. I couldn't see it at the time, but my last act of defiance was a bit like a metaphor for my entire time at the school—never good enough or bad enough to get noticed.

I tried my best in class and in sport but was just mediocre at everything, although I did learn over time that the harder I tried and the more I practised the better I got at everything. This was frustrating—other kids would be average without trying, then become awesome when they put work in. Me, I'd start at the bottom and end up average.

I'll never forget one evening as my fifth form year was coming to a close and the pressure of School Certificate exam stress was turning me into an emotional mess. I was more on edge than a heavily pregnant lady who had just watched *The Notebook* on DVD then found out her dog had cancer. Mum and Dad could see I was battling, so Dad pulled me aside and ran through a list of successful, high-profile people:

Thomas Edison
Benjamin Franklin
Albert Einstein
Walt Disney
Colonel Sanders
Ray Kroc
Ringo Starr.

All these history-making people had the same thing in common—they all dropped out of school. It was a nice spiel by my dad. He summed it up by saying I just had to try my best, and just because someone is not successful at school, it doesn't mean they won't be successful at life. It was a dangerous speech for a parent to be giving to their kid, because it was sort of giving me the green light to slack off. Fortunately, I didn't take it that way. I actually started to study even harder for School C . . . there was no way I wanted to end up like Ringo Starr.

My memories of my time at high school are kind of neutral—even the best of them would struggle to make a list of my top 100 life moments if I were to compile such a ludicrous document. On the other hand, my worst memories of school are nothing to write home about either. It was just secondary school—something that had to be done to fill the time until I was old enough to get a job.

One thing that stuck with me, though, and that I do think of on a reasonably regular basis, is the school's Latin motto—*Nihil Boni Sine Labore*. Translated, it means: *Nothing achieved without hard work*. I have found this to be true in all aspects of life . . . the exception being obesity.

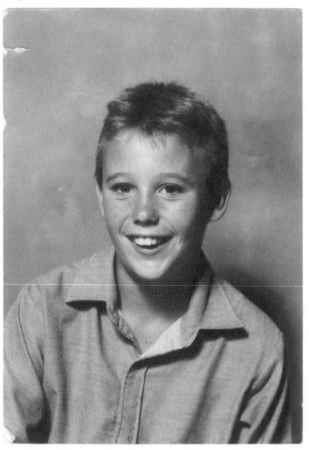

My third form photo, age thirteen. This must have been a really good photo. Mum and Dad usually returned the photos—only the exceptional ones ended up being purchased.

THE LONGEST RENOVATION

Dad has never been the home handyman type. His collection of tools included a hammer, a rusty saw, an axe and a couple of screwdrivers. Even basic DIY tasks like banging a nail into a wall stud were enough to leave him huffing and sighing under his breath. It didn't necessarily stop him, though. When we moved to Long Melford Road in Palmerston North, he even attempted some of the renovations himself, which seemed a bit ambitious from the start. This house was a three-bedroom, one-bathroom home made of those ghastly orange Huntly bricks. The people Mum and Dad bought it from were an old couple and it definitely looked like an old person's house. The garden was full of that red scoria rock which was a popular ground cover back then, especially with the elderly, and sitting on this bed of scoria there were more tyre swans than actual plants. Like scoria, tyre swans were reasonably popular for a time, mainly with the elderly. They were just old car tyres painted white and cut a certain way so they looked like a swan. The only problem was they didn't really look like swans at all. They always just looked like a painted tyre.

Mum and Dad had big plans for this place. Or more accurately, Mum did and Dad was just going along with it to keep the peace. To help keep costs down, Dad decided to do the wallpapering himself. What should have been a one or two weekend job ended up being stretched out over FOUR YEARS. Dad started stripping the wallpaper, then realised that removing the old paper from the plaster it had been glued to some thirty years earlier was way more difficult than he'd anticipated. So what did he do? He left it.

A couple of weeks later, Mum nagged at him to get back to it, so he got the tools required and did a little bit more before getting frustrated and giving up.

Another few weeks passed before Mum got on his case again—with the same result.

These reminders of Mum's got further and further apart as we all grew accustomed to our living room looking like a construction zone. It's funny, we would forget all about it until people came over and said something like, 'Oh, wow. Are you re-wallpapering?'

We also got used to the artificial snow on the ranch slider that led from the lounge onto the front porch. I'm not sure exactly what that white stuff in the can was but it was bloody difficult to remove. Mum got it from Woolworths, which later became Deka. She then went and sprayed it on the corners of the ranch slider and wrote 'Happy Holidays' in giant letters right across the glass.

It was supposed to look like snow but I don't think many of the neighbours were fooled—it was the middle of summer and sitting around twenty-five degrees most days. And snow is not typically known to form festive sentences as it falls. It was July before Mum finally went out with a razor blade to scratch all her fake snow off. This drastic action only occurred after an anonymous neighbour put a note in our letterbox asking if we planned to remove this eyesore, as it had been over two hundred days since Christmas. Mum was mortified. She was not the slightest bit concerned about what her friends or family thought . . . but disapproval from an unknown neighbour and she would spring into action.

One of Mum's biggest plans for the new house was to add a conservatory. She had been dreaming of a conservatory with slate tiles, brownish ones the same colour as autumn leaves. Anyone who had money in the mid eighties had a conservatory—all the wannabe posh people. They were usually made with brown or white aluminium and nobody seemed to notice (or care) that they rarely suited the property and just looked like a tacked-on extra room . . . which is precisely what they were.

Mum got her conservatory put out the back of our house. What was once our back porch now had a ranch slider, and a glass roof where the green corrugated plastic had been. The idea was to make this area an extra room of the house, a sun trap, where guests could stay or friends could drink tea. In reality it continued to be the back porch, a place where we would take off our muddy shoes and leave our sports equipment, but because it was now fully enclosed and waterproof, it also became a storage area for other big items, like old tables and chairs.

It was only used as a bedroom on one occasion. Bridget was made to sleep out there on a li-lo one night when she was sixteen, after she returned home drunk from a friend's party and was ruled too intoxicated to sleep inside. Mum and Dad were awoken by lights being turned on and noises in the kitchen. They got out of bed and went to investigate, only to discover Bridget squatting down next to the oven doing a wee. She had somehow mistaken the kitchen for the toilet in her drunken state. And that is how the posh new addition to our house ended up becoming a drunk tank. I suppose the luxurious brown slate tiles would have been easier to clean vomit from than the twenty-five-year-old pale green carpet inside.

As well as getting her slate tiles and conservatory, Mum also got another couple of big-ticket items as part of this not-so-extreme home makeover. One was a white wooden fire surround for the gas heater in the lounge. This thing was beautiful, ornate. It was made from wood and painted white with lots of carved swirls all over it. The only problem was it was far too over the top for the small lounge of this house. It would have looked fine somewhere else, like in the palace of a North Korean dictator, but for the lounge of a three-bedroom house in Palmy North? It was too much. But Mum and Dad both loved it.

I think it made Mum feel a bit posh and fancy. Like the rich people in her favourite TV show, *Falcon Crest*. She displayed her precious Lladró pieces on top of it, before she got the antique cabinet. And on winter mornings Dad would get out of the shower and dry himself in front of the gas heater while admiring the fire surround, somehow managing to block out the half-torn paper on the walls . . . and the other people in the same room.

Dad was comfortable walking round the house naked—too comfortable. On the mornings he was not naked, he would wear a bizarre nightshirt, which never seemed to reach any further than mid thigh, and always without undies. It was fine when it was just us Harvey kids at home (well, not *fine*, but you know what I mean). But on occasions this towelling-off procedure in the lounge would happen while we had sleepovers. Dad would always seem surprised and embarrassed when we shouted at him and told him we had friends over. Either he was going for a shock laugh or he literally did not know how many kids he had. Or what we looked like. Flashing someone else's kids was way less frowned upon in the eighties. It would probably get you a visit from the community constable or CYFS these days.

The treasured fire surround looked just as out of place as the giant medieval-looking dining room table. Again, too big for the space, and probably better suited to the props department of *Game of Thrones* than a small brick house in Palmy. Mum and Dad fell in love with this heavy wooden table with smooth hand-chiselled ripples all over the top of it. Not to mention the six throne-like leather-backed chairs that came with it. Seriously, it wouldn't have looked out of place to be drinking from brass goblets and staring at a pig's head in the middle of the table while sitting in chainmail shirts. But it was more likely we would be sitting there eating Mum's signature dish of that era, sausage casserole, off yellow plastic plates.

The Harveys on Christmas morning. Dad is still wearing his nightshirt, which was not quite long enough to cover his testicles. Thankfully, Bridget is blocking his genitals in this picture. If you look closely you can see the half-stripped wallpaper—the lounge remained like that for some years.

BRACES

Kids these days have no idea just how bloody lucky they have it when it comes to dentistry.

I know dentistry is nowhere near as painful or intimidating as it was in the eighties . . . but when I found out just how unintimidating a trip to the dentist is for a New Zealand child today, my mind was blown. I may have even had a small sulk in the waiting room after Jay-Jay and I took our adopted nephew, Sev, to the dentist when he was five. This posh Auckland dentist we took him to specialised in doing children's teeth. There was a TV screen hanging on the ceiling and Sev was given a choice of over a hundred kids' DVDs to watch during his appointment. He was even given a small toy afterwards for being so brave. I put on my condescending kid voice and praised him too, but inside I was spewing. What the hell was so brave about sitting in a fucking chair watching *Finding Nemo* for forty-five minutes? It was like awarding someone a Victoria Cross for killing a weta with a shoe.

Throughout my primary school years, dental appointments were held in the little building by the bike stands on the school grounds that everyone knew as 'the murder house'. The school dental nurse would come into the classroom with her clipboard and call out our names one by one. Everyone would put their head down in an effort to avoid eye contact, as if that was somehow going to make a difference. She would just work her way through the school roll and that was that. I don't even remember any notes being sent home in advance. The first my parents knew about my traumatic trip to the murder house was when I got home with a new silver filling in the back of my mouth.

There were no TV screens on the ceiling. No toy or patronising speech about how awesome we were afterwards. No, it was like we were cattle and this was the abattoir. There was screaming and crying, but the dental nurse would just power on through and do her thing. She was a busy lady. She had other kids to see. Her job was to take care of your teeth, not your feelings.

Most of these tears were caused by the drill. An implement with a high-pitched screechy sound enough to give goosebumps to any New Zealander whose molars got to experience its fury.

It was never the most comforting thing in the world, being called out of class and then waiting nervously outside the murder house while listening to a soundtrack of the unmistakable drill with vocals from one of your peers screaming and pleading for the nurse to stop.

*

Given my father's crippling fear of opening his wallet, it seems a cruel twist of fate that seventy-five per cent of his four children required costly orthodontic work to correct buck teeth. Bridget was born first and had perfectly straight teeth (bitch). The next three of us were not so lucky. I was six years old when Charlotte started teething and I remember Dad crying louder than her as the teeth broke through her gums in a wonky fashion.

Braces were expensive in the eighties. From memory, mine cost a couple of thousand dollars. I had two massive front teeth that poked out and rested on my bottom lip. I was subjected to the taunts you would expect all the way from primary school right up until I finally got the braces put on at fourteen—Bugs Bunny, Buckaroo, Beaver-face, Bucky. Nothing real clever or insulting, nothing that ever upset me too much. Primary school was a time when everybody got picked on for something. If it wasn't my teeth, it would have been something else. I count myself far luckier than poor old Travis, who I shared a desk with. He had the unfortunate nickname 'Pissy Pants', because he frequently wet himself on the class mat where we all sat while the teacher read a book out loud to us. Our teacher always had a jar of sawdust at the ready which she would sprinkle over the wet patch to absorb the moisture. On the Friday of a really bad week you would find as many as four little mounds of sawdust on the mat.

Travis and I were mates, we shared a desk together, but I called him Pissy Pants, too. I don't remember saying it to be cruel—we were all just filter-less kids. At that age you haven't started to become aware of other people's feelings or learned empathy. I feel embarrassed and a bit ashamed about it now and often wonder what happened to Travis. He was only at Riverdale School for a year before he and his family moved on somewhere else. I really wish I'd never called Travis Pissy Pants. I really wish I'd stood up for him and told others not to call him Pissy Pants. But even more than this, I wish the teacher had done more to look out for Travis and teach the rest of us to be kind to others.

*

At the age of fourteen, after one very brief consultation with the orthodontist, it was determined that I would need braces. I'm guessing Dad shopped around and Dr Claridge gave the cheapest quote, and that is why Char, Dan and I were all sent to this man. Maybe Dad even haggled and negotiated a better price than Dr Claridge's already bargain basement rates.

At my initial consultation, Dr Claridge put me in the chair and looked in my mouth, but really I think he knew that braces would be required as soon as my teeth walked into his reception, followed by me a couple of seconds behind them. It didn't take an orthodontist with seven years' study under his belt to figure that one out.

Four perfectly good teeth had to be extracted first. That was how much room would be required to accommodate the teeth once the braces had forced them back into a vertical position. I was given a local anaesthetic, an injection to numb the gums, rather than a general anaesthetic where they knock you out cold. I suspect a general anaesthetic was available, and probably even recommended, but Dad would have requested the cheapest option possible.

So I was sitting there with my little mouth stretched wide open while Dr Claridge, using a combination of medical know-how and brute force, wrenched out four of my teeth with so much force my whole head was pulled around. I will never forget the harrowing graunching sound it made. I wasn't in pain but I clearly remember thinking, 'Shit, my mouth is gonna be sore later when these injections wear off.' Again, you didn't have to be an orthodontist with seven years' study under your belt to figure that one out.

The upside of this was that I was unable to eat anything but instant pudding, ice-cream and jelly for the next four days. It was a fairly desirable diet for a fourteen-year-old to be living on.

Once the gums healed up, the braces could be installed. That was another level of pain again. Three hours it took to have these giant clunky metal things glued to my teeth. I was sent home with a warning that turned out to be the understatement of the millennium—'There may be some discomfort'—and told to gargle some warm salt water IF the braces irritated the inside of my mouth. Well, I'm not quite sure where that 'if' part came from. These things tore the inside of my mouth to shreds. It was painful enough to get the things on in the first place, but the ripped skin and ulcers from the metal just made things worse. I was in so much pain and felt so defeated that I quietly sobbed myself to sleep that night. I didn't want anyone else in the family to know just how deflated I was, but the thought of having these things in my mouth for anywhere between eighteen months and four years was too much to bear. I couldn't complain, though—Dad was as fragile as I was, on account of the cost, so whingeing about this big-ticket item in my mouth would have seemed ungrateful.

Having the braces on put an end to all previous nicknames. Bugs Bunny and Buckaroo were replaced, almost immediately, by a whole new range of unoriginal names reserved for those with braces—Brace Face, Metal Mouth, Tinsel Teeth, Train Tracks, Magnet Mouth and Cheese Grater. In hindsight, the braces were probably a good distraction—if it weren't the braces I was getting ridiculed for, it would have been something else, perhaps something I was far more sensitive about, like my lack of leg hair, which made me look like a hot chick from the thighs down. Pretty much everyone got teased by everyone. Teasing and getting teased was a rite of passage. The teasing was usually based on something visual and obvious—pimples (Pizza Face), weight (Fat Fuck), glasses (Four Eyes), facial hair (Bumfluff). You could usually find something to pick on, and if not you would just fall back on the classic combination of an offensive swear word teamed up with a gay slur—fucking fag, fucking homo, fucking cocksucker, queer cunt or fucking gay cunt. It was highbrow stuff, I tell you.

Every month I had to go back to Dr Claridge for an appointment called an 'adjustment'. He would tighten the braces and give me these little bags of rubber bands which would hook between the top and bottom teeth in both corners of my mouth. The tension from these rubber bands would help to pull my teeth back into the correct position. These adjustments were horrible, because for a few days afterwards my mouth would be in agony again.

There was another thing that made these adjustment sessions akin to hell—Dr Claridge's soapy fingers. Dentists all use rubber gloves now, a clean pair for each patient. I'm not sure when the use of gloves became a standard hygiene practice, but Dr Claridge always preferred to go in naked. In between patients he would wash his hands thoroughly with warm water and a cake of some cheap soap. You would end up with the taste and smell of his soapy hands all through your mouth, making an unpleasant experience even worse.

Dr Claridge seemed to hate kids, too. He was always grumpy. Which made me wonder why he chose this career path in the first place. Since the majority of his clients were children, it seems like one of the poorest career choices a kid-hater could make, right up there with teaching.

I would go home from these adjustments and plonk myself down in front of the TV and remind myself of why I was doing this. It was all for Nadine Garner. There was no way a girl as pretty as her would ever be interested in a boy with beaver teeth. I had a major crush on Nadine for the first few years of my teens. She was in my favourite afternoon TV show, *The Henderson Kids*. In this show Nadine played the part of Tamara Henderson. She and her brother, Steve, were forced to leave the city and move to a small country town called Haven Bay with their uncle Mike after their mum was hit and killed by a truck (charming).

I even had a not-particularly-well-thought-out plan of getting my braces off and going to Australia, where I would orchestrate a run-in with Nadine by hanging out at all the places I knew she frequented around Haven Bay.

Fortunately for me, the show was cancelled by the time the braces came off. My judgement had been clouded by the ibuprofen and my crush on Nadine, so I hadn't taken the time to think through a few fairly important points:

1. Haven Bay was a fictional place.
2. The places Tamara and her gang of friends hung out at were film sets.
3. International travel was expensive and I was earning eighteen dollars a week with a paper round.

Still, it was a nice fantasy to have and it did help me through some dark and depressing afternoons. The final month with the braces on was one of the most drawn-out months of my teenage years. I've never spent time in jail, but I'd imagine the excitement and restlessness I felt were similar to that of an inmate who's been told his release date. That day could not come soon enough. The feeling of running your tongue over your teeth is something you take for granted. For days afterwards I was addicted to doing this. I must have looked like some sort of sexual deviant to anyone unlucky enough to catch me reacquainting my tongue with the front of my teeth.

And credit to old soapy fingers, Dr Claridge—the teeth looked amazing. I was normal. Everything was falling into place for Dominic Mark Harvey. I had nice teeth, pubic hair, and had just scored an afternoon job packing groceries at Foodtown—a job which put me in contact with girls my own age, girls who lived in real Palmerston North suburbs and not made-up Australian towns. Life was good. It was my time to shine. Hello, ladies!

HELLO, LADIES!

The best and worst thing about going to an all-boys secondary school is the same thing: NO GIRLS!

Best, because it means you can spend more time concentrating on the reason for being at school in the first place instead of worrying about impressing chicks.

Worst, because it puts the young male students at a bit of a disadvantage when it comes to meeting girls their own age.

For proof of this you only need to examine my track record prior to starting secondary school. I was quite the young ladies' man, I think you will agree. I had my first proper kiss, a pash we called it, in standard three, when I was nine. By anybody's standards, that would make me an early starter. Then came my two years of intermediate at the co-ed St Peters. It was here that I had my first serious long-term relationship. Bronwyn Keegan and I lasted for two and a half months. That may not sound all that long, but when you're eleven it represents a reasonable chunk of your life.

It was also at intermediate that I had my first sexual experience . . . kind of. Ryan, the coolest guy in inter-mediate, and I went to the blue-light disco run by the local police. He got talking to a girl and they started kissing. While this was going on I was standing next to him, just watching and waiting for him to stop. I don't remember feeling awkward about it. I think I was yet to develop that sense of knowing when you should make yourself scarce.

Physical contact at the blue-light discos was not allowed, but these things were so popular that the number of kids always far outweighed the number of adult volunteers, so anyone who got caught would have to be pretty damn unlucky.

After maintaining this kiss for a couple of songs they stopped. Ryan then put one hand around the girl's shoulder and the other hand up her top, where I could see it dancing around from undeveloped boob to undeveloped boob. While this was occurring Ryan was chatting to me and his new friend and I was chatting to him and to her and she was chatting to us both. It was a perfectly normal conversation between three twelve-year-olds . . . except the only one in the conversation wearing a training bra was being subjected to a chest rub.

Eventually the biggest song in the world at the time came on, 'One Night in Bangkok' by Murray Head, so Ryan and his new friend went to dance. I lost Ryan after that and didn't see him the rest of the night. Monday morning at school he came up to me and explained what had happened—he and his new friend had been kicked out by an adult volunteer after they were caught making out on the dance floor. But far from being upset, Ryan was ecstatic: 'I got my first poke!'

He then offered me a sniff of his finger, presumably as evidence to back up his claim of digital penetration. It was unnecessary—I fully believed him—but I was not going to turn down such a generous offer. I inhaled and got a strong aroma of cheese, pastry and mince. By this stage it was fifty-six hours since the blue-light disco, so I'm assuming he'd had a mince and cheese pie on his way to school. I told him it smelt amazing, which was not untruthful. Then for the next five years of my life, until I finally got the chance to see a real-life vagina, a tiny part of me wondered if girls' private parts did smell like Cobblestone pies.

*

The first time I got to socialise with girls was when I turned sixteen and got an after-school and weekend job packing groceries on the check-outs at Foodtown. This was a massive coup. It was a shitty job with fairly poor pay . . . but I loved it. I loved everything about it, especially getting to mingle with girls who were not immediate family members.

The girls' uniform was a maroon smock that was probably designed to look as unflattering and unsexy as possible. On my first week on the job I got assigned to pack for Liz, a check-out operator the same age as me from Palmerston North Girls High School. Liz had huge boobs. I couldn't believe I was being paid to stand next to and talk to such a beautiful girl. Yes, I had to pack the groceries of annoying customers—irritating people who often wanted their ice-cream wrapped up in old newspaper and who complained when I put heavy items on top of their bread or eggs. But doing the job was a small price to pay for this nearly one-on-one time with girls. As Liz slid groceries over the scanner down towards me in the bagging area that day, I discovered the most difficult part of the job. I had to work the first hour with a full erection that refused to go away. I was so excited you could have hung a heavy bag of groceries off it!

*

It was not long before I developed a crush on another check-out operator, Ang. She had smiled and spoken to me and in doing so had given me the definite impression that she was keen to help me lose my virginity. We had a discussion about music. She was a big fan of the band Fine Young Cannibals, who had the number 1 song in New Zealand at that time with a hit called 'She Drives Me Crazy'. On payday I went into Foodtown to collect my wages, which were paid in cash in a small brown envelope. I think you could have your wages credited directly into your account, but cash in the brown envelope was still the option most staff went for. Ang was rostered on this particular afternoon and she waved and smiled as I walked past.

With that, I decided to do something crazy. Not the sort of thing I would normally do but the sort of thing I had seen in numerous movies, and in the movies these high-risk gambles usually paid off. This was going to be my John Cusack ghetto-blaster moment. *Say Anything* was one of my favourite movies at the time. In this movie, Cusack's character won a girl over by standing on her front lawn at night playing a Peter Gabriel song on his boom box. This was significant because earlier in the movie they had talked about this song. It worked a treat too—the movie ends with the couple holding hands on a plane. Sorry if anyone is mad that I gave away the ending, but since the movie is a quarter of a century old, I didn't feel it was necessary to offer a spoiler alert.

With my brown envelope full of notes and coins I ran over to the record shop in the Plaza Shopping Centre and splashed out on the Fine Young Cannibals cassette tape, *The Raw and the Cooked*.

I returned to Foodtown and went up to the check-out where Ang was packing. This was going to be epic. If it was one of the eighties movies I had watched for love tips, she would have kissed me right there in the store, then torn off her Foodtown name badge and told the predictably mean supervisor that she quit, before riding off with me on a motorbike while the credits rolled.

My expectations were far more realistic. I saw her being blown away by my romantic gesture, giving me a hug and maybe inviting me over to her house after she finished work to listen to it together.

Spoiler alert: neither of these scenarios took place.

I waited until Ang was in between customers and then approached her with the gift. She politely declined it. I politely insisted she take it. She less politely and more firmly declined it. I asked why. She politely said she didn't like me like that. I persisted. And that is when a customer turned up and began to unload her groceries on the conveyer belt, which was not ideal. But I was in too far to back out. My time was now. I gave the sort of speech Molly Ringwald's love interest would deliver to her in a pivotal scene:

'Ang, I like you heaps. I think you're wicked as. Please give me a chance. Please? I promise you won't regret it.

I want you to have this tape because when I hear that song I think about you. You drive me crazy.'

Okay, so maybe it was a bit more desperate and cringey than a movie speech, but it was delivered with the same level of conviction.

Before Ang even had the chance to respond to my all-cards-on-the-table spiel, the customer who had heard the whole thing, a woman in her thirties with a small child sitting in the trolley, spoke for Ang: 'Sweetheart, I'm sorry for eavesdropping, but I think you should just go. I don't even know you and I feel bad for you.'

I walked off feeling depressed. I was a bit sad that Ang had rebuffed me and embarrassed that a woman who chose to shop at the wrong supermarket at the wrong time had overheard it . . . but mostly I was gutted that I had spent almost half my week's wages on a cassette tape that I didn't even want. Fuck the Fine Young Cannibals.

STAR-CROSSED LOVERS

Before finding Jay-Jay in my late twenties and everything just sort of clicking into place perfectly, I had a couple of successful relationships, including a five-year on-off stint with Kim Lindsay, my first proper girlfriend and the girl I lost my virginity to. She deserves a bravery medal for that, or a mention on the Queen's birthday honours list at the very least.

Kim works for a car rental company in Palmerston North and gave me a free upgrade last time I flew in and picked up a car. I requested a compact Toyota and was given the keys to the newest Holden Commodore they had available. I think that means she has forgiven me for the Beachcomber Island incident. I travelled to Beachcomber in Fiji with my best mate, Robert Scott, for a boys' party trip. I got a couple of things for Kim from Fiji—a Swatch watch from the duty-free shop and a case of scabies from the Danish girl with limited English who I slept with in the bunk room.

Kim and I got on great. We argued a lot but we loved each other heaps. She even bought me a plush toy one Valentine's Day, a monkey holding a silk love-heart-shaped cushion with the words 'I Wuv You' written on it. If that isn't true love, I don't know what is!

*

I think Jay-Jay and I met at just the right time in both our lives. We were both on the dark side of our mid twenties. She'd had a few relationships that just never worked out and, as she puts it, she had to kiss a lot of frogs before finding a prince (awwww). I'd also had a few relationships that just didn't work out, but I didn't kiss many frogs along the way. Not through lack of trying!

I would have loved to be a skanky man-whore but just never had the necessary confidence to talk a G-string off anyone. Before Jay-Jay, I even committed low-level fraud as a way to make girls like me.

Right after leaving school for my first radio job in 1990, one of my tasks as the midnight to six am radio announcer was to stick around after my shift had finished to help produce the breakfast show—'Mike West in the Morning on 2XS FM'. Mike's real name was Blain Yarrell, but outside of family and really close friends nobody called him that. He started his radio career in the early eighties, a time when a lot of broadcasters would change their name at the program director's suggestion if it was thought their actual name was not catchy enough. This is uncommon in the radio industry these days, but it still happens occasionally. I was in a mate's car the other week when a guy came on the radio called Richie Hardcore. I could be wrong, but it sounds like a made-up surname to me.

One of the most popular segments on Mike West's show was his morning horoscopes at around quarter to eight. Women in particular loved this part of the show. A lot of women based their day, what they wore, ate and did, around what their horoscope was for that day.

Being a little old radio station in Palmerston North, we naturally didn't have our own astrologist on site. And reading horoscopes straight from that morning's paper wouldn't work. We did try it, but people complained that they were the same as the ones in the paper. It seems that people who believe in bullshit like to get their bullshit from a variety of different sources. To give this crock-of-shit segment some credibility, we would buy twelve different horoscope books each year, one for each sign, written by some famous astrologist. The books had a fairly lengthy and detailed prediction for every day of the year. One of my jobs was to look at the books and then write a punchier, more radio-friendly summary for each star sign.

By the time I handed the prepared horoscopes to Mike West for that morning's show, it would be a hand-typed sheet of A4 with twelve predictions like this:

Aries: Be careful when chatting with colleagues today. Things you say could easily be misinterpreted, which may lead to trouble.

See, what the hell does that even mean? It's so broad and meaningless, but some people live by these things.

I hated this job so I belted them out as fast as I could. Even then it still took about half an hour a day.

It was around this time I met Nicole. She worked in the Plaza Shopping Centre and was really good-looking. You would see her walking around and wonder if she was from Wellington or Auckland, because she just didn't look like the other girls in the area. This particular year, most of the girls studying at Massey University in Palmy wore the same outfit—those patchwork Canterbury rugby shorts, short-sleeve checked shirts with the collar popped up and a fob chain. It was a very rural look and not something that ever caught on internationally, or even nationally. If the girls were getting glammed up for a night out, the rugby shorts would be replaced with three-quarter pants, called pedal pushers, and their accessories would be carried in a little black backpack. From memory, the only thing Nicole had in common with the majority of the Palmy population at the time was the fob chain.

We got on really well and started to hang out a lot. She had some boyfriend doing his OE in London. As far as I was concerned, that meant she was single and ready to mingle. This was a time when a phone call from New Zealand to London cost about eight dollars a minute, so letter writing was still the most popular way to communicate. Fax machines had been around for a couple of years but were still just business tools. So there was no way I was going to let old Mr Imaginary Boyfriend all the way over on the other side of the world put me off the hottest chick in Palmy!

As my luck would have it, Nicole was one of those girls who lived by her daily horoscope.

Out of desperation, I started to manipulate her daily prediction, so it would work in my favour. On a Friday, her star sign, Taurus, might have gone something like this:

Any plans you already have in place should be reconsidered when another invite comes your way. You may have way more fun than you expect.

Or, if she had been talking to me about old Captain Imaginary over in London, the next morning's horoscope might have said something along the lines of:

It could be time to cut ties in a relationship that is not working for you. Someone better will be just round the corner.

My self-serving horoscope tweaks were about as subtle as a bright orange Hummer. I pity any listener who happened to dump their partner only to discover there was no one waiting just around the corner.

Nicole never said anything about her daily horoscope readings mirroring her life, but she must have had her doubts about them. Some were just too blatant not to arouse suspicion.

Eventually, Nicole left Palmerston North to fly over to London. I cannot believe she had the courage to fly out . . . her horoscope on the morning of her departure warned it was unsafe for Taureans to be flying that day.

*

Nicole leaving signalled the end of my manipulation of the astrological charts but opened up a whole new chapter of humiliation. Most people would have taken the hint if someone told them they were flying for twenty-four hours to be with their boyfriend. I'm not sure how I managed to misread the situation so badly, but I still thought there was a chance for me and Nicole. I thought the connection we had and the groundwork I had laid down were so awe-inspiring that she would get to London, realise what she had left behind in New Zealand and then fly straight back home . . . like a scene from a John Hughes movie.

That didn't happen, surprise, surprise. But a couple of weeks after she departed, I did receive a postcard from London which I read, over and over. I can't even remember what it said, but it was fairly innocuous. I showed it to other female friends and got them to analyse what it meant and what I could read into the 'XOX' she signed off with. The general consensus was that it was just a fucking postcard, there was no hidden meaning in the message and I should stop trying to find one and just forget about her. Being far wiser than all of my well-meaning friends, I decided to do the opposite. I made her a mix tape. I got a brand new C60 blank cassette and filled it up with songs that we both really liked. And since I worked at a radio station as an announcer and had professional recording equipment at my disposal, I decided it would be more personal to talk through it—introduce the songs and explain why they had been included. I have tried to block out the memory, so I really have no accurate recollection of what I said, but I am sure it was fucking horrible. If this tape still existed somewhere I would pay a substantial sum to have it destroyed. I would rather get a notoriously painful traditional Samoan tattoo on my scrotum than have to sit down and listen to this recording. However, at the time, it seemed like the smart thing to do.

Nicole loved it. She thought it was the cutest thing ever. By the way, the C word is not a word any guy wants to hear from a girl he is hoping to dominate in the bedroom. I know she thought it was cute because she told me in a letter she sent me. The paragraph about the mix tape went something like this:

'That tape was just too cute. I loved it. I listened to it over and over and each listen made me feel a bit more homesick.'

Good start, I thought. Then came the bit that made me want to punch myself in the Adam's apple:

'We went on a road trip to Paris with our flatmates and blasted it all weekend in the car. We all loved it.'

So this quite personal recording, something which I envisaged would be listened to in private with headphones on, had been playing on a fucking car stereo to a fucking audience! And it turned out the invisible imaginary boyfriend was a real-life human, with ears. That was karma, I reckon. He'd been overseas while his girlfriend was being chipped away at by some pimply broadcaster in Palmerston North. He ended up keeping the girl, and the prick got the last laugh too.

That was the last mix tape I ever made for a girl. I suppose I should just count my blessings that this was in an era well before YouTube and Facebook. This was a time when 'going viral' meant that four flatmates in a car on a road trip would get to hear you make a dick of yourself. I had gone viral early nineties style—today a similar act of awkward embarrassment in the name of love would hit a million views within a couple of days.

*

I'd say the threat of going viral after making a dick of yourself on a global scale is the only aspect of being a teen now that is worse than being a teen in the eighties and nineties. Apart from that, teens today have got it so good. Nobody needs to get rejected face to face or even voice to voice on the phone these days, so asking someone out is an ultra-low-risk situation. My teenage years would have been so much more fun with an iPhone loaded with Tinder, Snapchat and Facebook. Written communication would have worked in my favour way more than face-to-face stuff. Also, rejection is way easier to swallow if it arrives as an abbreviated text message a couple of sentences long. The only real pitfall I can see is that if I'd had access to the tools young men have these days, there would probably be many thousands of photos of my penis clogging up the internet.

Young lads today will never experience that awkward first meeting where you are sweating bullets trying to think of more shit to ask to fill any uncomfortable silences. All that stuff can be done with messaging now, so when you finally have some face time the ice is well and truly broken.

Young lads today will never need to rehearse a conversation, practising their tone and delivery. I did all this stuff. I'm sure I wasn't alone, was I? Oh shit. Yes, now that I write it down, 'conversation rehearsal' definitely does sound a wee bit creepy, and something that may not have been all that common. Once I was happy I had nailed the right tone—a bit blasé, not too eager or needy—I would clear my voice and dial my unlucky victim's landline. It wasn't called the landline then, though—it was just called the phone. And in our house these calls were never private. Ever. We only had the one phone and it sat on a little table in the hallway, meaning every conversation could be heard by everybody in the lounge, depending on the volume of the TV. If you rejoined the family in the lounge after being on the phone there was a 97.5 per cent probability that someone would ask: 'Who was that on the phone?'

That figure dropped significantly a few years later when we finally became a two-phone household—not because it gave us more privacy, but because a second phone made it easier to listen in on other people's calls. Invasive espionage meant there was no need even to ask who was on the damn phone.

We still had the phone in the hall, but now we also had one next to Mum and Dad's bed. Being a two-phone household was a pretty big thing. A phone in the bedroom was right up there with a fourteen-inch telly in the bedroom and having an ensuite. Now when someone was on the phone, Mum would go to her room and discreetly try to pick up the bedroom phone and listen in on the chat. It was not easy to do and the odds of being caught were high. The handset had to be lifted slowly and gently, like you were playing a game of pick-up sticks, so the phone would not make this clicking noise that was a dead giveaway.

Funnily enough, the only way to ensure total privacy was to bike round the corner and use the payphone in the red New Zealand Post Office phone box.

LAWN PRICKLES

Not only are kids softer these days—so are the lawn prickles. These things used to be ferocious. Not bee-sting ferocious, closer to real-hot-sand ferocious. Bad enough to make most of us barefoot kids tread with caution across lawns as if we were walking across a field of landmines in Mozambique. We would cross particularly prickly lawns awkwardly on our heels, since they were the toughest patch of skin on the bottom of our feet.

It was not uncommon to finish a lawn walk and then spend a couple of minutes sitting on the front porch, footpath or driveway carefully removing the numerous prickles that had pierced the skin.

Yes, we could have just worn shoes or jandals. But it was summer and our feet were hot. And shoes reminded us of school and church and other more formal situations where Mum had forced us to wear shoes and keep them on. Probably for good reason, too—if we took our shoes off somewhere, we would inevitably lose a sock, or both socks. Occasionally the shoes AND socks would be left behind. This irresponsibility is a perk afforded to the young and carefree—it starts to wear off when you have to replace these misplaced items with your own hard-earned money.

Lawn prickles and balls being hit over the fence were the two biggest hold-ups New Zealand kids faced in backyard cricket in the 1980s. The prickles are not as much of an issue anymore.

Unfortunately, a solution has not been found for the ball-over-the-fence scenario. Not even the introduction of the six and out rule has done much to cut the number of balls being hit into the next property on the full.

WHITE DOG POO

It is entirely possible that if you are a reader of a certain age, you would never ever have seen a white dog poo in your life. Proper white, like Shane Warne's teeth. In the 1980s it was everywhere. You would find it hard to walk a hundred metres without spotting a white dog poo on someone's grass verge.

When I was five and living in Galway Place in Hastings, one of the slightly older kids in our cul-de-sac convinced me this white stuff was not dog poo at all but cloud poo. I was open to this suggestion because I hadn't really thought too much about it—it was poo, that's all I knew. What creature (or troposphere) it came from was not something I had ever bothered looking into.

I was a fairly trusting/gullible child, as most five-year-olds are, but he seemed to have an answer for all the questions I had. He explained that rain was wee from the clouds, the thunder was a cloud fart and this hard white stuff was cloud poo. When I asked why we never saw it land on the ground, he told me that the clouds only did their poo at night-time. Sounded plausible, even considerate on the clouds' part.

For the next couple of years, anytime I was outside after dark I was mildly petrified about being shat on by a thunderous cloud above . . . and walking home from school in winter getting soaked in cloud urine did not exactly fill me with joy.

I have an unexplored, unscientific and un-googled theory on the white dog poo: I reckon it must turn white after a certain period of time, say a couple of weeks. And because dog owners picking up their pets' waste was a foreign concept in the seventies and eighties, poo was just left out in the elements to transform from a repulsive-smelling, warm, soft brown thing into this hard piece of white shite . . . but nobody ever really noticed the metamorphosis while it was in transition. So maybe dog poo still ends up white after a period of time, but these days it is never left out long enough for the whitening process to occur.

Thankfully, these days dog owners always take a plastic bag out with them and pick up after their dog (at least, when it is daylight and they know other people can see them!), but back then there was no expectation or responsibility at all to pick this stuff up.

I can't say I ever touched the stuff, but I do know it was as hard as a rock just from the sound it made when Dad would run over one with the lawnmower. White dog poo being mowed made the same *clunk* sound as the popular red scoria rocks from the garden. Come to think of it, you never see too much scoria used in landscaping anymore. That was replaced by bark chips as the ground cover of choice and nowadays scoria is about as rare as white dog poo.

The white dog poo situation got so bad in the mid eighties that Kiwi home owners started doing what was, in hindsight, an irrational and counterproductive thing to stop the dogs defecating on their lawn.

Someone suggested that dogs hate to poo anywhere near fresh water. I can't remember where, maybe it was on *A Dog's Show*. This was one of New Zealand's most popular telly shows—every weekend for half an hour you would watch as farmers whistled at their dogs to get them to herd sheep into little pens. Not surprisingly, the concept was never picked up by TV networks in other countries.

I don't know if this dogs-and-fresh-water theory is true or not but a trend began to fill old soft drink bottles with water and place them on your lawn. It started with just one or two houses in a couple of streets, mainly old age pensioners, placing a bottle on their front lawn and a bottle on the grass verge out front. It didn't take long before this theory reached critical mass and almost every home had old bottles of Mello Yello, Leed, Coke and Fanta all filled with water littering the front lawn. Some houses had so many bottles dotted around their lawn it would have been an effective way to keep the squatting dogs away . . . because there was so little visible grass left for the dog to go on!

Eventually, this practice disappeared. Maybe because New Zealanders came to their senses and realised that:

1. The bottles of water were about as effective as making a hissing noise to scare away a cat.
2. One white dog poo on the lawn was easier on the eye than seventeen old plastic Fanta bottles with rain- and sun-faded labels.

THE FIFTY-CENT MIX

One of the greatest pleasures of being a child in New Zealand in the 1980s was the fifty-cent mix. This was the name given to a little white bag of lollies you could buy at the dairy. There were pre-prepared bags under the counter, but any self-respecting kid who was lucky enough to be in possession of a giant heavy old fifty-cent piece would want to select their own sweets to make up the fifty-cent mix.

It did not stop there, either. You could go higher or lower. You could get a dollar mix or a twenty-cent mix. This was a time when a Popsicle sold for twenty cents and a Trumpet was only fifty-five cents, so a twenty-cent mix could be a reasonably substantial bag of lollies.

All the dairies had an area with a glass counter top and a slide-out drawer underneath. This drawer had maybe twenty or so square compartments, which each contained lollies of different values between one cent and five cents each.

The five centers were big things like Pineapple Lumps and bubblegum in the shape of a spinning top that spun. The mid-price lollies were things like Glo Hearts and raspberry drops. And right down in the one-cent row were sweets that were the cheapest for a reason—most commonly, imitation pebbles. These looked just like the delicious Cadbury Pebbles but were made from cheaper ingredients and left a horrible aftertaste . . . not that it stopped us from buying and eating them. The other staple in the one-cent row were powdery, tasteless lollies made to look like NZ coins. In hindsight, swallowing a real coin would have been tastier, and possibly better for your digestive system.

I don't remember the shopkeepers ever using tongs or wearing gloves. They just weren't required, since this was before the invention of germs.

Often, this coin (actual currency, not the tasteless sweet) was the reward for going to the dairy on behalf of a parent or uncle to get whatever it was they required but couldn't be arsed getting themselves—milk, bread, the newspaper or smokes. I don't know if it was legal or not for shopkeepers to sell smokes to kids, but we were always sold smokes at Mr Horman's dairy because he came to know Mum and us kids. For any dairies we were being sent to for the first time, Mum would usually give us a note to hand over to the shopkeeper, like a permission slip.

Mr Horman ran our local, the College Street dairy. It was about six hundred metres from our house and we didn't have to cross any roads to get there, so we were allowed to bike there any time we came into some money.

Poor old Mr Horman—every time a child went into his dairy with a coin in hand you could tell he would die a little inside. Deciding what lollies to get in your mixture was a decision not to be made lightly. Some contestants on *Who Wants to Be a Millionaire?* spend less time deliberating their answer than it took us to select the final sweet to go in our bag. Mr Horman would sigh and tap the glass and, if he got really impatient, tell us to hurry up because he didn't have all day. The funny thing is, he *did* have all day. He lived in a house out the back and only came into the dairy when the buzzer went off and he heard someone walk through the flappy plastic fly-curtain at the front door.

I remember him doing all this stuff, but I don't remember ever being bothered or rushed by it. It wasn't just the lollies that got Mr Horman angry. He was always shouting at people, kids and adults, who had the audacity to open up the iceblock fridge before they had decided what they wanted. And on his watch, I don't think any customer ever got to hold a magazine for longer than fifteen seconds before he asked them if they planned on buying it.

Eventually we stopped going to his dairy and biked the extra three hundred metres to the Rugby Street dairy instead. It was not a protest or anything. We were not taking our business elsewhere on account of Mr Horman's rudeness. The Rugby Street dairy was under new management and word spread fast that the new owners, the Clouts, were generous with their lollies, sometimes even chucking one or two extras in for free. They also got a reputation as making the biggest ice-creams in the city.

The Clouts were friendly as well. They seemed like cool grown-ups. They were in their twenties, I suppose. They never hurried us or complained about not having all day. It was as if they understood the magic that was occurring—the magic of being a kid, the magic of having some money to spend, and the magic of getting to make a decision for yourself at an age where most decisions are made for you.

DURASEAL COVERS

I think these things were compulsory. They must have been. Otherwise I cannot imagine why any right-minded person would have kept giving it a crack year after year.

At the beginning of each school year, Mum would go to a shop called McKenzies, which later became Deka and is now nothing more than a sign still standing in Huntly, and buy all the exercise books we needed for the school year.

I don't see any real difference in the exercise books available today, but for some reason putting your own cover over the book's actual cover was considered very important back then.

If you were a kid who was hoping to be bullied or ridiculed, at the start of the school year you could get your mum to cover your books in some sort of recycled paper from home, like old wallpaper, Christmas wrapping or even an old page from a newspaper. These were like the tight-arse alternative to Duraseal. How I avoided this fate is a mystery to me. Mum usually seemed to get a sadistic pleasure out of sending us to school with the uncool alternative—if all the kids in class were wearing Nomads, Mum would buy me a pair of Charlie Browns.

And when it was time for a new bike and I really wanted a BMX, I was given a far more sensible bike called a Cruiser, with an emasculating carrier on the back. For sports prize-giving, when we had to bring along a plate of food, I'd be sent to school with a well-buttered date loaf that would always remain on the table uneaten.

When I complained about these things, Mum would tell me that the other kids teased me because they were jealous. It was reasoning that made no sense—why would the student who brought along the tray of Rice Bubble cake be jealous of me and my food offering that was so repulsive not even the sparrows would eat it when it was eventually thrown out on the lawn?

I'm not sure how Duraseal managed to stay in business, given it was impossible to use. Nobody ever managed to get it on free of air bubbles and other unsightly creases and folds.

Every year Mum would spend hours covering all our books, and I'd estimate each book she covered reduced her life span by a week, that's how stressful it was. Rocket science and brain surgery are probably easier than putting Duraseal onto the cover of a 1B5 Warwick.

But Duraseal still served its purpose and protected the cover of the book. Sadly, nothing could protect the lined pages inside the covers, so clean and pristine at the start of the year. When the Christmas holidays rolled around each December, the Durasealed cover of the book still looked decent, compared to the shabby dog-eared pages filled with work so untidy you'd think the author did most of his schoolwork while sitting on the back tray of a ute being driven over bumpy terrain.

SPORTS AND ME

Do PE teachers still do that awful thing where two class-mates are chosen to be team captains and then get to pick their team members one by one until that humiliating moment when one fat kid is left standing? For a lot of the less sporty kids, I'd say the only thing more humiliating would have been the shirts v. skins games when you were on the team who had to remove their shirts. Surely both these things have been discouraged, so the kids who are terrible at sports or have early-stage moobs don't end up with hurt feelings, or melanoma.

I would stand there full of nerves, my self-esteem plummeting further every time a name was called out that wasn't mine. I was reasonably lucky, too. I was never the very last to be picked. Then again, I was never the first to be picked, either—even when friends of mine were given the role of team captain (thanks for the support, guys!).

I always had mixed emotions as I looked at the last kid standing. Naturally, I felt a bit embarrassed for them—it *was* humiliating. But I was equally relieved I wasn't the one left standing there awkwardly, unwanted. My reputation as a liability to the team was well deserved. Anybody who had played with me before knew about my limited hand-eye coordination. I was physically fit, always running around doing stuff, but my clumsiness was legendary. The way I moved around, with long limbs flailing all over the place, I looked much like a newborn giraffe attempting to walk. It got to the point where I was simply unable to play any weekend team sport because the really competitive kids in the team would just get too annoyed with me.

I hung up the rugby boots and retired from Saturday morning footy at the age of nine. This was my first year of wearing boots, too. Before that we had been forced to run round the frosty parks on Saturday morning in bare feet. It stung for the first few minutes . . . but then your feet would go numb and the pain would stop. I think I would have stuck it out for another season or two if Mum and Dad had got me some boots like all the other guys in the team had. Instead, I was made to wear hand-me-down boots . . . Dad's old ones from when he was my age back in the 1950s! The boots are long gone now—I didn't feel the need to keep them as an heirloom and pass them down to any sons I might father for a further generation of teasing.

This certificate is the only proof I have that I ever played our national sport.

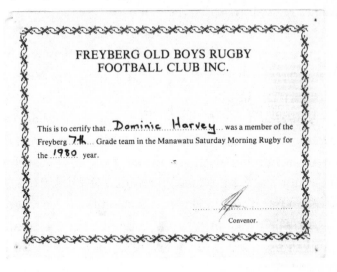

I wanted to give up earlier, but Dad made me stick it out. There were two massive problems. The first was that I hated rugby. The other big problem was this weird handicap I still have to this very day—I can pass the ball to my right, but not to my left. If I was standing on the left side of the field, I would be fine—but when I found myself down the right side or had no teammates to my right, I had to do this bizarre manoeuvre where I would turn around so my back was facing the other team and *then* pass the ball to my right. It worked. But it did slow the game down quite considerably, it meant I had to pass the ball while stationary, because running backwards and passing was too difficult. By the time of my premature retirement, my teammates were so fearful of what could happen if the ball came to me that I would often go entire games without touching the ball.

It's funny how you forget these things and bury them away somewhere until something occurs that reminds you. For me, that trigger event was the NRL Nines in February 2013.

New Zealand rugby league legend Monty Betham was putting together a NZ media team to play a game of touch rugby against an Australia media team as the curtain-raiser for the NRL Nines grand final at Eden Park. He asked me if I wanted to be involved and I said yes without hesitation. It was one of those situations where I didn't really think things through before saying yes. If I'm being completely truthful, I was a little bit starstruck at being asked by Monty.

Saying yes to things without properly thinking it through is something I seem to have a bad habit of doing . . . as long as whatever I'm being asked to do is far enough in the future. Monty asked in November 2013. At that point it felt like February 2014 was a whole year away.

For most Kiwi males, this would be a boyhood dream fulfilled—playing at Eden Park in front of fifty thousand and with a potential TV audience of millions. For me, it was the stuff of terrifying nightmares. Letting down my primary school teammates and hearing parents on the sidelines snigger at the gangly kid who couldn't pass the ball to the left was one thing. But to let down a legend of the game and be booed at by such a massive audience was not something I really fancied at this stage of my life.

Sunday evening, 15 February 2014, I presented my player accreditation to a security guard and walked through the tunnels of Eden Park with my teammates. Both our team and the Australian team were a combination of members of the media and former NRL stars, including Wairangi Koopu, Richie Barnett, Gorden Tallis, Andrew Johns, Wendell Sailor, Danny Buderus, Brett Finch, Steve Turner and Tim Brasher. Most of the media guys were lapping it up, basking in this chance to rub shoulders and play alongside some of the game's greats in front of a big home crowd. I was shitting my pants.

We got to our team changing room and Monty handed everyone their uniform. I put mine on then went to the toilet and threw up. It was only a small amount of vomit but it burnt the back of my throat and left a lingering awful taste. It was unpleasant, but I could deal with that—I just hoped nobody else in the team had heard my retching. That would be embarrassing.

Monty then gave us a team talk. It was very shouty and sweary. First he said some stuff about representing our country. Then he said something about beating those cunts. It was all very emotive. Then he reminded us that it was all good fun and we should enjoy ourselves. I went and threw up again. What the hell had I got myself into?

The ground announcer called us out onto the field one by one, then the game commenced. I had a mantra that I repeated to myself as we waited for the game to start: *DON'T FUCK IT UP! DON'T FUCK IT UP! DON'T FUCK IT UP!* Given my ability on the sporting field, this is what I would consider a positive affirmation.

It worked. I did not fuck anything up. It would have been incredibly unlucky if I did, though, since I only got to touch the ball once. Someone passed the ball to me and I just had to pass it on immediately to the teammate to my right, *the side I can pass to.*

I narrowly avoided being humiliated in front of an audience of millions in the second half, when I was out on the right wing marking one of the Australian guys. This guy caught a real long pass and had a lot of open space—he just had to get past me and he would have been off with a certain try. I should have been in the moment, all super focused. Instead, all I could do was repeat my mantra:

DON'T FUCK IT UP!
DON'T FUCK IT UP!
DON'T FUCK IT UP!

He started running down the sideline with the ball in one hand. I managed to get in front of him with my arms out wide. He ducked back away from me and did this funny little pretend-to-sidestep-and-do-a-fake-pass move. Then, as he was about to shoot off in god-knows-what direction, I managed to reach out and touch him. I TOUCHED HIM. The euphoria and relief was indescribable. This was as good as scoring a try.

Immediately after the game, which we won by a point, I went home to watch the replay on TV. I just wanted to see how I'd managed to escape fifteen minutes of guaranteed humiliation. When my touch came on, this is how the commentators described it:

'Brasher back. Brasher. Here he goes . . . Oooooh, great touch, Dominic Harvey. Superb work from Harvey, catching Brasher in full flight!'

I had no idea if this bald bloke Brasher was a former player or just an Aussie media hack, so I googled him. Turns out he's kind of a big deal. A legendary player who had played for Australia, New South Wales and Balmain. And I had stopped him from scoring a try. Me. The kid from Palmy who gave up on team sports thirty years earlier because I had been traumatised by moments far less daunting.

I went down to the supermarket to grab a bottle of wine, a little something to try and get my adrenaline down a bit. The Indian bloke who served me said, 'You look happy tonight, mister. Did you win the Lotto or something?'

I gave him the truth: 'It's better than Lotto, mate . . . I didn't fuck it up!'

The funny thing is that if I knew the guy I was marking was some big legend, there is no way I ever would have made that touch. But I had done it! I had conquered my team sports demons.

TENNIS COURTS AND JOGGING SHORTS

Tennis was a big sport in our family. Dad played most weekends and was in the Manawatu rep team. I think he was quite good, which is surprising given the weakness of his serve.

When Dad served he had none of the grace or poise of the world's best when they throw that green ball high into the air with total concentration. Nor did he have their ferocious power. When Dad served, it resembled an odd tribal dance—like there was a bug on the ground he was trying to squash, and if there was a headwind his second serve would sometimes fail to make it all the way over the net.

It was just luck that Dad's rival for the title of Palmerston North's best tennis player was a fat bloke called John. John's nickname for my dad was 'Slim'. He moved fast for a big fella, John did, so they had some great battles.

Because Dad played tennis we always had racquets and balls lying around the house and all of us ended up playing a little bit. Daniel was by far the best of the Harvey kids. I lacked the coordination required, so my racquet ended up getting more use as a weapon to kill bees mid-flight and a pretend guitar. Neither of the girls embraced the sport. Dad would have liked Bridge and Char to be a Caucasian version of the Williams sisters, and they were both reasonable players, but neither of them had the competitive drive needed. Bridge and I even teamed up one Saturday for a club game of mixed doubles. We won the match but sat in silence for the entire car ride home. She was furious at me for telling her off on-court. To be fair, I *was* in the wrong . . . but I became really frustrated when after every point we lost, she put her racquet between her thighs so that her hands would be free to applaud our opponents. I'm all for fair play and good sportmanship but it was like she was the president of their fan club!

Dad was so confident of his ability that he even lay down a challenge when we were kids—the first one of his children to challenge him to a game and beat him would win a hundred dollars. Since this offer was made in the mid eighties, it was a substantial sum of money. I think Dad extended the offer knowing he would never have to pay up, and he was right. Dan may have won the odd game or set against Dad but never managed to beat him. I intend to be the first. As far as I'm aware, the offer had no expiry date, so I'll just wait another couple of years, until Dad turns seventy . . . then challenge. Some might say that would make it a bit of a hollow victory, since he's now an old man and hasn't played tennis in twenty-five years, and they are probably right . . . but I don't care! I'll take it. And even though a hundred dollars doesn't have anywhere near the spending power it had when the offer was first made, I still reckon tears might well in my father's eyes as he hands over that crisp red Lord Rutherford.

Mum never got into tennis. Even if she had an interest in it I think it would have been too hard for both her and Dad to play on the weekends. So she became a tennis wife and looked after the four of us kids as we travelled to different tennis clubs to watch Dad play. Some of these days were achingly long and excruciatingly boring. There is that saying about being bored to tears? Well, I can tell you, one weekend we went to Masterton to watch Dad play an interclub tennis match and I did actually cry in sheer frustration. On the upside, by the time Sunday night came around I was fairly excited about going back to school for the week.

Mum's sport of choice was jogging. She jumped on the jogging bandwagon when it became popular in the eighties, round about the same time Charlotte started school.

Nowadays it is just called running and lots of people do it. But before the 1980s, very few people ran unless they were actually running away from something, like a house fire. Then jogging came along and was the trendy thing to do for a while. Mum was in a jogging group with some other housewives. They would meet up and go for a short run then sit around for hours and gossip about whoever failed to turn up that week. It was a great way to guarantee good attendance numbers—if you didn't go, your life would be fodder for the rest of the group.

Unlike other fitness fads of the same decade, like Jazzercise, leg warmers and aerobics in front of the TV with Jane Fonda videotapes, running has stood the test of time and seems to be here to stay. Mum becoming a jogger is how I got onto the sport. Most kids in the eighties were naturally fit—we were always active and running around doing stuff. Since there were only two TV channels, and no computers or gaming consoles, going for a run with Mum seemed like the best of two lame options—stay inside and be bored or go for a run with Mum and be slightly less bored.

Because I had been so badly burnt from being dragged around tennis courts to watch Dad play tennis every weekend, I was not going to fall into the same trap with another parent. So when Mum started entering five- and ten-kilometre fun runs that were popular at the time, I would sign up to run too.

Doing the run was way more fun than driving around the course to cheer Mum from a selection of random vantage points. There are not many sporting events more tedious and difficult to be a spectator at than a running race. You have to get yourself into a position to cheer and then hope like hell the person you are supporting hasn't already gone past. Then, if you're lucky enough to catch them as they run by, it's only for a few seconds and then they're gone again. So whenever Mum was running I would often partake as well.

Sometimes I did this in shoes not really designed for running, like Bata Bullets or the Para Rubber classic Commando-M's. Other times I'd just run in bare feet. Since so much of my childhood was spent wandering around without shoes, the soles of my feet were thick and hard.

One of these runs was the eighteen-kilometre annual Feilding to Palmerston North run in '82. I was nine at the time and wasn't allowed to take part because someone had told Mum and Dad that it was bad for kids to run long distances—something to do with bone development or some other nonsense. I was miserable, sulking. I didn't even bother getting out of the car to watch the start. I was very good at holding these dark moods, too. I could stay grumpy for hours, maybe even the whole day if I really put my mind to it.

Dad got back to the car after the run had commenced and just gave in. 'If you really want to run, just go and run! Go on!'

So I did. Not expecting this outcome, I was wearing my short-sleeve button-up pyjama top with cartoons of planes and trains, a little pair of shorts and no shoes—not what you would consider running attire. The fact I was allowed to leave the house in this state of dress has got to be put down to poor parenting!

I think Dad must have weighed things up and decided it was better to risk long-term damage to my skeletal system by letting me run than to spend the next hour and a half trapped in a car with a little bitch of a kid.

By this stage I was a long way behind the four hundred or so runners who had been sent on their way a few minutes earlier, but I got out of the car and ran. The rough gravel of the open road proved to be a bit of a challenge for my feet, which were more used to smooth footpaths, but I ended up completing the distance. I didn't even finish last, thanks to the very big ladies I passed along the way, the sort that you see and say, 'Good on them for getting out there!'

I had a huge blister on the heel of my left foot for my trouble. This thing was massive, the biggest blister I have ever seen, like the size of an egg yolk. Mum popped it with a needle that night and the liquid inside it shot about a metre across the sofa. It was spectacular and repulsive in equal measure. It didn't put me off running, though. I still run to this day, marathons. And the bones seem to have developed just fine, too. I took to running again after a decade-long break from it, an era I like to call 'the fat years'.

I peaked at 112 kilos. I didn't really feel or think I had turned into a fatty boomstick—it just crept up on me. I'd be home from work by lunchtime each day, so I got into a habit of stopping by Foodtown on the way home and picking up a 1.5 litre Coke, a loaf of white toast slice bread and a pack of cheese Sizzlers. I'd cook the whole pack of Sizzlers and end up eating the lot throughout the afternoon. I really feel sorry for people who are gluten intolerant . . . I fucking love the stuff.

The turning point, where I knew I had to take some drastic action, came one morning when I got out of bed to go to the toilet. I looked down and, because of my bread-baby, I could only see the last three centimetres of my penis.

FAKE IDS

The drinking age was still twenty when I finally came of age in 1993.

I don't know why I bothered with the 'finally' bit in that sentence. By the time I was legally entitled to enjoy a cold beer, my liver had already sustained enough damage to make it unfit for the organ donor program.

I was still under twenty when I had my bad rum experience that so many of us seem to go through. One of those nights where you drink so much Bounty that you wake up the next morning and, after breaking the crusty seal of vomit on the corners of your mouth, utter those words: 'I am never drinking rum again.'

For me the rum experience came courtesy of the world-famous-in-Palmerston-North-all-you-can-drink-twenty-dollar Friday nights at Exchequer nightclub. At the time, this was the most popular place in the city for seventh formers to drink, partly because of the twenty-dollar drinks-all-night deal and partly because they were prepared to let in and serve under-ager's.

This place was disgusting, though at the time we all thought it was like a magical kingdom. I can still remember the feel and stench of the carpet. It was permanently sticky and had a smell not unlike foot odour—a mixture of alcohol, industrial cleaning chemicals and vomit. They eventually ripped up the carpet and put some new stuff down, but only after the pool party theme night of 1992. A four-metre round pool was placed on the dance floor and filled with water. Because, I mean, who doesn't take their togs and a towel out with them when they go nightclubbing, right?

The pool remained unused until about 1 am, when the first customer was thrown in by his mates. That started a wave of copycat throw-ins. It must have been between 2 and 3 am, in the last hour of business for the night, when one of the pool's panels finally gave way, causing thousands of litres of water to gush everywhere. A wave swept across the room as girls raced to put their handbags on higher ground. By the time the pool was fully drained there must have been almost a centimetre of water covering the floor. It was one of the most epic and memorable nights out in my entire life.

My underage drinking only ever got me in trouble once, and that was with my parents and not the police. After a suitable amount of nagging and pleading on my part, I was sent up to Auckland for a week in the Christmas holidays to stay with my cool uncle, Robert. I was about a month off turning seventeen at the time. I was already a fairly prolific drinker, thanks to my training at Exchequers, so had no trouble keeping up with Uncle Robert, his mate and his girlfriend, Leonie, as we went out for dinner then hit a couple of Auckland nightclubs. I think my undoing was that Robert was a Steinlager Blue drinker. I'm not exactly sure what this shit was. It was beer, and it was Steinlager, obviously, but I can tell you for free, no brewery ever discontinues a product on account of how awesome and delicious it is!

So Robert, his friend and I were all drinking these ghastly beers can for can, while Leonie stayed sober so she could drive. It was only when we got into Leonie's pride and joy, a Honda Prelude, for the ride back to her home in Epsom that my world started to spin around me. I felt real sick, real fast. As bad luck would have it I was sitting right behind Leonie, the car's only sober person. I hit the button so the window would go down. Unfortunately, it was one of those really slow automatic ones, so it was only about a third of the way down when I leaned towards it for a power-chuck.

I can't be certain, but I would like to think I got some of it outside the window. The little bits of brown stuff stuck to the exterior paintwork afterwards would suggest I got at least some of it out. But the bulk of it went on the inside of the window, on the seatbelt and in Leonie's hair. So, after a night out carting around her drunk boyfriend and his equally pissed mate, and her drunk boyfriend's irritating teenage nephew from Palmerston North, she now had a car and a head that stunk of vomit. She was furious. Pretty unreasonable, I thought.

Luckily for me, the following day was my prearranged departure date. Unlike the vomit in her vehicle, the conversation between Leonie and me had dried up by that stage. I did my best to clean up the mess I'd created in her car but I think we all know that smell never really leaves, no matter how many cleaning products you douse it with. That's why I have always found the soiling fees charged by taxi companies fair and reasonable—$150 to totally destroy someone's office seems like a bargain.

Leonie and Robert dropped me at the bus station. I told them I'd see them again sometime. Leonie mumbled something under her breath. I'm not sure what exactly, but it was two short words, so it might have been 'hope not', 'please no' or a sarcastic 'yeah, right'.

I shook Uncle Robert's hand and gave Leonie a hug. I didn't like that very much—her hair smelt like a mixture of Sunsilk shampoo and my stomach lining.

I got on the bus for the excruciatingly slow trip to Tauranga, where I was being reunited with my family. Mum and Dad were waiting when I got off the bus and their greeting was about as frosty as Leonie and Robert's send-off. Turns out that while I had been travelling on the loser cruiser, wallowing in my own hung-over shame, Leonie had called Mum to tell her about the small matter of me vomiting in her hair and car. Fortunately, Mum and Dad didn't give me a ranty ear-bashing, which could have made me sick all over again. They just gave me the old 'We are not mad at you, we are just disappointed' spiel. I could live with that. That speech is a heart-stabber for kids who are not a disappointment, but for the rest of us you just get immune to it.

It was in 1999 that the drinking age changed from twenty to eighteen, causing thousands of seventh formers to legally raise their glass of champagne in jubilation. (Bernadino Spewmante is champagne, isn't it?)

Jenny Shipley was the prime minister at the time. Her kids were around that age and she thought it seemed outrageous that they and their equally sophisticated friends could not be trusted to enjoy a wine over a meal with some quality conversation. She was right, too. If your mum is the PM, chances are you're not the teen who is going out on a Saturday night playing whizz-boing-bounce with a 1.5 litre Sprite bottle filled with rocket-fuel and carrying on till you throw up on yourself.

I reckon it's a lot harder to get your hands on alcohol now if you are underage. Everything seems so tightly enforced. I'm not naive—I'm sure plenty of under-agers are getting their hands on the stuff, drinking until they're off their tits and doing the same stupid shit in stolen supermarket trolleys as we did in the nineties. But, other than pinching it from the piss cupboard of a sloppy parent or having it purchased for you by an older friend, I can't imagine where they would be getting it.

Even though the drinking age was twenty back then, it seemed to be more of a rule of thumb. It was not long after my sixteenth birthday that I first purchased my own alcohol from the Albert Street bottle store in Palmy. I wasn't much of a fan of beer, so I nervously walked up to the counter with my four-pack of Miami wine cooler—the closest thing to an RTD at the time. Yes, it was considered to be a 'ladies' drink', but it was also very sweet and delicious, so I tolerated the name-calling that came with being a male consumer of wine coolers—although it is probably no coincidence that I didn't lose my virginity until I bowed to pressure and switched to beer after my eighteenth birthday.

So there I was at the counter, my face dotted with angry red pimples, the sort that look sore to touch. I was feeling nervous as hell, and said as few words as possible in a put-on deep voice that sounded nothing like my real one:

'How's it going?'
'Just these wine coolers for the missus, thanks, mate.'
'Beauty. Cheers.'

And I was off. Feeling very mature, feeling like I had just pulled off the heist of the century. My impression of a twenty-year-old man had been successful!

This approach was hit and miss. Some places were stricter than others. But word got around quick about what places were soft targets and what staff members never bothered to ask for ID.

There was always a way to get your hands on alcohol. As an absolute last backup, we would get our mate Pete to buy it. Pete was twenty-two, wore a black leather jacket and a gold necklace, had black chest hair that crawled out the top of his shirt towards his Adam's apple and drove a Mazda RX-7. We all thought it was amazing and not the slightest bit odd that this twenty-two-year-old wanted to spend his Saturday nights in the company of a group of sixteen-year-olds. He never gave off a creepy vibe or tried anything untoward. I think he was maybe just a bit immature for his age and felt like he slotted in better with kids a bit younger.

Even without Pete and his useful maturity, most of us had at least one form of fake ID. This was when driver's licences were about the size of a postcard and were made from this waxy paper that would fold up and go into your wallet. It had no photo on it—just your name, details and date of birth. I recently found my old licence, and even though it is no longer legal and hasn't been for many years, it *still* has four decades to go before it expires!

Anybody lucky enough to have an older brother or sister of the same sex would just use theirs. The rest of us would just alter the year of birth on our own driver's licence. So for me, a crude scrape with a pair of scissors could make a 3 look like a 1, so 1973 would instantly become 1971. Genius! An eighties version of what is now known as a life hack.

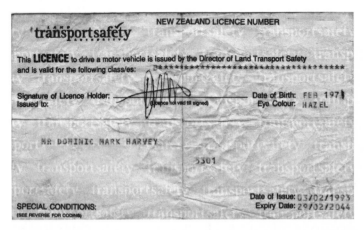

IN THE NAVY

It was during one of the school holidays when I was nine that I decided I wanted to be in the navy when I grew up. My uncle Patrick was in the navy and he took us for a tour of the ship he worked on. That was it. Mind made up.

I did worry about the uniform a bit, though.

I was an extremely clumsy and messy eater, still scooping up my peas with a spoon at this stage, so it would have been very difficult for me to keep a white suit clean, but I was confident I could sort my eating issues out and consume a sausage wrapped in bread without the sauce spilling onto my clothes by the time I reached school leaving age. Unfortunately, I was wrong about that—I only just managed to master the fine art of eating an ice-cream in warm weather without it dripping everywhere when I was thirty-two.

My dream was crushed only a couple of years later, when my uncle Pat told me you had to be really good at maths for a career in the navy. Suddenly it all just seemed unobtainable. I could have found a way around the white uniform dilemma, even if it meant wearing a bib at mealtimes, but since maths was my most hated subject I thought there was no chance of me ever being accepted. I never looked into it, so it's possible Uncle Pat just made up the thing about maths to try and steer me away from the navy. He was fairly high up, and when he saw how interested I was he possibly started to panic that I could tarnish his good reputation if I got a job there.

That NZ Navy vessel was the second coolest boat I got to go on that particular holiday . . . but in terms of amazingness, no boat could beat the swinging Pirate Ship ride at Rainbow's End. This was a time when going overseas to Los Angeles or even the Gold Coast was just not something that middle-class kids got to do, so going to Rainbow's End was something we had been looking forward to for months. A trip to Auckland was as good as it got for most Kiwi kids. As well as Rainbow's End, Auckland also had MOTAT (the Museum of Transport and Technology) and the Footrot Flats Leisure Park in Te Atatu. The Footrot Flats park isn't there anymore. I'm not sure why it went belly-up. Maybe it had something to do with basing an entire theme park around a cartoon comic strip from the newspaper.

MOTAT is still operating and still looks exactly like it did when we went to visit in 1982. Back then it was a museum. Now it feels like a museum OF a museum. I'm pretty sure the only new exhibit that has been added to MOTAT since I went as a nine-year-old is the old scooter Helen Clark used to ride to university on.

Mum and Dad saved the really good theme parks overseas for themselves. I'm not sure if it was planned this way or just a coincidence, but they generously shouted themselves a trip to both Disneyland in Los Angeles and

Dreamworld in Australia when all four of their children were at ride-friendly heights. Then on their return home, looking relaxed and tanned, explained all the rides they went on to us kids in great detail.

I still have the souvenir my parents got me from their child-free trip to Dreamworld on the Gold Coast—it's a plate with a picture of them on it. They're sitting in what looks like a log flume ride, grinning from ear to ear. I know I shouldn't be ungrateful, but come on! Even a fucking clip-on koala from the airport would have been better than that! Also visible in this plate photo is my father's ballpoint pen, poking out from the teal blue polo shirt he was wearing. Dad is NEVER without a ballpoint pen, ever. He even takes it to places you would never have any need for a pen . . . like an amusement park.

I often wonder if the Air New Zealand slogan 'Being there is everything' was thought up by someone in advertising who, like me, had to sit through hours of cruel stories from his parents about how much fun they had at Disneyland while their kids were sent to their uncle and aunty's farm.

Still, us kids who went without while our parents spoiled themselves with lavish holidays will get the last laugh when we select a rest home with mean staff who feed the elderly residents jelly meat.

The closest I got to a proper theme park as a kid—a souvenir plate from my parents when they went.

AN IDIOT GETS A JOB

Not long after my navy dream was torpedoed, we had a class field trip to 2XS FM, the Palmerston North radio station. It was here where I first thought about radio as a job. During our tour of the station we got to have a look through the glass window of the studio and watch the announcer at work. The job looked easy. And fun. The DJ had a cigarette burning in an ashtray and was wearing shorts and jandals, clothes my dad only got to wear after work and on weekends. This looked like a hobby rather than a job—sitting in a chair in comfortable clothes smoking a fag while listening to music. I'm not sure why, but the thought of wearing casual clothes to work really appealed to me. I only bought my first suit when I got married at thirty-two and may be the oldest person in the world who has no fucking idea how to do a necktie!

The seed had been planted. But because I was still only twelve and had a voice that sounded more like a horse jockey than a disc jockey, I had to keep my options open. I quite liked the idea of being a cop as well. That could have been a challenge, given how appalling I was at maths:

> 'I pulled you over today, ma'am, because my radar clocked you at sixty-four kilometres an hour and this is only a fifty kilometre an hour zone. That means you were going about twenty-two kilometres over the limit. SLOW DOWN!'

I decided I wanted to do radio and nothing else when I was fourteen. It was on a school trip to Nelson for the New Zealand Secondary Schools Cross Country Race. I had taken up running because after trying my hand at numerous team sports requiring hand-eye coordination, I'd realised that running would be ideal for me because:

1. I would not be letting any teammates down with a poor performance.
2. It required minimal coordination, since it is essentially just extreme walking.

I wasn't a natural at it, or even particularly fast, but I worked hard for my mediocrity.

One of the other, more gifted runners from the school team was my mate Shawn Retter. He had a cassette that he played on the tape deck of the Hertz mini-van. It was a whole lot of prank calls by this Auckland radio announcer called Kevin 'Blackie' Black. It was unlike anything I had ever heard before and it blew me away.

All young kids had a go at prank calls. The most popular one was to call a stranger and ask them if their fridge was running . . . *Because I just saw it going for a jog past my house.* But it was just a juvenile pastime that peaked in the school holidays; it was not something anyone was doing on the radio in Palmy at the time.

I had been so caught up in the idea of wearing a pair of stubbies and a T-shirt to work that I'd never paused to think about the actual job in hand and the things you could say or do on the radio:

Fire Service: Hello, Fire Service?

Blackie: Ahh, yes. Hello. I have a fire that I was hoping you guys could put out for me.

Fire Service: Yep, sure thing. How do we get there?

Blackie: What? Don't you have those big red trucks anymore?

(Fire Service hangs up)

It seems fairly basic now—today's crop of youth would no doubt hashtag it as #lame—but this was groundbreaking radio. Blackie was an innovator, a radio entertainer far superior to anyone else on the airwaves back then. In another prank call on the tape, Blackie called a guy who had applied to become a police officer, to tell him there were some results from his blood test he should be aware of: 'Do you know that you are a homo sapien?' The guy was mortified. He protested, saying they must be wrong because he was married. The guy was on the verge of tears when Blackie revealed to him that homo sapien is the Latin term for human being.

There was no way we could pick up Blackie's station, Radio Hauraki 1476AM, in Palmerston North, so I dubbed a copy of Shawn's tape and listened to it over and over. I even wrote Blackie a letter telling him what a big fan I was and asking him if he could send me some tapes of his prank calls. He never replied. Years later I got to work in the same building with him and we became mates. I told him about the letter I had sent him some twenty years earlier. Without even a pause, he said, 'Ah, yes. I'm in the middle of writing back to you right now. Be patient. The reply will get there shortly.'

After that it became a bit of a running joke. Whenever we spoke he would inform me that the reply was coming along nicely and it wouldn't be too much longer before it was done. Unfortunately, I never did get the letter. Kevin Black died on 17 February 2013. He was sixty-nine. He had been a guest at my fortieth birthday party just twelve days earlier and I had commented on how good he was looking. I never got the reply, but I got something far more amazing than that—the friendship of an incredible broadcaster and a great bloke.

After being inspired by the prank calls of Kevin Black, radio become my single focus. I was obsessed to the point where I ditched my mates Andrew and Mark and began riding the five kilometres to Boys High all by myself. This was so I could practise my radio DJ voice as I rode. This was a time when everybody on the radio had a deep, velvety voice and all sounded the same. If this was going to be my future, then I too would need to develop one of those golden voices to fit in. I would chat away to myself nonstop on these rides, out loud and in my new DJ voice, reading street signs, car numberplates, business signs and letterbox numbers. If there was nothing at all to read, I would just commentate what I saw. I hadn't wanted something so desperately since I was seven and nagged Mum and Dad for a View-Master.

There's a famous saying, 'It's not what you know, it's who you know.' Unfortunately for me and my radio aspirations, I didn't know anyone who could help me out. I saw an opportunity to change that when I started the sixth form. I took 'work transition' as one of my subjects. I'm not sure this is a thing schools do anymore, but I loved it. Students who took this option would be interviewed by Mr Leighton, the teacher in charge of this subject, to find out what they wanted to do when they left school.

Mr Leighton would then ring around to find suitable workplaces where the students could work as unpaid employees for blocks of four to six weeks to gain some work experience. It was a bit like school-sanctioned truancy.

For me, Mr Leighton teed up 2XS FM. So each Thursday I would get to skip school, with permission, and hang out at the radio station instead. The jobs they had me do would most definitely not help me follow in the footsteps of Blackie. They had me clearing out the unkempt storage room and filing records back in the station's music library. The work was mundane and monotonous . . . but I loved it. I got to work alongside everybody at the station, and because they all felt a bit sheepish about the shit jobs they were asking me to do, they were nice to me. When my six weeks of work experience were over, I managed to convince the school and the station to let me carry on. And so it continued for the entire year. I now knew people in radio, which, as the saying goes, was more important than what I knew.

Did these 'contacts' of mine like me? I'm not sure really—my heart was in the right place, but I must have been so fucking annoying. I made a total pest of myself with my persistence and eagerness. But at least I was now on their radar if something suitable came up.

And it did, the following year. Steve Rowe, the station manager, had been out at a function and came into the station on his way home. He walked past the reception area and, after hearing a commotion, looked up and noticed one of the giant ceiling panels had been moved, exposing a big hole. On the ground beneath it was a stool. After a bit of time a pair of legs dangled from this hole and then the overnight announcer dropped to the floor, right in front of Steve. It turned out he had been climbing through the ceiling cavity into the locked prize cupboard and taking whatever he could get his hands on (cassettes, concert tickets, VHS tapes, etc.). It was always going to be tough to come up with an adequate answer on the spot to the station manager's question: 'What the fuck are you doing in the ceiling cavity?'

He 'fessed up and was dismissed. In his defence, he did claim he was not a dealer. He admitted he had a crippling Wilson Phillips addiction and all the tapes were for personal use. It didn't matter. He got no sympathy from Steve Rowe and was dismissed immediately, leaving a vacancy for the most undesirable job at any radio station. The mid-dawn (midnight to dawn) shift was horrible—the worst hours, the worst pay and a smaller audience than a Ja Rule concert. I wanted it more than anything in the world.

As soon as I heard about the vacancy, I went into the station after school and spoke to Steve Rowe. In a roundabout way he told me he wasn't going to give me the job. He told me it was far more important for me to see out my seventh form year than to think about getting a full-time job. Rodger Clamp, the station's program director, seemed a little more open to the idea of me getting the job. I mean, it was filling six hours of airspace at a time of day where the only listeners were shiftworkers and insomniacs. They could have got a monkey to do the job . . . but a desperate wannabe broadcaster was a more affordable option.

During our most recent family summer holiday to Whangamata I'd had a caricature done of myself by this bloke on the street, one of those cheesy things you get done while strangers stand around looking at his easel, then looking up at the subject, then looking back at the easel with a facial expression that says, 'That looks NOTHING like you.' This caricature artist had asked what I was interested in and I said radio, so he drew me in a studio with a microphone in front of me and headphones on. I used this ten-dollar street cartoon as the cover of my CV. I'm not sure what else I had in there to flesh it out. I had just turned seventeen, so apart from some school reports and fun run certificates, I really had nothing else to back up my unproven claims to awesomeness.

As it turned out, Steve changed his mind, and I got the job—but it wasn't till some years later that he told me why. He'd taken a box of CVs home with him, and one night in bed while he was flicking through them, his wife, Linda, picked mine up and laughed at it. She then told Steve he should give me the job. So he did. I owe my entire career in radio to that lady.

It was Rodger Clamp who told me the good news and informed me what I would be earning. I reckon Steve was too embarrassed to tell me the amount so delegated that job to his deputy. I was put on a starting salary of $12,000 a year, which was shit money even back in 1990. Not that I was concerned. I would have done it for free. I even told Rodger that. Then he gave me my first piece of advice about handling negotiations: 'Never ever ever ever tell your employer you will do something for free. They might just take you up on the offer.'

*

I could not believe my luck. I had just turned seventeen three months earlier and I had a full-time on-air radio job straight out of school. The radio legend Mark

Harvey had been born. Mark is my middle name, so I went with that because I thought it sounded catchier than Dominic. I had plans to take over the city. This was my destiny. People in Palmerston North would be changing their sleeping patterns just so they could stay up through the night to hear the most talked-about radio show in the city. I had it all planned out in my head.

Then I started and that is when reality hit—I sucked.

I was truly bad. Even at $12,000 a year I was overpaid.

I knew I was terrible but I had no idea how I could make myself suck less.

It was devastating. I had landed my dream job and discovered I was useless at it.

Radio was way different then. Everyone talked in a pretend voice and consequently all radio announcers had the same sound. So I had this fake name and this weird put-on voice and was simply unable to do the job. Rodger told me to keep it 'Tight, Bright and Real'. This was a big rule that all radio stations followed at the time.

Tight: Don't talk very long. Start the song, then start talking and stop before the vocals.
Bright: Sound upbeat and friendly. Talk with a smile on your face.
Real: Be yourself.

The problem with 'Tight, Bright and Real' was the 'Real' bit. If you are having a real day-to-day conversation with someone, you don't have to pretend you are happy and attempt to communicate your message over a twelve-second intro to an MC Hammer song! Rodger continually told me to slow down and to talk on the air like I talked to him. It was an instruction that I could just not get my head around. If I talked in my normal voice I wouldn't sound like a radio DJ, and I couldn't slow down because I was trying to cram all this information about the radio station's promotions over the intros of songs:

> 2XS FM with Mark Harvey at 2.46 am. Make sure you join us this Sunday at Himatangi beach for the annual 2XS FM beach dig starting at 2 pm. We have major spot prizes including a fourteen-inch Akai TV from Manawatu TV and Sound and an Ansett mystery escape weekend to somewhere in New Zealand. It's going to be loads of fun, so come down with your family. Now here's Heart and 'All I Wanna Do Is Make Love to You' on the station with Manawatu's best music, 2XS FM.

It was terrible stuff. On the songs with really long intros, I'd start off fast and slow down towards the end when I realised I had time to spare. That particular Heart song I just mentioned above had a seventeen-second intro—I can still remember twenty-four years later!—so it was always a bit of a mad sprint that sounded like a horseracing commentator calling the Melbourne Cup rather than a friendly guy on the radio inviting you to a fun event at the beach.

*

One of the duties of the mid-dawn announcer was to stick around from 6 am till 8 am to help the breakfast show host out by answering phone calls. Mike West was the breakfast host at 2XS FM in those days. Had it not been for that guy, I'd say my radio career would have been shorter and less memorable than the musical career of Milli Vanilli. Mike and I struck up a friendship almost immediately, and it was not long after I started that he had me on his radio show from time to time. He called me Baldrick, a reference to the TV show *Blackadder*, with Rowan Atkinson, which was very popular at the time. Because I was essentially the radio station dogsbody, one of the sales reps had given me the nickname and it stuck. These moments on the air with Mike West, using an even more unrealistic name than my already fake radio name, made the six hours of overnight self-loathing worthwhile. Instead of shooting off home at 8 am when my day was officially over, I'd stick around until Mike's show finished at 10 am. I was always tired and had pale skin from lack of natural daylight, but I loved it.

It was while I was still on mid-dawn that I got my first written warning from Steve Rowe. I'd always rather be in the studio with Mike than sitting at reception answering phone calls, but if Steve arrived at work and there was a ringing phone, he would be furious. He was so hung up on customer service that he would call the studio line any time, day or night whenever there was a song playing, just to count the number of times the phone would ring before the announcer picked up. Any more than seven and you'd be in the shit. It kept everybody on their toes— every time the phone light lit up in the studio, you would answer it immediately . . . just in case it was the general manager!

Steve would often arrive at work between 7 and 8 am when I was supposed to be sitting at reception manning the phone. Mike would often call me into the studio, which would take me away from the phones, and if Steve arrived at work while I was in the studio and the phone happened to ring, I'd get a bollocking. So I came up with a brilliant plan. Whenever Mike yelled at me to come into the studio, I would first mute the phone unit at reception, so the red lights representing each phone line would light up . . . but there was no sound. It was a fantastic scheme . . . until that fateful morning in September '91 when I forgot to unmute it—a mistake that was not noticed until much later in the morning, by which time dozens of phone calls had been missed. Steve was outraged. Customers had been calling and their calls had been neglected. Steve had a good point. I was way out of line. But the truth is I just did not care about that part of the job. I wanted to be on the radio and make people laugh, like Blackie. The last thing I wanted to do was an impression of the world's ugliest receptionist, dealing with callers with ridiculous requests like these:

'What was that song that was played between seven and nine last night? It was a male singer and was something about being in love.'

'My cat has gone missing. I was hoping I could add it to your pet patrol feature? She is a brown and white tabby missing in the Milson area who responds to the name Julie.'

'I'm calling to check the serial number for this week's lucky five-dollar note?'

This was a regular feature the station ran, where if you found the correct five-dollar note somewhere in circulation in the city you would win whatever the cash jackpot happened to be. It was regional radio at its finest. I don't think many people ever gave it much attention, because the jackpot was hardly ever struck. Oddly enough, the people who did take part and call to double-check the serial number were always the sorts of people who would never have a pen ready when I repeated it to them. But without a doubt the most phone traffic came in for the daily birthday call list at ten to eight. And these people were always hard to brush off.

> **Caller:** Can you please say happy birthday to Hayden, who is eight-years-old today?
> **Me:** Absolutely. And shall we say lots of love from the family?
> **Caller:** Yeah, yes please. That's love from Mum, Dad, Katrina, Molly, David, Uncle Rob and Aunty Sonja . . .
> **Me:** Okay, shall we just say love from the whole family then?
> **Caller:** Yes please. Also Nana, Poppa . . .
> **Voice in background:** Did you say Juliana? Don't forget Juliana!
> **Caller:** Juliana. And the Williamsons.

Then they would call back and complain when their laundry list of all the family members' names (sometimes the names of pets as well) was not read out. It was after one of these calls that I decided it was in the best interests of both the radio station and me if these calls were just left unanswered—which was why I muted the entire phone system. It was a move that almost ended my radio career just sixteen months after it started, as this letter from Steve demonstrates:

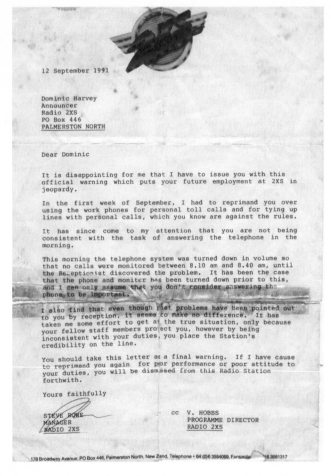

12 September 1991

Dominic Harvey
Announcer
Radio 2XS
PO Box 446
PALMERSTON NORTH

Dear Dominic

It is disappointing for me that I have to issue you with this
official warning which puts your future employment at 2XS in
jeopardy.

In the first week of September, I had to reprimand you over
using the work phones for personal toll calls and for tying up
lines with personal calls, which you know are against the rules.

It has since come to my attention that you are not being
consistent with the task of answering the telephone in the
morning.

This morning the telephone system was turned down in volume so
that no calls were monitored between 8.10 am and 8.40 am, until
the Receptionist discovered the problem. It has been the case
that the phone and moniter has been turned down prior to this,
and I can only assume that you don't consider answering the
phone to be important.

I also find that even though past problems have been pointed out
to you by reception, it seems to make no difference. It has
taken me some effort to get at the true situation, only because
your fellow staff members protect you, however by being
inconsistent with your duties, you place the Station's
credibility on the line.

You should take this letter as a final warning. If I have cause
to reprimand you again for poor performance or poor attitude to
your duties, you will be dismissed from this Radio Station
forthwith.

Yours faithfully

STEVE ROWE   cc V. HOBBS
MANAGER   PROGRAMME DIRECTOR
RADIO 2XS   RADIO 2XS

178 Broadway Avenue, PO Box 446, Palmerston North, New Zand, Telephone + 64 (0)6 3584069, Farsimile   )6 3561317

It was not long after that letter was written that I was
taken off the mid-dawn shift to work full time on the
breakfast show with Mike West as his sidekick and
producer.

I was hard-working and eager to learn . . . I just wasn't
very good. Generously, Mike appreciated the effort. As

Mike West and Baldrick we had an incredible radio partnership that ended up lasting ten years. Most years we won the NZ Radio Award for best regional music and entertainment team and we enjoyed number one ratings year in and out in the radio surveys.

With this success came all the spoils a local celebrity could expect to enjoy.

I could get a table at any restaurant in town without booking first. Although, in hindsight, I now accept it was because none of the restaurants in Palmerston North were ever fully booked.

I could park in a thirty-minute zone for a couple of hours and still avoid getting towed, although I now accept it was because there were probably no tow trucks in the city.

And I could call the city council and be put straight through to the mayor. But yes, I now accept that it is possible everybody who called got this treatment, because the city's limited budget meant the mayor did not have his own secretary.

As well as the great chemistry Mike and I had on air together, we were best mates outside of work, too. Especially after Kim and I started our four-year relationship. Kim is the younger sister of Mike's wife, Amanda, which meant our work life and personal lives crossed over. It was fantastic, though I'm sure to some outsiders it must have seemed like some weird keys-in-the-bowl-banjo-playing scenario.

Despite all my numerous work-related cock-ups, I can only recall one particular incident that made Mike want to punch me in the throat. We had been invited to officially start the city's annual Tour de Manawatu cycling event, held on a Sunday morning at some ungodly hour. Hundreds of locals on bikes would be there to participate: lycra freaks, mums, dads, kids, a couple of people on penny-farthings, all sorts. It was a great opportunity for us to put our faces in front of a couple of thousand people, potential listeners. The organisers had come up with a plan that we would lead the ride out, the two of us on a tandem, then after a kilometre we would pull out and the race would officially start.

I went out the night before and ended up having a far more epic time than I'd intended. After stopping by Golden Takeaways at 3 am for one of their world-famous-in-Palmy fish burgers, I walked home (my financial position at the time meant I had to choose between the taxi fare home or the world-famous-in-Palmy fish burger). So, after getting into bed still dressed at four-ish, I somehow slept through my 7 am alarm . I was supposed to be at the start line in time for the 8 am start. It must have been about ten to eight when I was woken by my flatmate banging on my door to wake me up. Mike was on the phone wanting to know where the fuck I was. The perk of sleeping in my going-out clothes was that the job of getting dressed was already done. I got my flatmate to give me a ride to the start line and put my shoes on as she drove. We sped there with the windows down—I stunk. And looked like shit.

As we pulled up we could see the back end of the bikes already well up the road from the start line. We must have missed the start by about ninety seconds, I reckon. So close. I waited at the start and a couple of minutes later I could see my old mate Mike in the distance, riding back towards me. He was on our tandem bike. All by himself.

I couldn't help but laugh out loud when he got closer: 'Mate, you wouldn't believe how fucking funny that looks! The empty seat makes it funny as.'

Mike was furious. He ripped me a new one. He didn't find it funny that I had turned up late and drunk leaving him to start the ride alone, and I can't say I blame him. Having seen it with my own two eyes, I can assure you— there are few things in the world that look sadder than a grown man all by himself on a bicycle designed for two.

Amazingly, after spending a few minutes letting me know just what a useless piece of shit I was, Mike put it behind us. No grudge. What a guy.

*

I only got one other written warning from Steve Rowe. This one came five years and one logo change after the first one. Don't get me wrong—there were loads of verbal warnings. But the written warnings were incredibly uncommon. I have a hunch this may have been because Steve and the station's accountant, Catherine Parsons, ran such a lean operation that they hated to waste the station letterhead.

828 AM ★ 98.6 FM

20 August 1996

Dominic Harvey
35 Kingston Street
PALMERSTON NORTH

Dear Dominic

Yesterday I received a complaint by phone call from a lady (Helen) who was disgusted by some of your comments made to Michelle Terry and guest last Friday 16 August.

I understand Michelle was demonstrating karate kicks, and that you made comments about her not wearing underwear and about her having nine husbands. The way it was said and your repeated low level comments have spurred her to take her complaint to the Broadcasting Complaints Authority

I have spoken to you on more than one occasion about you making obscene and sexually offensive comments. Your again total lack of judgement and inability to know where to start and stop has probably lost you more female listenership at a critical time when it all counts not just for you, but affects everyone at 2XS.

Take a good look at your 25 - 39 year female audience. You dominate this group but if they start to leave you it will really hurt. Classic Hits is already targeting them musically so if they leave you, it will take more than prizes to get them back.

You basically have a 'gutter mind' and I strongly advise you to get your brain together and start thinking about the longevity of your show and your own personal future. If this goes to the Complaints Authority it will hurt the show and 2XS FM right in the middle of survey

As I said when we signed up for the contracts, if you damage the show by your actions involving obscenity and low life humour you will have to go, and have no doubt that I mean it. Take this as a serious warning.

Yours faithfully

STEVE ROWE
MANAGER
XS RADIO LTD

XS Radio Limited. 178 Broadway Avenue, PO Box 446, Palmerston North, New Zealand, Telephone + 64 (0)6 3584069, Facsimile + 64 (0)6 3561317

The written warnings were bad. But I reckon the verbal telling-offs were way worse. Without a hint of exaggeration, if I was given the choice at the time of a) Going into Steve's office for a verbal warning, or b) Having my wisdom teeth removed without anaesthetic WHILE getting punched repeatedly in the balls by an ex-girlfriend, well, I'd have to say that option B would usually have been the easier of the two choices (depending on exactly what I had done). Steve would be bright red in the face, incandescent with rage. If I'd had a stick and a bag of marshmallows with me I could have toasted them in the angry glow of his face. I can't remember what any of my verbal warnings were for now, but I have no doubt they were all perfectly justified.

Steve and I are great mates these days and I think he feels a bit embarrassed about the written warnings and his management style in the 1990s. I have told him he shouldn't. He was exactly the boss I needed at exactly the right time. What I needed was a good kick in the arse, and Steve Rowe was a man who knew how to administer such a punt.

Steve and I left 2XS within a few months of each other. He took up a radio management job in Australia. I went to work with my girlfriend, Jay-Jay, on *The Edge*. I was petrified about the change. I was almost thirty and was leaving the job I had held since I left school. It was also the station I grew up listening to, in the city I grew up in and came to love, in spite of its dullness and lack of character. What the landscape of the city lacked in character and vibrancy, the people more than made up for with theirs.

THE SUNDAY DRIVE

Dad always had a job that came with a company car so it made sense to make the most of this perk of the job and use it on the weekends to transport the family around. We were a family of road trippers. We would often go for a Sunday drive as a family, a trip that usually involved sharing a spread of fish'n'chips sprawled out on the bonnet of the car. We ate them straight from the paper they were wrapped in, often pre-read newspapers complete with crosswords that had been partially filled out by the reader.

These on-the-go meals were a bit of a frenzied affair. Our weekly meal of fish'n'chips at home was much more formal, with the food portioned out and given to us on plates. We would each be allowed to order one big thing, like a hot dog, a pineapple fritter or fish, and we would be allocated a serve of chips. It was all quite a civilised affair. Well, as civilised as greasy finger food can be.

The piles of chips had to be dead even. I recall a couple of times that Mum went to the extent of counting out the individual chips to make sure each child had the exact same amount, after cries that one of us had been short-changed. It seems silly now, but at the time this seemed like a fair and reasonable way to distribute them.

On road trips, though, it was a bit like *The Hunger Games*—every man for himself—so us kids would pile the chips away as fast as we could to avoid missing out. The fear of getting painful indigestion was far less of a concern than the fear of missing out. Anyone who ate politely, slowly and with their mouth shut—in other words, 'normally'—would risk going hungry. A family of pigs eating grain from a shared trough was probably more dignified than the Harveys sharing three scoops of chips from a takeaway bar in Foxton with a C-grade hygiene certificate.

This food was usually washed down with a shared two-litre bottle of fizzy. And despite Mum's constant and ongoing pleas for us to make sure our food was completely swallowed before taking a gulp, this carbonated beverage ended up looking like a murky soup by the time the bottle was half drunk. I'm not sure why Mum didn't just learn after a few outings and keep some plastic tumblers in the glove box.

This promise of lumpy soft drink and food with no nutritional value was the clincher needed to get everybody to cram into the car together for a drive. The destination was never that breathtaking—usually somewhere within an hour's drive of Palmy. Popular spots included Dannevirke, Eketahuna, Masterton and Wanganui. Occasionally it would be a drive to Taihape, ninety minutes away. There we would stretch our legs, use the public loo, and walk up and down the main street window-shopping, since these were the days when nothing was open on Sundays. Then we would have a feed and drive back home again.

Because we sampled fish'n'chips in all sorts of small towns and from places with varying degrees of hygiene and quality control, a bad batch of takeaway would sometimes play havoc with Dad's intestines. He just was nowhere near as good as us kids when it came to processing fatty foods. When Dad had 'crook guts', as he called it, the trip home was repulsive. After farting, Dad would wind down his driver's window a few millimetres to let some fresh air swirl around. Of course, after a while we learned that this sudden rush of noise and air from the outside meant Dad had grossed himself out and needed to clear the air before the smell spread to the rest of the vehicle, exposing his repugnant secret. The problem was that the blast of fresh country air coming in seemed to have the opposite effect, and facilitated the circulation of the stench around the car, causing us all to gag. For some minutes afterwards we would all be breathing through our mouths while holding our T-shirts over our faces, only returning to breathing normally again when we could be absolutely certain the air had cleared.

In the last few minutes of these Sunday outings, Dad, who was tone-deaf, would break into song, singing an original composition with repetitive lyrics:

Thank you, Daddy, for the wonderful drive
Thank you, Daddy, for the wonderful drive
Thank you, Daddy, for the wonderful drive
Thank you, Daddy, for the wonderful drive.

This was our cue to thank Dad for what he perceived to be a wonderful day. Whether or not it had been was an irrelevant detail. After a while we all cottoned on and learned to thank him and sound like we meant it. Ignoring the song or saying thanks in a sarcastic tone would only increase the length and the volume of his song.

PRE-DIGITAL CAMERAS AND PHOTOGRAPHY

The average teenage girl in possession of an iPhone probably takes more photos of herself on an average day than I have of my first twenty years of life.

Am I bitter about this? Yes, a little bit. The entire collection of photos I have from my first quarter century on earth can comfortably fit in a shoebox . . . with room left over to put one of the shoes back in the box!

Almost everybody has a high-quality camera on them at all times these days, meaning very few precious moments will be missed out on. And lots of incredibly boring moments will be captured too. I mean, how many 'duck face' selfies does one person need?

I was out the other week with my wife and some of her friends when they decided a group photo would be a good idea. I volunteered to take it. Immediately three of the other women who were about to be photographed reached for their phones and asked me to take one for them too. 'Yeah, of course,' is what I said. What I was thinking was 'Fuck off! I'll just take one and you can all share it on your Facebook pages.'

In the end three of the four photos were ruled unsuitable for sharing and were subsequently deleted. The reasons were:

1. 'My eyes are closed.'
2. 'Eewwww, gross. My right arm looks fat.'
3. 'Oh my god! I've got three chins.'

So, after all that, the girls decided that the one photo they could all sort of agree on would be posted to Instagram and copied by whoever else wanted it. This is the curse of camera phones—they have killed the magic of photography. Photos are no longer a treat, a surprise. Back in the day they were a one-take-wonder lucky dip. You wouldn't know about the arm fat or collection of chins until you picked up the envelope from the camera shop and flipped through the photos, sometimes months after the actual photo was taken.

Mum got her first proper camera in '87. It was a point-and-shoot Ricoh thing but it would still have cost a few hundred dollars. She got it to coincide with a trip she was taking to Rome with her mum and a couple of siblings. Naturally, she wanted some good-quality snaps to remember this trip of a lifetime. But having a good camera most definitely did not mean taking a shitload of photos.

It was about cost. Once you had the camera, you had to buy the film to go in it—and a twenty-four-shot roll may have cost, say, ten dollars, which was a lot of money at the time. Then, once the roll was finished, it would cost more than that again to get it developed and processed at the pharmacy or photo shop.

Because of these additional costs, in our house it was not uncommon for a roll of film to last a year, or even longer. Then, once it was removed and replaced with a fresh film, Mum would sometimes keep the undeveloped film in the top drawer of her dresser until she had the money to take it in for processing.

Most of these places offered a one-hour service, but that always cost the most money, so Mum would usually go for the five-day turnaround. Mind you, I suppose a five-day wait for a few photos didn't seem that long, since the film had sometimes been sitting in the corner of an undie drawer for years!

The top of Mum's camera had a little display that let you know how many shots you had taken. This was a handy thing to know, because after the very last photo on the roll had been taken, the camera would automatically roll the film back into its casing. It could then be popped out and replaced with a fresh one. The problem with this automatic winding function was the noise. It was a loud whirring sound that lasted for ages, a good thirty or forty seconds. So for the last photo on any film you definitely wanted to make sure you were somewhere suitable, to avoid drawing too much attention to yourself. This is something Mum discovered after she used the final shot on a film during the vows at a family wedding.

It was the wedding of Mum's younger brother Matthew and his soon-to-be wife, Claire. And because we were immediate family, we were in the front row. So close to the bride and groom that we could hear the vows without the need for microphones. Likewise, they could hear Mum's camera. They turned. To be fair, they were probably relieved when they saw Mum burying her camera in her cardigan to try to muffle the sound, because for a moment it is entirely possible they thought someone in the church was starting up a chainsaw!

Mum's answer to the question 'WHY WOULD ANY PERSON TAKE THE TWENTY-FOURTH PHOTO ON A TWENTY-FOUR-SHOT FILM DURING THE VOWS OF A WEDDING?' was that sometimes the film manufacturers put a couple of bonus shots on the film. She was right, this did happen. But still, why would you chance it during the most special moment of someone's most special day?

One person who I'm real sad never got to live to see digital cameras and smart phones is my granddad, who died in the late nineties. Granddad Williams loved photos but hated the cost involved. After he retired from his life-long career as a school headmaster, he and Nana went on one of those seniors' bus tours of the South Island, where they got to experience firsthand all the stunning scenery New Zealand has to offer, including the breath-taking Milford Sound. To save money on photos for this trip, Granddad just grabbed as many free brochures as he could get his hands on, cut out the glossy professional photos and stuck them into his photo album. Naturally, there were no photos of Granddad or Nana in this album, but with all the cash Granddad was saving, he didn't care. His sales pitch to Nana was that they both saw each other every day . . . it was the scenery they needed in the album.

It was a genius plan, he thought, and every time he flicked through this album he smiled as the memories came flooding back—memories of all the beautiful things he had seen, and the money he had saved by using brochures.

I wonder from time to time what is going to happen down the track with photos. Growing up, we had way less photos, but the photos we did have were lovingly catalogued in photo albums. These stacks of albums were treasured possessions. Ours were kept in a hall cupboard and only ever brought out occasionally, but whenever we went through them it was always a good laugh. The way things seem to be now is that everybody just has their collection of photos stored on their phone or computer without many actual physical copies anywhere. Maybe I'm showing my age with my lack of trust in computers, but if something happened to my iDevices, I would be iFucked! All my precious memories from the past five years would be gone, including an irreplaceable video of our first-ever Christmas with our adopted nephew, Sev, who was five years old at the time. In this video he is sitting in the lounge with the lit-up Christmas tree behind him, wearing nothing but a pair of red Spiderman undies unwrapping his present. If I somehow lost this video, his twenty-first birthday party would be substantially less humiliating for him.

The earliest recording I have of myself is a rather unflattering video of me vomiting up vast quantities of what looks like lumpy DB Draught after finishing the traditional yard glass at my twenty-first. This video would be a badge of honour if I had drunk the yard of beer in a reasonable time—less than five minutes, say. My good mate at the time, Neil Wagener, was at the top of the yardie leader board for our group of friends. He did his in fifty-eight seconds without spilling a drop. Neil was born to binge drink. He was a big guy for his age, had a good tolerance and was blessed with one of those throats that are perfect for drinking games, a throat you can open up and pour liquid down without having to gulp or swallow.

Me, on the other hand, I ended up in the wooden spoon position on the yardie honours board, with a snail-paced twelve minutes. What are the chances? The earliest video recording I have and it is me looking like a complete arse—binge drinking and vomiting . . . and doing it poorly to boot. Definitely not something I'd bother transferring to YouTube for future generations to see.

SCHOOL HOLIDAYS ON THE FARM

My favourite cousin and best friend, Carmel Saulbrey, lived on a farm. Carmel's parents are my Uncle John and Aunty Robyn. Robyn is my mum's slightly older sister. Both Aunty Rob and my mum got married around the same time and had the same number of kids at around the same time. This was incredibly convenient for inter-family visits—it meant all the Harvey kids had a cousin to buddy up with. Often in the school holidays, I would be sent to the farm to stay, sometimes for quite long stretches, like a few weeks at a time. These farm stays gave me some of the best—and worst—memories of my childhood.

I loved being with Carmel and my other cousins, and they had a pool, too. It was one of those ones from Para Rubber that sit on top of the ground, so it was nothing too flash, but in summer we would spend hours in it. It was better than the equivalent we had back at our place in Palmerston North, which was putting on our togs and running through the sprinkler on the lawn. Don't get me wrong—the sprinkler run was fun. And Mum and Dad would even let us do it during dry summers when water restrictions were in place. On these occasions we had to follow two strictly enforced rules, to ensure that neighbours and busybody dog walkers wouldn't find out and dob us in to the council:

1. Absolutely no noise.
2. Don't have the tap on full, otherwise the neighbours might see the fountain of water.

From experience I can tell you there is only so much fun you can have when you're running and jumping through a spray of water so small it would not wet more than a two-metre circle of grass.

I can't remember if I was asked if I would like to go to the farm or just told I was going to the farm. I suspect I was told. Kids back then rarely had a say in anything, and rights were something you didn't earn until well into your teens. If we were asked to make a choice, it was usually a lose–lose situation:

'What do you want for tea? Rissoles and peas or chops and peas?'

'Would you like a drink? You can have water or watered-down Raro.'

'What punishment would you like? Your mouth washed out with soap or a whack on the backside with the belt?'

The farm stays did have a downside, and that was the sheer amount of work involved. I hated it. Uncle John would wake us up at what felt like the middle of the night, but was probably more like seven-ish, to help him out. Still half-asleep, we would be in our farm overalls and gumboots hosing out the cowshed or standing on the back of a tractor feeding out hay while a combo of mud and cow shit sprayed up onto us from the wheels.

In the Christmas holidays, while my friends in Palmy were loitering around Wizards, the biggest (and only) spacies parlour in the city, asking passers-by for twenty cents, which was the going rate for a game, I'd be busy helping my cousins hoe entire paddocks of swedes, or haymaking, or doing some other equally unpleasant outdoorsy job while breathing in the putrid sweet stench of silage. We were like the little kids making Nike sneakers in the sweatshops . . . except at least they got paid a couple of cents an hour for their labour!

You have heard the popular saying 'Make hay while the sun shines.' But from firsthand experience of making bales of hay on some of the most intensely hot days of summer, I can tell you, I would rather be poor and live by the less well known saying I invented at the age of ten, which never really caught on—'Just chillax and set fire to ants with a magnifying glass while the sun shines.'

I did have a tendency to complain a fair bit, which my Uncle John found either amusing or annoying, depending on what mood he was in. He would call me a city slicker, which made me feel rather important, like I was somehow a wee bit cooler than my country cousins, who I was sure were terribly envious of my pristine fingernails and velvety soft palms. Looking back, since I was not all that slick and the city I was from was Palmerston North, I think it may have been an ironic joke at my expense. Like when he would call me 'Princess', even though I am not a royal, or a lady.

Uncle John was fun and intimidating in equal portions. Part of this had to do with his big commanding voice. From the breakfast table in the farmhouse you could hear him singing Engelbert Humperdinck songs in the cowshed over the noise of the machinery, about a hundred metres away. He loved Engelbert, especially 'Ten Guitars'. He also loved the radio station 2ZB and Lindsay Yeo, who did the breakfast show. Nobody would dare touch the dial of his radio in the cowshed. Even after I started on the radio, he only ever heard me after 2ZB changed format to Newstalk ZB and Lindsay was replaced.

Whenever I arrived at the farm he would give me a tutorial on how a man should greet another man, including the importance of eye contact and a good firm handshake. He had big rough hands. And when you went in for that handshake, it was imperative that you positioned your hand correctly. His grip was so firm and tight that if he ended up just grasping your fingers there was a real chance of bones being fractured—or even worse, you might let out a high-pitched whimper of discomfort.

As well as doing his bit for handshake etiquette, another one of Uncle John's big crusades was the behaviour of men in front of women. If any man ever swore or told a rude joke in front of Aunty Rob, or any other women for that matter, Uncle John would tell them to watch their language. If his advice was not taken on board it occasionally resulted in a fistfight, or a 'dust-up' as John would call it. These things were all rather civilised. Well, as civilised as fights can be. They would always take place outside, with both men involved removing their jackets first before putting their dukes up. Nothing like fights today, which often seem to involve unwilling participants being kicked on the ground and lots of broken glass.

Despite all the work, I enjoyed these farm stays. The best thing about them was getting to spend heaps of time with Carmel. I didn't even mind that she was a girl, unlike the girls I went to Riverdale School with in Palmy, who all us boys thought of as lesser citizens. I don't remember ever busting out this popular playground nursery rhyme to Carmel:

Girls are weak—chuck them in the creek.
Boys are strong—like King Kong.

I remember the bizarre feeling of total confusion and sadness the day Carmel and I were no longer allowed to sleep in the same bed. We were both prepubescent twelve-year-olds. She hit puberty a couple of years down the track. Me? I was still a good five years away from making the transformation from a boy into a young adult.

As all my mates around me started to develop, my own lack of change became more and more obvious to me. The body part I used to gauge my progress was my armpits. It became a mini-obsession. I would check them out on a daily basis to see if the small wispy blond hairs there had grown at all. When they eventually started to go black and sprout in length, it was a period of immense joy. I can say with a reasonable amount of accuracy that I was the only sixth former in my year at Palmerston North Boys High School who had no armpit hair. I know this because for PE it was compulsory to wear a singlet, and I was so obsessed with my own lack of development that I was always aware of what was going on in everyone else's armpits. Fortunately for me, these hairless pits of mine were an easy enough thing to hide, so it's not like I was teased for it. In hindsight, I probably didn't need to be so self-conscious . . . I doubt any of the other kids in my class were as interested in what was going on under anyone else's arms.

The decision to separate Carmel and me and put us in separate rooms came, I think, after a parental panic that we were becoming sexually curious. Aunty Robyn and

Uncle John had this big book they kept under their bed called *The Joy of Sex*. It was a big hardcover thing that had lots of realistic drawings of an adult couple having sex in every position you can think of . . . and many positions you wouldn't be able to think of even if you tried. All us kids knew about the book and Carmel and I would often sneak into Robyn and John's room to have a flick through and giggle uncontrollably at all the drawings of these naked adults with such an abundance of hair everywhere. They had hair for Africa. Actually, the lady had hair that kind of looked a bit like the map of Africa as well.

Our favourite picture was the one where the man, who had long hair and a beard and looked like a 1980s Ashton Kutcher, was lying on his back while the lady was kissing him on the penis. From reading a part of the text we found out it was a thing called a blow job, and we wondered if she was trying to inflate him. At our ages it made perfect sense—why would the book say it was a blow job if she was actually sucking?

We found this book and all its pictures hysterical. And gross. We knew it was something a bit naughty, but it definitely did not make us curious. If anything, it made us feel a bit sick—especially the picture where the man was kissing the lady on the bottom. 'Eww, what if she does a blow-off in his face?' Carmel asked earnestly, before we both laughed hysterically.

We never got caught in the act of reading this book, but we must have put it back incorrectly or left some clue that we had discovered it, because one day, without any discussion, we were told we would be sleeping in different rooms. I was so unhappy—I missed my best mate. We thought we must have done something really bad but had no idea what it was. It all makes sense now. The grown-ups were probably just freaking out because the thing we called 'top'n'tailing' was remarkably similar to the thing in their secret book called a 'sixty-niner'. They had nothing to worry about. Even if I'd been more sexually aware, there is no way I'd have been shagging my first cousin. Second cousin? Who knows. Probably not, but never say never.

THE CHRISTMAS HOLIDAY ROAD TRIP

The last full family road trip we did together was just before Bridget, the eldest, got her driver's licence at the age of fifteen. I'm pretty sure she had her licence test booked for bang on her fifteenth birthday—on the actual day itself. That was how desperate she was to escape these family trips. The main problem was that Dad's company cars were never designed for two adults, four children and ten days' worth of luggage and supplies—he usually had a Ford Cortina or something similar. When we were all small, this was do-able, but as we got older the back seat became a hotbed of tension and unrest.

We set out on that last trip on Boxing Day 1985, after getting up in the middle of the night to beat the rush. Dad was all about driving at off-peak hours to avoid the holiday traffic. The odd thing is that he wasn't even a speeder—quite the opposite, in fact. Dad would drive at the exact same speed at 4 am on a clear road as he would at midday with a caravan, a camper van, a logging truck and an elderly couple in a Toyota Starlet all behind us. I think he just enjoyed the freedom of not having a big line of cars in front, without feeling the need to use this clear road to get to our destination faster.

By this particular holiday all us kids were over it. We didn't hate each other, per se, but the thought of a nine-hour trip with my brother's right thigh stuck to my left thigh with a mixture of our leg-sweat didn't thrill me. Pretty sure it was mutual, too. Or if Dan did enjoy having his leg joined to mine with combined bodily fluids, he certainly put on a very convincing act of being repulsed by it.

It didn't help that this was before cars had air conditioning. They had heaters with a 'cold' option, which meant on a warm summer's day the only viable option was to have the windows down, because even on the coldest setting the heater would still be blowing warm air at you.

Mum came up with a solution. Charlotte, the not-so-babyish baby of the family, aged eight, would sit on the floor of the front passenger seat, in between Mum's legs. Us three older kids, aged eleven, thirteen and fifteen, all shared the back seat. Even with this extra space in the back, it would still be impossible to avoid leg-sweat, given our ages and size, so Mum, ever the problem-solver, came up with another winner idea to make the trip bearable—we would travel with two pillows in the back seat to keep our legs from touching. In hindsight, the three of us older kids must have really kicked up a fuss for Mum to risk Charlotte's life and sacrifice her own leg room just so we could travel with a little bit more space. Then again, there were never more than three seatbelts in the back seat of these cars, so in the event of a head-on collision on the open road, I guess Char was probably fucked in the front or the back.

I do recall one year Dad had a station wagon as a company car. This made things a bit more comfortable. Daniel's preferred seat was in the boot next to the big CNG tank. Back then we referred to this as travelling 'doggy style', because for dog owners with station wagons, this was usually where the dog went for trips in the car. I can't remember who told us that travelling in the boot of this type of vehicle was known as doggy style—possibly one of our uncles. But none of us Harvey kids had any idea of the innuendo behind it. And thinking back, I don't recall Mum or Dad ever sniggering in a knowing fashion or reprimanding us for using that phrase. Maybe the term was a little more underground than it is now.

For as long as we had the station wagon, Dan would climb over the back seat into the boot anytime we went anywhere. This was a win–lose situation for poor Dan. Yes, he got the luxury of space, having the entire boot area all to himself, but he was prone to terrible bouts of carsickness and would often end up violently ill after staring out the back or side window for hours on end. Instead of sympathy, or an offer to switch seats, we would just give Dan grief for stinking out the car with his vomit-breath.

But before you feel too sorry for Dan, it's worth mentioning that we all took turns at being the tormentor and the tormented. It wasn't a formal roster system, but it all ended up even, I think. Charlotte, being the youngest, was exempt from most of this. Also, she was a bit of a crybaby, so there wasn't much sport in making her cry and we usually left her alone. But it was rare that all three of us older kids would be getting on at the same time. So on any given day Dan and I would tease Bridget, Bridget and I would rip into Dan, or Dan and Bridge would rip into me. Our parents were in the front seat and could hear it all, but Mum was usually too busy plucking her pubic hair to worry about what we were up to. As far as she was concerned, if Dad was there, he was the disciplinarian . . . even when he was driving.

Dad wouldn't get involved until someone said, usually in that drawly whingey voice: 'Daaaaaaad, the others are being mean.' Seeking a referee was never a good idea, though, because it usually resulted in everyone being punished further, including the victim. Dad would just shout and tell everyone to stop or he would make us get out and walk. Obviously, we knew this was not going to happen. We were on State Highway 1 somewhere between Turangi and Taupo—a drop-off would not only be impractical and dangerous but also highly illegal. On other less busy roads, Dad did sometimes pull over, and a quick roadside smack would be administered before we all piled back into the car, upset and stinging, and the drive would continue. Other times, he would keep driving, looking forward with one hand on the wheel, while his free hand swooped wildly and blindly round behind him, looking for someone's leg to connect with—anyone's would do. This attempt at discipline was rarely successful, but it did usually shut us up for a while afterwards.

The problem was the boredom. Today you can pop a DVD on or load a movie onto a tablet to shut the kids up for a road trip, but we had none of those luxuries. We would usually read a book until we started to get a headache and feel sick. Then we would switch to a more traditional game, like I-spy or That's My Car!

That's My Car! was an incredibly uncomplicated game—we would go turn and turn about in order from oldest to youngest and shout out, 'That's my car!' when a car came in the opposite direction. Because we travelled off-peak, we could often go for minutes waiting to see another vehicle. The fun part was laughing at the others when they ended up with some old shit heap of a car, but if it was Charlotte, she would often burst into tears. This was Mum and Dad's cue to tell us to wrap it up.

These all-inclusive make-your-own-fun games stopped the year Bridget was given a Nintendo Game & Watch for Christmas. I could have got one too, I suppose, but that was the year I got a new cricket bat. In some more generous families, where the parents were nicer to their kids, I might have been able to get both the cricket bat and the Nintendo Game & Watch, since only one was a toy. I mean, come on, a cricket bat—IT'S A PIECE OF SPORTING EQUIPMENT!

You'd think parents would buy their kids sports equipment during the year, because it encourages them to play sport instead of getting up to mischief, like my mate Patrick, who I caught the bus to St Peters Intermediate with. He got on and off in Highbury, the shit area of town with all the state houses and its very own youth gang—the unoriginally named Highbury Hoods—who were very big fans of glue sniffing. Patrick played no sports and every morning amazed and frightened me with stories of what he and his Highbury mates had got up to the night before. Even at eleven I recall being disturbed by a story he told me about catching frogs in the Mangaone Stream and lighting small fireworks like Double Happys and Tom Thumbs after poking them into the frog's bottom. Maybe he was just making it up to be cool or whatever. Who knows. Even if he did make it up, it's still a pretty twisted thing for a kid to have even thought about.

So I foolishly prioritised a cricket bat instead of a cool new electronic toy. The bat was awesome . . . it just didn't work. Some may put that down to human error, but I'm blaming the bat. It has to take some responsibility for the fact that I only scored a total of seventeen runs for the whole season.

I was disillusioned by that bat. It was this thing with no shoulders called an Excalibur. It was the best damn cricket bat in the world and looked completely different to every bat every decent cricket player in the world was using . . . apart from Lance Cairns! Lance used this bat and he was hitting sixes all over the park. One particular game had made me decide this cricket bat would make a better Christmas present than a Nintendo Game & Watch. New Zealand (dressed in beige without a hint of irony) were playing Australia at the MCG, and Excalibur and his assistant Lance smashed six sixes off only ten balls, including this spectacular one-handed shot. I HAD to have that bat, and Santa kindly delivered. Bridget got her Donkey Kong Game & Watch at the same time. The envy and regret were more or less instant.

They're terribly lame by today's gaming standards, but at the time the Nintendo Game & Watch was the most awesome thing any of us had ever seen. Bridget hogged this device and never offered it to anyone else, even when she wasn't playing with it. I only got a turn every now and then when Mum or Dad intervened. Donkey Kong was in an orangey-brown case that flipped open to reveal two small LCD game screens. It had two buttons, one to jump over the barrels the gorilla kept throwing down and the other to move you up the scaffolding towards him. When you got to the top, you had to jump to reach a crane. Then you would start at the bottom and do it all over again. It was such a simple game, but I couldn't even begin to guess how many hundreds of hours we all (but mostly Bridget) got from it. It ended up breaking—a cracked screen—when Bridget left it on the car seat and a friend of Mum's from her jogging club, a larger woman who had just taken to the sport in an attempt to lose all her baby fat (and there was plenty of it), sat on it. It was as sad for Bridget as any break-up with a boy she went through down the track.

Even after this piece of electronic history had been judged unfixable by the repair shop Mum took it into, Bridget still hung on to it. It seemed sad to throw out something so cool . . . even though it was now little more than a decorative paperweight.

The very last stages of the road trip were always trouble free. We could see glimpses of the blue Pacific Ocean as we turned various corners and knew a leg stretch and some personal space were not far away. Given our early departure, we usually arrived just after lunch, which meant we would have all afternoon to swim in the motel pool while Dad cracked open a longneck beer and turned on the telly. Mum took all the luggage out of the car boot and into the motel unit. Jobs like this just sort of happened around us. We were so excited to be at our destination that we were oblivious to this work going on. I don't think Mum minded too much, though—she was probably not quite ready to put her togs on just yet, due to the angry-looking red raised bumps on her inner thighs.

THE CHRISTMAS HOLIDAY IN WHANGAMATA

Every boxing day we travelled from Palmerston North to Whangamata on the Coromandel Peninsula for the annual Harvey family summer holiday—I described a typical journey there in the previous chapter. Dad was never the camping type; actually he was not much of a beach type either. So a happy compromise was to book a motel unit. This would allow Dad to pretend he was still at home and the rest of us to enjoy a holiday at a great beach.

Dad would sit out of the sun inside the motel unit, close to his crate of DB, and either read a book or pull the curtains to keep the sun's reflection off the screen and watch whatever cricket was on the telly. Mum would supervise us kids as we swam in the motel's kidney-shaped pool or down at the beach. I use the word 'supervise' very loosely. The perk of having four kids was that Mum could put her towel down, chuck on her Le Specs and worry about her tan, safe in the knowledge that one of her children would come and alert her if one of the others got swept out to sea.

Every year for god-knows-how-many years we would book out the same dates and stay in the same unit at the same motel. It was the two-bedroom unit at the end of the block at the Whangamata Motel on Barbara Avenue. Mum and Dad would share the room with the double bed and the girls would have the single beds in the second room, leaving the fold-out sofas in the lounge for Dan and me.

Next to the motel was a walkway that took you down to the beach, and on the other side of the walkway were the camping grounds. We used to wander to the beach most days and look at all the different shapes and sizes of tents enviously. The adventure of sleeping in a tent and the novel idea of sharing showers or, even better, not showering at all, appealed to the younger me immensely.

Because of Dad's aversion to the idea, camping is not something I ever got to experience, and I am too set in my ways to bother trying now. As a young kid it seemed like fun, but as an adult the idea does not appeal at all— communal toilets and showers, drunk people walking past tripping over your tent pegs, walls so thin you can hear the morning flatulence of the bloke two camp sites down, waking up early because the tent is warmer than a Bikram yoga room, waking up early because there's a storm and everything is wet, and sleeping on an air bed that goes down more frequently than a Kardashian on heat.

If I'm being completely honest, I'm even worse than my dad ever was—I'm a hotel snob. There is no way I would ever spend ten nights in a three-star Best Western with limited facilities like the Whangamata Motel in the 1980s. Thanks, Mum and Dad, you have created a monster. I have inherited my father's loathing of camping and my mother's love of spending money—a dangerously expensive combination.

I'm also largely incapable of following instruction manuals and doing pretty much anything myself. I place the blame for that squarely on my dad's shoulders, too. I'm even incapable of putting snow chains on car tyres— I'm one of those mugs you pass on the side of the road who pays someone twenty dollars to do this five-minute job because I'm unable to do it myself. So even if I were to attempt this camping lifestyle that so many Kiwis love and swear by, I doubt I would be able to erect even the most basic tent.

Dad was terrible at all this stuff. Every appliance in our house with a digital display would permanently flash 00:00 because Dad would try to follow the manual and end up in a flustered rage, before throwing the booklet into the drawer with all the other booklets and vowing to try again another time—just like all the other times, with all the other electronic appliances. Even the clock in his car was incorrect for half of each year. It was right in summer, but then, when daylight savings finished in April, he would be running an hour fast. It may have caused panic for any clients or co-workers he was driving, but Dad and the rest of us just instinctively knew that in winter the clock was off by an hour.

Intervening and offering to fix it was not an option, either. Dad was quite happy with the clock being right half the time and correct after some basic addition for the other half, so he insisted nobody play with it. I really think he thought, 'I'm a reasonably smart man . . . if I can't work out how to set this clock, nobody can!'

I think I'm slightly better than Dad at this stuff, but that may just be because stuff these days is far simpler to operate. With My Sky, for example, you just have to select a show and press the red button and it will record. Hell, if you select a show and press the green button, it will record every episode of the show for the entire season. Easy. The early video recorders were a different animal altogether. Even a ridiculously smart human being like Stephen Hawking would have left his home in the eighties not entirely confident the VCR unit would switch on and start recording at the time he had set it to do so.

*

It was in the build-up to one of these Harvey family Christmas holidays at Whangamata that I suffered a humiliating and incredibly painful knee injury that made me the laughing stock of the wider family on Christmas Day and meant that for the first few days of the holiday I could only swim if I had a plastic grocery store bag taped around my left knee to keep the bandage dry. When you are fourteen and still yet to hit puberty, and you are holidaying in a hot beach town where there are lots of girls your age in bikinis and other attire offering minimal coverage, the last thing you want is to be seen limping into the ocean with a rustling white plastic bag on your knee. Finally, it meant I was getting noticed by the girls . . . but it was not the sort of attention any teenage boy would seek.

It was only a couple of days out from Christmas when I saw an ad on TV for Foodtown supermarket, announcing they had two-litre bottles of Coke for only $2.50 each. I loved Coke, and since my only source of income was from my *Evening Standard* paper round, this offer of my favourite beverage at such a steal of a price was too hard to pass up. I begged both Mum and Dad for a ride into Foodtown, but they turned me down, claiming it was because Coke was gutrot and they didn't want to encourage me drinking it. The real reason was that they just couldn't be arsed driving me in, as I discovered when I asked if I could ride there on my bike. They were both fine with this suggestion and immediately stopped being so concerned about the possibility that I might rot from the inside out.

I had twenty dollars, so I purchased as much Coke as I could—eight two-litre bottles. I had the staff at Foodtown put four bottles in each bag, and then double bag them for strength. Then I hooked each heavy bag with its eight litres of liquid over a handlebar and started the four-kilometre bike ride back home. I must have looked absurd. It is just lucky for me that hardly anybody had a video camera back then and, even in the highly unlikely event that someone with a camera did happen to film me, the only way to share clips of people humiliating themselves was by sending them into the TV show *America's Funniest Home Videos.*

It was not an easy journey home. With every pedal stroke the bags would swing a little bit, making the handlebars sway. But against the odds, I made it. Well, more specifically, I made it onto Long Melford Road, where we lived. I was no more than two hundred metres from home when some dickhead travelling in the opposite direction did a U-turn in his car. The driver then slowly crept up behind me and blasted his horn with a long, loud BEEEEEEEEEEEEEP. The noise gave me a fright and I turned around to see what was going on, causing the bags of Coke to swing so much that I fell off my bike and onto the road. Fortunately for the rest of my body, my left knee took one for the team and hit the road first. Unfortunately for my unselfish left knee, there was a loose piece of gravel right on that very spot and it ended up embedded deep in my flesh.

To make things worse, three of my eight bottles of Coke had split open—so there I was, sitting in a pool of my own cola, in a world of physical pain, heartbroken at my loss, and I still had to figure out how I was going to get myself, my bike and the ten litres of soft drink that had survived the crash home. In my dazed state I decided to stash the undamaged bottles in someone's front garden and limp home while wheeling my bike.

I was relieved when I walked in the door. My knee was killing me and by this time so much blood had trickled down my shin that my sock was drenched red. The response from Mum and Dad was not exactly what I was hoping for: 'Serves you right for being greedy!' Yeah, I suppose they were correct. But it would have been nice if they'd felt just a bit guilty for not taking me in the car to help me feed my sugar and caffeine addiction.

After some crude home surgery by Mum, using Dettol, a pair of tweezers and a needle from the sewing kit, the Jaffa-sized stone was finally removed from my knee, leaving a hole big enough to put the tip of my little finger into. Now I could limp back up the road and retrieve my stashed bottles. While Mum was digging the stone out, these lonely unguarded bottles were all I could think about. The pain of my injury was bad enough . . . but it would pale in comparison to the sting of losing all my Coke.

*

On these holidays we had the same lunch every day—ham sandwiches.

Every Christmas without fail, Granddad Harvey would give us a family present—a giant ham. I assume it was some sort of a deal struck between him and my dad that made the day as easy as possible for all concerned. Remarkably, it took my siblings and me about four Christmases to notice this trend. On Christmas Day Granddad would go to the fridge and bring out this big cold thing wrapped in festive paper. The four of us kids would tear into it, wondering what the devil it could be, and what sort of a silly granddad would use his fridge as a hiding place. Eventually Bridget picked up on the pattern and cracked the code. After that, Granddad even gave up on wrapping the damn thing in Christmas paper.

Since we didn't have a chilly bin, Mum had a way to make sure the ham would survive the eight-hour road trip in a stinking hot car and still be fit for human consumption. I'm not sure where she learned this trick—in the pre-internet days, this sort of information was all word-of-mouth stuff—but she would get her three oldest tea towels, tea towels that were still being used to dry dishes but had definitely seen better days, and then run them under the cold tap and put them in the fridge overnight. Then, just prior to leaving in the morning, she would wrap them around the ham and put it in the car. Probably not a technique many Food and Hygiene officers would recommend, but we never got sick. We got sick of the ham, but not sick FROM the ham.

I grew up believing that ham was a seasonal thing, like strawberries, because the Christmas holiday was the only time we would have it . . . and have it we would! It was delicious for the first few days, but by the time the holiday came to a close, the thought of another ham sandwich was enough to make me blurt out something highly inappropriate and offensive: 'Oh no! Not another ham sandwich. Can't I have something else on my sandwich? Like peanut butter or honey or something?'

On paper this seems like a reasonable question, but in the eighties, a child saying something like that to an adult was considered as outrageous and out of line as it would be today if a kid of any age told an adult to fuck off. As punishment I would usually be subjected to bread with nothing on it. I never said this out loud, but after ten consecutive days of ham sandwiches, two pieces of dry white bread with nothing on it was a treat for my incredibly unsophisticated palate.

*

As far as activities went, all there really was to do in Whangamata was play minigolf or go on the hydro slide that used to be in the main street. Or, if it was a wet day, go to the movies and watch something so fucking old that you'd probably seen it when it first came out in your town but so long ago now that you had forgotten the plot. From memory, the Whangamata cinema only got *Dirty Dancing* in as a new release after Patrick Swayze died.

I only recall ever seeing a few movies in all our years of going to Whangamata. The other stuff we did a lot, though. We loved playing minigolf as a family. We only stopped going there so much out of sheer awkwardness, after Dad got caught stealing. From that time on, Dad never went back. He wasn't banned or anything, he just felt too stink to be seen there.

It was pretty pricey to play there for a family of six. I don't remember how much it cost but I remember it being steep and Dad always sighing and looking distressed as he pulled his wallet out from deep inside his pocket. As he handed over the required notes he'd be muttering under his breath, but still loud enough for anyone within a metre to hear: 'Bloody unbelievable!' The funny thing is he said that every time. You would think after seven or eight visits he'd be used to the high cost of playing there, and the bloody unbelievable would become the bloody believable. Not my old man, though—it got him every time.

Then one year Dad devised a plan so he wouldn't feel so bad about the money he was forking over every time we played. On the final hole, when the ball went in, it disappeared down some long pipe and travelled all the way back to the office. When we got to the eighteenth hole, Dad called everyone in and told us we would all get what's known in golf as a 'gimme' for our final shot on this hole. In other words, we just had to putt the ball near the hole. We wouldn't take another shot, causing the ball to travel back to the office—instead, Dad would pick up the different coloured balls and put them in the pockets of his pleated corduroys. Even though Dad was a keen golfer, I don't think he would have ever used the balls, which were not great quality—I think he just felt like he should get to keep them since he had forked out so much money to be playing minigolf in the first place.

We all agreed and Dad positioned himself by the hole with his back to the office. One by one he scooped up the balls until he had three in each front pocket. We walked back past the office and hung up our putters, then walked back onto the main street. We can't have been more than twenty metres down the street when one of the staff from the minigolf place came running after us, saying, 'Excuse me!'

He was a youngish surfie-looking dude, maybe early twenties, probably earning minimum wage, tasked with the terribly unpleasant job of asking a middle-aged man on a family outing if he had stolen some putt-putt balls. He awkwardly asked and Dad awkwardly confessed, then the two fistfuls of golf balls were returned, and gratefully received with an instruction to please let them go down the hole in future.

Dad made the right call not to return—it would be terrible to be that customer who the staff in the office all talk about:

'Pssssssst. Hey. Don't look now . . . but the old guy over there on the fifth hole. With the pen in his shirt pocket. Wearing the cords with jandals. That's the guy who stole the ball back in 1985!'

The hydro slide was another costly activity, but it was a good way for Mum and Dad to get rid of us for a few hours of silence. It was not some fancy water park or anything. It was just this wooden platform with what seemed like never-ending flights of stairs, then a single slide that wound its way down to a rectangular plunge pool at the bottom. Fairly boring by today's standards, but a shitload of fun that would keep us going for hours. The hardest part was the waiting. We would have our fifteen-second ride down, then spend ten minutes in the long line on the stairs waiting for our turn again. All because of their stupid rule about riders going ten seconds apart, for some stupid reason like safety or something. I would always try to sneak off a second or two behind Daniel. I would then lie down as stiff as I could to streamline myself in an attempt to catch him. If I caught him, I could then give him a surprise push on his shoulders with my feet. It was a huge amount of fun for one of us.

We got banned from going on the hydro slide after Mum heard a story that I'm sure is just an urban myth. The hydro slide eventually closed down for good and is no longer there. I do wonder if its demise had anything to do with the story Mum heard and the panic it caused. The rumour was that someone had gone down the slide and stopped themselves halfway, then carefully stuck some razor blades into the joins of the pipes. The next few kids in togs who went down got slashed, or 'cut like a hot knife through margarine' as Mum explained. Sounds like total BS to me now, but we were banned from that day onwards. And, I must confess, even now when I go on a hydro slide, the razor blade story does still sit in the back of my mind.

*

Our last year going away as an entire family came about as the 1980s drew to a close. I was a month away from turning sixteen, that awkward age where I was too young for a holiday with my mates but too old to still be going on a motel holiday with my parents and siblings. I'm pretty sure this holiday would have been just as miserable for Mum and Dad as it was for me.

This was during the time I call the grunting years, a period where anything Mum or Dad asked me would be met with a grunt. Part of this probably had to do with me finally going through puberty and the fear of my voice breaking mid-sentence, something which always got a laugh from any adults who happened to be within earshot. On top of that there was my inflamed face, which was covered in acne—real angry, red-looking pimples. I never seemed to have less than fifteen or twenty at a time, and there were always a couple on the go that were inflamed and painful to touch.

I tried almost everything to get rid of my pimples. I don't know much about today's equivalents and whether or not they are any good, but in the eighties, there were numerous products . . . none of which worked. I know because I tried all of them—this liquid from the pharmacy called Ten-O-Six, which I'm sure was just turps in a smaller, fancy-looking bottle; Oxy 10 cream; Topex; Clearasil; even some herbal remedy my nana suggested called witch-hazel. I did make an executive decision to draw the line at rubbing my own semen on my pimples. This was suggested to me by a good schoolmate of mine at Boys High. Who knows, maybe I would have contemplated it if Andrew had nice clear skin. The fact that his face was more of a mess than mine told me his unorthodox method was not only vulgar, it didn't even work.

This was the year we travelled to Whangamata in a two-car convoy. Mum, Dad, Dan, Char and I were in one car, and Bridget and her best friend, Ingrid, followed us in another car. Bridget was almost eighteen and had just finished at high school, so this was quite a bit of freedom she had been afforded by our super strict parents. It didn't end there, either—they got to set up a tent right outside our motel unit and sleep together in that.

On the first morning, when Dad was making himself a cup of tea at some ridiculously early time, he opened the kitchen window in the motel unit and yelled out towards the tent the popular catchphrase from this dreadful TV show, *Hi-de-Hi!*, that was popular at the time: 'Hi-de-hi, campers!'

I can't be sure but I think Bridge and Ingrid may have even mustered up the energy to reply with the expected response, as per the TV show: 'Hi-de-ho!'

Dad has never known when to bail on a joke, though. So this became his tedious routine every morning for the duration of the holiday. By day seven, I think Bridget and Ingrid were plotting ways to stab Dad to death with a tent peg and make it look like an unfortunate accident.

WHERE ARE THEY NOW: MUM

From the time Charlotte was about fourteen, Mum used to say, in the most Kiwi of accents, 'After Charlotte's twenty-first, I'm breaking up with ya father!'

We all knew it needed to happen but were not sure it ever would. They broke up a lot over the years, Mum and Dad. I remember the first time Dad left. I was nine and in standard three. Divorces and one-parent families were nowhere near as common in the eighties as they are now. There were three 'minorities' represented in my class that year—Melee, the only Chinese girl; Crystal, the first girl to reach puberty and need a bra; and Craig, the kid whose parents had divorced.

I remember running up to Craig quite excited on the first morning after Mum and Dad sat us down for 'the talk' and telling him my news. I should have been heart-broken—my world was falling apart, after all. But being nine and not very emotionally advanced, my focus was not on losing a parent, or the absolute shit Mum was dealing with, having to hold together a household with four kids who were all too young to appreciate what she was going through. All I could think about was what I was going to gain from this situation.

You see, Craig was all I had to go on, and his situation seemed pretty damn awesome. Everyone in the class was jealous of Craig. He would see his dad every second weekend and the Monday afterwards he would always have good stories for morning news about the cool stuff they did and the things his dad bought him. Not being much of a forward thinker, it didn't occur to me that my dad would be just as much of a tight-arse as a single guy as he was as a married man. In hindsight, I suppose what I really needed was for Mum and Dad to stay together but for me to spend every second weekend with Craig's rich dad.

I can't remember how long Mum and Dad broke up for. Time seems to move differently when you're nine. I don't think it was very long, though—maybe a month.

After that, a predictable cycle developed: the fighting would escalate, Mum and Dad would tell us they were breaking up, then they would get back together and a period of short-lived bliss would follow. I remember one particular shouty night where they both ended up screaming and crying in the kitchen. It was loud enough to wake us all up. I remember this one because it was on the night before my fifth form School Certificate maths exam. As I've already mentioned, maths was my absolute worst subject, so part of me was wondering if there was some way I could use this massive domestic dispute as an excuse for the poor results I would inevitably get for the following day's exam.

Mum and Dad managed to work through whatever had caused this incident far more skilfully than I worked through the maths paper—although in my defence, it took them most of the night. For my maths exam, I only needed eighty minutes of the allocated three hours to answer all the problems to the best of my ability.

Eventually Charlotte turned twenty-one, and not long after that, as promised, Mum and Dad went their separate ways. For good. Ultimately, they were just better people as individuals than as a couple and nobody can accuse them of not giving it an honest crack. That was over fifteen years ago now and Mum is still single.

I would like to believe Mum and Dad only joined genitals on four occasions, each resulting in a pregnancy. The thought of Mum and Dad having sex with anybody—each other, other people or even by themselves is just too repulsive to consider.

I know Dad has done okay with the ladies over the years, far better than a man with that much visible nostril hair deserves. But I was convinced that the only man Mum had ever been with was Dad. The theory made sense—she got married as a nineteen-year-old Catholic girl and had been single since the break-up. That theory was blown out of the water during some stupid on-air segment that backfired a couple of years ago.

We were running this segment for Mother's Day, asking adult children to call us and guess the last time their mum had been intimate. We would then call the contestant's mum, and if the answers matched they would win a prize worth way less than they deserved after such an embarrassing revelation, like a Michael Bublé CD or something equally undesirable.

As a dummy run, to demonstrate to the audience how the game would work, I took part as the very first contestant. After guessing that the last time my mum had sex was in 1998, we called her for verification. And that is the precise moment that me, my siblings and around 400,000 New Zealanders discovered that my mum had a one-night stand sometime between breaking up with Dad and now. I was mortified. A part of me was a little bit stoked for Mum, but I was mostly mortified! Charlotte was even more mortified and didn't speak to me for three (glorious and blissful) days.

Mum is now in her early sixties and I will never ever inquire about her sex life, on or off air, ever again.

My mother is remarkably fit. She still runs marathons and is just coming to terms with the reality that her times are getting slower and slower with age. We all try to tell her it is an achievement that she can still run that distance. She only gave up smoking a few years ago after much pestering from Billie, her eldest granddaughter. Mum loved her ciggies, but it did always seem to be a bizarre combo of passions—distance running and tobacco. She would go out for a thirty-kilometre training run on a Saturday and then, still in her sweat-drenched gear, sit on her balcony and light up a Dunhill blue.

Mum replaced her smoking vice with an even more addictive and dangerous habit—talkback radio. Now when we catch up she no longer smells of smoke but she is continually quoting Sean Plunket and what he has to say about that week's big current event. Occasionally I remind her that I, too, do a radio show and am on the air at the same time as some of the presenters she quotes.

She is incredibly proud of having a son who has enjoyed moderate success as a radio personality. I know this because every now and then she will tell me she met someone in passing, like the guy who sold her a Lotto ticket at the mall, who is a fan of our radio show, and I always wonder how she managed to work the fact that she is my mum into the conversation with this stranger during the forty-five seconds it took to buy the ticket. I can go for months at a time without meeting anyone who knows or cares who I am . . . yet Mum seems to run into these people in the most unlikely of places all the fucking time!

Auckland is a big sprawling city and for a while I was the only member of the Harvey family living in the big smoke. Then a few years ago Charlotte moved back from London with her young family and into a place about a kilometre away. After Char, Mum moved back from the Australian Gold Coast, where she had been living for a few years. A move back to New Zealand was long overdue. I'm convinced that one more blistering summer on the Gold Coast and Mum would have turned into a giant raisin.

As luck would have it, Mum moved into an apartment right around the corner from us! It was only four hundred metres away from our place—a good, convenient distance, since I am her unofficial tech support. It would have been incredibly annoying to have to crawl through the Auckland traffic for an hour each way only to discover that Mum's DVD player wasn't working because she'd taken the plug out earlier that day when she did the vacuuming!

*

When Mum and Dad broke up they both walked away with a bit of money each, but not enough to buy a place. For Dad, this is fine. He is possibly less materialistic than the Dalai Lama. As long as he has a room with a bed, a bedside table to put his library book on and a fridge to keep the beer cold, he is a happy man. Mum, on the other hand, has always liked the security of having a place she could call home and decorating it with photos, Lladró and things that mean a lot to her. Seriously, how these two survived almost thirty years together is a mystery to me!

In late 2013, Jay-Jay and I signed new five-year contracts for our radio show. With a bit of certainty about our futures in what is considered to be a fairly unpredictable industry, we bought two apartments—one for Jay-Jay's mum and one for my mum. Nothing fancy, just basic, small-ish apartments, but still a place they could each call home without fear of being turfed out on the street. They are both really hard-working, salt of the earth Kiwi women who have raised families but, through divorce and a bit of bad luck, had ended up without places of their own. I'm always sceptical of that lame old cliché about it being better to give than to receive because, quite frankly, I love getting shit for free! But when we unlocked the doors and told these incredibly important women in our lives that these places were theirs and they were home and they could stay there for the rest of their lives, seeing their tears of appreciation was an absolute privilege. Jay-Jay and I consider ourselves lucky that we had this opportunity—and anyway, it was either that or eventually chucking a couple of little granny flats out on the back lawn, and there was no way in a trillion years I wanted Mum living in my backyard . . . four hundred metres is close enough, thanks very much.

Mum has been alone for years now. I think she likes her own company, but I do worry a bit about her being lonely. It's not something we ever chat about. She's got four kids, so I figure one of the others can take care of the deep and meaningful conversations and I'll take care of all her IT and electronic set-up needs. But who knows what the future holds. I'd like to think that one day Mum will run into a nice guy and fall in love again, hopefully with some bloke who is rich and who loves her and will look after her. I'm not sure if this will happen—she's pretty fussy these days.

My main wish would be that she is happy, whatever that entails. She does stress about money, so I was pleased we could take away a little bit of that pressure by buying her a place to call home. I imagined that with the extra money she'd have she would get to live life a bit more—travel, work a bit less, stop buying cask wine. She hasn't done any of those things yet. What has she done? Bought more fucking Lladró!

WHERE THEY ARE NOW: DAD

Dad is currently in a relationship with a very nice lady, Michelle. I can't imagine he will ever remarry. If he did, there would have to be some coupon cut from the newspaper involved. The wedding would have to cost nothing and he would have to be getting something out of it other than a new life partner.

I think in some small way I am responsible for helping Dad and Michelle get together. Dad called me one day to tell me he was trying out internet dating and was on a website called NZDating. I think he'd been on this site for a while but was telling me now because he wanted my help. Internet dating and meeting people through phone apps like Tinder is no big deal now, but when these services were first introduced, I think there was a certain stigma attached to them, particularly for older generations.

Dad was trying it out but was disappointed with the lack of hits his profile had been getting, so he wanted to know if I could give them a boost by mentioning it on my radio show. This was when I found out a couple of very interesting things. Things so hilarious that I had to immediately text all three of my siblings to tell them what I had discovered:

1. Dad's username was 'Fitasafiddle'.
2. Dad was an NZDating gold member.

Firstly, that username. It was more than a little bit misleading. Unless he was referring to the way a fiddle just sits there and doesn't do anything until someone picks it up and plays it. The gold membership surprised me too. You could become a member for free or pay different amounts for varying levels of privileges. Dad hates spending money, so it was hard to believe he had paid for the most costly membership package available. Almost as hard to believe as the part in his profile about how much he enjoyed tramping and bushwalks. Apart from the very occasional walk along the Palmerston North Esplanade, a short gravel path surrounded by trees and shrubs with a miniature railway running through it, a walk that can easily be done in jandals, I can't say I had ever known about Dad's hidden love of tramping!

So after we spent the best part of a week giving Dad shit on the air about the mistruths in his username and dating profile, his hits had gone through the roof. Unfortunately for him, they were mainly just people visiting out of curiosity, wanting to see his profile picture—something else I had given him arseholes about, since the photo was at least fifteen years old. But a Wellington listener called Michelle, who was not on NZDating, quite liked the sound of the guy behind the inaccurate profile, the real Stuart Harvey. She set up a profile just so she could message him, and they hit it off.

I don't think Dad closed down his Fitasafiddle account straightaway. After paying for a full year's member-ship up-front, I don't think he could bring himself to do that. And because Michelle knew just how frugal my old man was, I think she let him remain a member until that twelve-month cycle was up. It was a brave chance she took, but in that time there were no other women looking for love online who were swept away by the man in the picture who claimed he was forty-five years old and as fit as a musical instrument, who spent his weekends doing things like yoga on the beach at sunset.

Another bonus for Dad was that Michelle had her own place, which meant he could save on rent and living expenses. This is one area where Dad has never wavered as he has got older. If anything, my dad's love of money is stronger than ever. It would be cruel to the tight-arses of the world to call my dad a tight-arse. I have never known someone who can survive on such tiny sums. Just last year he stopped drinking alcohol after he developed painful gout. His doctor put it down to his drinking. I put it down to what he was drinking. He was a beer man and would drink for price rather than taste. So whatever was the cheapest dozen available is what he would go for. This would usually mean he was knocking back Ranfurlys from Liquorland at eight dollars a dozen, Rheinecks from PAK'nSAVE at eleven dollars a dozen or something equally as undrinkable. I'd imagine he was able to put the hideous taste aside and draw immense pleasure from each can knowing it only cost him sixty-seven cents.

A couple of years ago he came up and stayed at my house. As I dropped him off afterwards, he thanked me for the hospitality and told me he had left a token of his appreciation in the fridge. When I got home I opened the fridge and expected to see, I don't know, maybe a box of chocolates or something similar. I knew I wouldn't open the fridge door and be buried by an avalanche of those expensive round gold Ferrero Rocher chocolates, but I thought he might have left a box of Roses or something similar. Instead, sitting at eye level in the middle of the top shelf, were two cans of Double Brown beer. Dad must have overestimated how much beer he would consume on this visit when he stocked up on his arrival, and these were the cans he didn't get round to drinking. He must have been devastated by this overestimation and poor planning. For the next few texts after that he would ask if I had drunk the beers yet. Eventually, I said I had drunk them and they were delicious, lying twice in one text message.

Whenever Dad comes to Auckland from Wellington to visit, he always flies. He also arrives and departs at the most inconvenient times for just about anyone anywhere! This is because he books his flights so far out from the travel date and goes for the cheapest flights possible. He will come up whenever he can go on the Grabaseat website and get a one-dollar flight. I don't think he has ever paid more than forty dollars to fly from Wellington to Auckland return!

This was a major pain in the arse before Dad turned sixty-five. It would mean dropping him off at the airport at 2 am on a Sunday (or some time equally as inconvenient). Now that Dad has officially become a senior citizen, things have got a lot better. He has this thing in his wallet called a Gold Card. It is a card that all senior citizens get that entitles them to free train and bus rides. So now when he visits he would rather bus, for free, out to the airport than have me drive him out. As he gladly points out in a rather gloaty way, the petrol I'd use to take him to the airport would cost more than his whole flight. After fifty-odd years of being a taxpayer, Dad is determined to get as much of it back from the government as possible.

Some weekends he will even phone to skite about it.

Dad: You'll never guess what I got up to today.

Me: You're probably right. What did you get up to today?

Dad: I went to Otaki and back on the train.

Me: Oh, that's nice. Is your car at the mechanics or something?

Dad: No, no. The car's fine. But with the Gold Card I can get on the train for free, so I'd be mad not to use it.

Me: Excellent point. So . . . what did you do in Otaki?

Dad: Nothing really. Just wandered around. Got a sausage in bread for a dollar from the sausage sizzle outside the mall, then got the train back. So the whole day out only cost me a dollar! Can you believe it?

I told Dad I couldn't believe it even though I could. It sounded like a terrible day out to me—a free ride on public transport to a destination you don't really need or want to go to in the first place!

It's not all free rail travel to uninspiring locations, though. Dad got a mountain bike last year and started doing some cycling to get rid of the beer belly that had developed after years of punishing his vital organs with so-called beers that taste like contaminated water from a pond in Mozambique. He posted a photo of himself on Facebook, on his bike, dressed in just a regular pair of shorts and a tight lycra cycling top . . . in tartan print. I think you'd struggle to find a Scotsman who'd let this fabric anywhere near his body!

After I asked where he'd acquired such a top, Dad told me he found it on a sale table in the mall and managed to get five of them for only $2.50. He offered to send me one of them, an offer I declined. I thought it would have been unfair of me to take him up on that offer, since the postage would cost more than the top. He then asked me if I could believe it, that he got these five tops for only fifty cents each.

Again, I told Dad I could not believe it even though I could. I wonder if the cashier who served Dad had a similar conversation at home that evening:

'You know those tartan lycra cycling tops I was telling you about ages ago? Well, the funniest thing happened today. This man came in and bought all five of them! CAN YOU BELIEVE IT?'

I think it was one of my uncles who described Dad to me by saying he was always the first person to get out of the taxi and the last person to get to the bar. I was just a kid and I didn't get it. He told me I was too young to understand what it meant but assured me I'd laugh one day when I figured it out. He was right. And he didn't even know the big family secret about the most extreme example of Dad's tightness. Actually, nobody outside of the immediate family knows this. (Sorry, Dad!)

Back in the eighties it was way more common for friends to just knock on your door without ringing first. The 'pop in' is almost unheard of these days but was considered no biggie at the time. If this happened when Dad had an open beer on the table next to him, he would hide the big brown bottle and his glass of beer around the back of the sofa before going to answer the door. One of his worst fears was being forced to offer a free drink to a visitor who turned up unexpectedly and without their own beers.

I reckon Dad will be around for a long while yet. Apart from the gout and his irritable sphincter, Dad is in good health. Granddad Harvey lived into his nineties, so he has good genes on his side.

When the time comes, it wouldn't surprise me if we found out Dad was worth millions and millions of dollars that he had made and not spent. If this proves to be true, I just hope he doesn't do something stupid with it like give it all to a charity. Even though his kids are all middle-aged adults now, we will gladly become trustafarians—but a charity is welcome to his collection of cycling shirts.

Dad and his fifty-cent tartan lycra cycling top.

WHERE ARE THEY NOW: BRIDGET, DAN AND CHARLOTTE

The last time all four Harvey children were in the same room at the same time was Christmas Day 2004. The following day, a massive tsunami hit the Indian Ocean region. I doubt all four of us being in the same room at the same time had anything to do with the tsunami . . . but you never know.

I'm proud to say we have all done okay for ourselves. We all have jobs, there are no criminal convictions between us and only one of us has spent a night in a jail cell. That was Dan, after he got drunk at his flat in his late teens and hit a wall, prompting his flatmates to call the police, who locked him up overnight so he could sober up. The next morning Dad went in to pick him up and drove him to the golf course, where he played in a tournament representing Manawatu. They had just enough time to swing by his flat and grab his golf gear, but not enough time for Dan to shower or brush his teeth. Hung-over, smelly and with a sore neck from an uncomfortable night's sleep, he still managed to shoot a two over par round to win his match. Remarkable.

Bridget went to Massey University straight after school to study psychology and now works in this profession in Perth. She has a really good job and is extremely capable at it. Clearly her clients and patients don't know as much about her innermost secrets as I do. If they had access to her teenage diaries, I doubt they would be paying her to listen to their problems.

Bridget moved from Palmerston North to Australia at around the same time the internet became popular. I think these two events were related, because Bridge was notorious for making up statistics, studies and survey results to back her up in any family debate. Whatever the argument, if she wanted to end it she would pull out an outlandish made-up statistic to suit her. The sentences always started the same way: 'Well, according to a recent university study . . .'

At this point Bridget was the only member of the Harvey family who had gone to university, so I think she was feeling pretty chuffed about that. I'm sure it was Bridget who made up the line about there being a whole golf ball of fat in every pie. But since the internet made it easier for us to verify these sorts of claims, she left and moved to a small town near Byron Bay in Australia that had very slow dial-up internet and people who were not motivated to double-check her made-up facts anyway.

She has three cool kids: Billie, Felix and Nell. I don't see Bridget and her family all that often, but when we do we always have a good time and enjoy each other's company. She and I last caught up at our nana's funeral in Levin in 2013. I suppose that's the thing about living in different countries—your face-to-face catch-ups are usually at a family wedding or a funeral! But even given the unpleasant circumstances, we had fun in Levin. Bridge, Char and I shared a motel unit and had a couple of reasonably big nights with cousins we hadn't seen in years. It was nice to catch up with the girls— we drove past our old houses, reminisced, gossiped and laughed. It would have been cool if Dan had been there, too.

I am terrible at keeping in touch. I have never been into lengthy phone conversations with anyone, and I've never got into the whole Skype chat thing in a big way. Though we don't talk often, there is a lot of love and respect there, and we know that we would be there for each other if needed.

*

Daniel also lives in Perth. He's there with his wife, Amie, and their three sons: Jayden, Jesse and Koby. They were living in Christchurch, but after the big earthquake in September 2010, Dan had one of his hunches that there was going to be another earthquake, a bigger one. I've always given Dan a bit of shit about his hunches—he's a gambler, loves to have a punt on the horses, and so he often has these 'hunches' and they often lose me fucking money. This hunch, however, turned out to be true, and in the following February, Dan and Amie watched it all unfold from the comfort of their home in Perth. I got a voicemail message from Dan that night:

> 'Yeah, how ya goin? Just me here. Jesus, what about that fucking earthquake, eh? See? Didn't I say this was going to happen? Fucking knew it. Fuck that shit.'

It was the ultimate I told you so. I'm sure his swearing has got worse with age, and his Australian accent.

It took Dan ages to figure out what he was doing with his life. He dabbled with golf for a while around school-leaving age. He got real good, real fast. Eventually he got bored with it, though, and gave away the idea of pursuing it as a viable occupation. I think he just got sick of the tediousness of whacking balls over and over on the driving range. Oh, and he owed a large sum of money after he made a bad bet on a horse and had to sell his golf clubs to Cash Converters to pay for it.

After that he worked in horse stables around the country. He loved working with the horses. And much like he has picked up the Australian accent since moving to Perth, while working in horse stables he started to speak like a jockey . . . just not quite as high-pitched as some of the tiny blokes in silk jackets and pants. It was very funny.

Dan met his wife Amie at a bar where she worked in Christchurch. The story goes that one day he went up to the bar and, with all the coolness of a sauna, wrote his number on a five-dollar note, scrunched it up and threw it towards her, with the instruction to give him a call sometime. I'm not sure why he chose to write his contact details on legal tender—presumably he wanted her to think he had plenty of money to throw around. Whatever the thinking, it worked. And if it hadn't, no big deal—it only cost him a fiver anyway.

Dan hasn't thrown a punch at me in years. I was never really a fighter, but Dan had quite the temper on him. Our age gap seems like nothing now, but when you're in single figures, two years feels like a lot. When Daniel would blow a fuse and start attacking me, I would usually just fend him off, grab his flying fists or laugh and let him hit me (until his punches started to have a bit of force behind them).

Another thing that's changed is that neither of us tries to compete with the other anymore. Or more accurately, we can compete with each other without someone being strangled or sports equipment being broken. We were terrible opponents growing up, especially me.

The problem was that Daniel would copy me, since I was the older brother. I should have been flattered by this adulation, this hero worship, which wore off the minute he developed a sense of self. But instead of being stoked about him wanting to be me, I was pissed off, because he was better.

It was a terribly soul-destroying cycle I was living in.

I'd take up tennis. A year later he would take up tennis. Six months down the track he would beat me.

I'd take up running. A year later he would take up running. Six months down the track he would beat me.

I'd take up cricket. A year later he would take up cricket. Six months down the track he would beat me.

Sometimes it wouldn't even take him six months to beat me. I was so bad at golf that he beat me at his first attempt. Then again, even the drummer from Def Leppard would have given me a run for my money playing golf.

We don't get to see each other much, due to the distance. We had a brothers' weekend in Melbourne for his thirty-ninth birthday in 2013, though. His wife shouted him a trip there for the Melbourne Cup and I flew over to meet him. We shared a room, just like old times. It was amazing how different we are these days, considering our upbringings were identical. For his toiletries, he had packed three items: a razor, toothbrush and deodorant, which he laid out on the bathroom vanity in the hotel. Next to them were my shaving gel, shaver, deodorant, aftershave, eye gel, moisturiser, exfoliating face scrub, body soap, nose and ear trimmer, ear buds and eyebrow tweezers. When Dan saw all this stuff, his first response was: 'Is someone else staying in here with us?' Nope, it all belonged to me.

Apart from me now being a full-blown metrosexual Aucklander, we had a fantastic time. We had a couple of great nights out—losing money at the casino, going out for dinners, talking shit, drinking wine. One night after dinner, Dan went back to our hotel room for an early night while I went all by myself to a classy establishment called Kittens, where I made a number of generous donations to help some vulnerable young women pay for clothes. I went all alone, though—Dan didn't come with me. (*See, bro, promised I'd never tell anyone.*)

Everything has sort of fallen into place for Dan in the past decade. He has a great job, loves his wife, adores his boys and is in pretty good health. If he dies early, it will be from a heart attack while watching his beloved rugby team the Hurricanes get thrashed in a game. Watching televised sports is about as wound up as Dan gets these days.

*

Char and I see a lot of each other. She lives just around the corner, only about two k's away, so we catch up a few times a week. Before we got the swimming pool put in at home she would pop over for a visit maybe once or twice a month. But I'm sure the pool being built and the dramatic increase in the frequency of her visits are just a coincidence.

She is married to Nick, a bloody good artist and an incredibly tolerant and patient bloke. They got married on the third of February, which also happens to be my birthday. That was incredibly thoughtful of them. Out of the 365 days of the year they obviously chose that one because it is such a significant and important day that they wanted to make sure they would never forget it. Foolishly, they asked me to be the toastmaster at their wedding, so I made sure I hijacked it and made the day as much about me and my birthday celebration as possible. At one point I got a candlelit birthday cake brought into the venue and had all of Charlotte and Nick's guests sing 'Happy Birthday' to me. That earned me a death stare even more ferocious than the time she found out I shagged one of her friends.

They have two adorable daughters Edie five and May three, and, at the time of writing, a third on the way. I'm not quite sure how Char is going to cope being a mum of three, as she gets really stressed really easily, but there are few things in the world that give me more joy than seeing my baby sister having a full-on argument with her three-year-old daughter.

Char and Mum are as thick as thieves and see each other most days. I'm not quite sure when this transition took place, but Charlotte is now the one who tells Mum off—it's as if the baby has become the boss. When these two are in the same room, Char comes out with gems like this:

'Go home and get changed. You are dressed so inappropriately for a woman your age.'
'I think you might be an alcoholic. That's your third glass of wine.'

'Why have you got an iPhone? You should give me your iPhone. All you use it for is to take photos and put them on Facebook.'

'Stop commenting on all my Facebook posts or I'll be forced to un-friend you. You are embarrassing yourself.'

'You need to take your role as a grandparent more seriously. You haven't been over to see the girls for two days now.'

It's nice having both Char and Mum living in the same city, and so close, for the company as well as the incredible entertainment they provide.

Char is quite neurotic. She always has been. Mum used to call her a 'worrywart' when she was little, but I reckon it has escalated with age. These days she won't drink a coffee after 2 pm for fear it will keep her awake all night. She cries a lot less than she used to, though.

I remember one time when Char was about nine and we were in the car together at the traffic lights and an old man crossed the road with a bundle of newspapers. He dropped them and the wind blew them everywhere. Char felt so sad for him that she cried as Dan and I laughed at the poor guy's misfortune. Then, weeks later, from out of nowhere, Char burst into tears. When asked what was wrong she said she had just been thinking about the poor man who dropped the papers. That sort of sums up Char really—underneath that bossiness is one of the most generous and caring people you'll ever meet.

There is an old saying that you can choose your friends but you can't choose your family. I like that saying. Would any of the four of us Harvey kids be friends or even like each other if we weren't related? Hard to say. We are all so incredibly different. But we all love, accept and appreciate each other for these differences. We're not incredibly close like some siblings, but then again we haven't had any major falling-outs. The longest spell of silence was the year and a half that Dan and Char didn't speak after a Christmas Eve blow-up, when she told him he shouldn't have any more to drink. I think he misheard her and thought she said, 'You should get all shouty then storm out with your suitcase and take the next flight back to Christchurch.' That made Christmas the next day a bit awkward, but we all appreciated the extra pavlova that we got to eat in Dan's absence.

WHERE ARE THEY NOW: ME

I survived. When I look back at some of the stupid things I did and risks I took, it really does have more to do with luck than anything else that I am now a middle-aged man writing about my middle-class childhood.

Growing old is a funny thing. Some mornings I look in the full-length mirror in our bedroom and, for a split second, find it hard to register that the old bloke looking back is me. While standing there I ponder, was that hair grey yesterday or did it change colour overnight? How the hell did those hairs get inside my ear? And when did my scrotum start to hang lower than my penis? Seriously, my balls have not aged all that well. (Was I supposed to moisturise them or something?) If you saw a picture of just my balls and were asked to have a stab in the dark at their age, you would probably guess sixty-something, maybe even early seventies. Gravity is a bitch.

I'm lucky in a lot of ways. I still run, always in shoes these days and never in my pyjama top. I love to run marathons. I'm considerably slower than the Kenyans but can still complete the forty-two kilometres in about the same time it takes to watch the *Titanic* movie. At my age I reckon that's pretty cool, and lucky—lucky because I'm sure it has more to do with genes than anything else.

I'm okay with the wrinkles (not that I have a say in it). If they really bothered me, I could always do something about it, but I think it's better to roll with it than look like some tragic in denial about his age. And anyway, the laugh lines are a fair trade-off for a life full of laughs and happy moments.

These days, the time goes so fast. I remember weekends growing up in Palmerston North so excruciatingly boring they felt like they would never end. Housebound days in the school holidays where the biggest spike of excitement was going to check the mail after the postie rode past. I wasn't expecting anything, but it was just something to break the monotony, something slightly more exciting than being killed by boredom indoors. We literally had nothing to do.

Just like we used to do, Sev often complains of being bored. I usually respond by rattling off a list almost as long as Santa's of all the options open to him. If I'm not in the mood to remind him of all the awesome mod cons he has, I tell him that I'm his father, not his personal activities coordinator. It's a bit of a dad joke, and not even a very good one, but I think it's still better than Mum's standard answer whenever we complained of boredom: 'Go and play outside!'

That's not a suggestion most parents would offer these days—far too risky. When I was Sev's age, all we really had to think about was a thing called Stranger Danger and rubella. Both these things had their own ad campaigns. Stranger Danger was all about kids not getting into the cars of strangers who offered them lollies. I don't know how many Kiwi kids were abducted by strangers before that, but presumably it was enough of an issue to warrant its very own ad campaign. It must have been an effective one, because I still remember it now. And even though I was never approached by a confectionery-wielding molester in an appropriately rapey vehicle, say a white van or a station wagon, if I had been, I probably would have accepted the offer, had it not been for the extensive advertising. We didn't get a lot of sweets at home, so it would have been very tempting.

The rubella immunisation campaign ran in the middle of the eighties. Rubella is a type of measles—you don't hear too much about it these days in mainstream media, but New Zealand must have had a real struggle to contain it. The ad did a pretty shitty job of explaining the basic facts: it had a kid on a swing in the playground and he was furiously rubbing one of his eyes. For years afterwards, anytime anybody rubbed their eyes, people would ask them if they had rubella.

These days everything is a worry, but it's not such a bad thing, I think. Parents just want to take the best care that they can of their kids. I must admit, every time Sev tears off down the footpath on his scooter or bike, I have to hold my breath for fear of a reversing car smacking into him, even though I used to do the same thing . . . minus any protective gear. And I hate the thought of him loitering unsupervised down at the creek in our park, exactly like I used to do when I was his age.

Parents in the seventies and eighties still wanted to take the best care of their kids, but there was definitely way less risk management in place. Maybe that's why bigger families were more of a thing—parents had more kids because they assumed they might lose one or two along the way.

I always planned to have a decent-size family. I love kids, and would have loved to have had at least a couple—someone to call me Dad. Life throws you some funny old surprises, though, so that's not how things have worked out for us, Jay-Jay and me.

In 2005, while running the Auckland marathon, I ended up collapsing with off-the-chart blood pressure after only five kilometres. When you're feeling like a total arse only five kilometres into a forty-two kilometre run, it's never a good sign. Long story short, this nine-centimetre-round tumour was found hidden around my stomach somewhere. It was taken out in a seven-hour-long operation that saved my life, but it came at a bit of a price—I can't have kids as a result. In the big scheme of things, it was a small price to pay, a fair trade-off.

We got balls-deep (literally) in IVF and underwent years of fertility treatment without any success. In the middle of all of this, we became guardians of Jay-Jay's nephew, Seven. Sev is now eleven. He called us Jay-Jay and Dom for the first four years with us, then out of the blue started calling us Mum and Dad, which is beautiful, but at eleven he is already at an age where he pulls out his trump card during tantrums: 'You're not even my real dad!' So the teenage years should be a hoot.

I think I'm doing an okay job as a dad and Jay-Jay is exceptional as a mum. But since we gave up on IVF I have had to rethink my whole life. I always thought my purpose in life was to be a dad. After twenty years of working my arse off on morning radio, a job where every morning you have to try your hardest to make an invisible audience like you enough to keep listening, I just wanted that unconditional love that comes from kids just as a result of being a decent parent. It's been a strange few years coming to terms with all this. I feel like a bit of a moaner even bothering to write it down, given there are tonnes of couples who choose to not have kids. I suppose that's the big difference, though—it wasn't my choice. But as the saying goes, at least I've got my health.

Apart from having kids, I don't think there's anything in my life I would change. Life has been bloody good to me. Even the people I've met along the way who have turned out to be dicks have taught me something useful, even if it was just making me better at spotting dicks from a mile away. Neither Jay-Jay nor I have had anything handed to us, but we have worked bloody hard (well, 'hard' by broadcasting standards—it's not exactly rocket surgery) to create a good life for ourselves and our boy.

My name is Dominic Harvey and I survived the 1980s. My mum smoked while I was in the womb and then every day of my childhood. I never had a car seat, rarely had a seatbelt, got the belt at home and the cane at school, never wore sunscreen, shared bathwater, stood on lawn prickles as ferocious as landmines, fell from jungle bars onto the concrete floor below, was billeted on sports exchanges and stayed at homes of complete strangers, walked to school in winter in bare feet, was made to ride a Cruiser instead of getting a BMX—and somehow, I managed to pull through—all without wi-fi!

I'm not special, either—most of us made it. If you missed living through all of this firsthand, count yourself lucky! You don't know how easy you had it! Still, I think we were pretty fortunate—we were raised in a special time. It wasn't better or worse, it was just different . . . nah, actually that's bullshit! It was way better! I doubt there would be too many school-aged kids in this country now who get to take jelly crystal sandwiches to school every Friday!